Predatory Nuns

Predatory Nuns

Sexual Abuse in North American Catholic Sisterhoods

BRIAN TITLEY

Exposit

Jefferson, North Carolina

ISBN (print) 978-1-4766-8957-9
ISBN (ebook) 978-1-4766-4717-3

LIBRARY OF CONGRESS AND BRITISH LIBRARY
CATALOGUING DATA ARE AVAILABLE

Library of Congress Control Number 2022024581

© 2022 Brian Titley. All rights reserved

No part of this book may be reproduced or transmitted in any form or by any means, electronic or mechanical, including photocopying or recording, or by any information storage and retrieval system, without permission in writing from the publisher.

Front cover photograph © 2022 Kraken Images/Shutterstock

Printed in the United States of America

Exposit is an imprint of McFarland & Company, Inc., Publishers

Exposit
Box 611, Jefferson, North Carolina 28640
www.expositbooks.com

Table of Contents

Preface   1

1. Syllabus of Errors: The Church and Its Sexual Predators   5
2. Foolish Virgins: Novice Nuns and the Vow of Chastity   22
3. A Laying On of Hands: Older Nuns and Younger Ones   39
4. Sorrowful Mysteries: Orphanages   56
5. Weaknesses of the Flesh: Missions to Native Americans   76
6. Unfaithful Servants: Catholic Schools   94
7. Days of Reckoning   115

Conclusion   127
Chapter Notes   131
Bibliography   149
Index   157

Preface

I am often asked why a male secular historian would write about Catholic nuns. The question is understandable. It only makes sense when I explain that nuns and convents were part of the landscape of my youth growing up in Ireland. Even my own education began at the hands of the Sisters of the Presentation at their Douglas Street convent in Cork, the first to be built by Nano Nagle, the founder of the order.

For girls of my generation, the encounters with nuns were much more prolonged and profound than anything I experienced. It would not be amiss to say that the cloaked menace of the nun cast a long shadow over the lives of Irish women, young and old. Convents were everywhere and were often unavoidable—if you sought an education, for example. In the absence of a public school system, there were no alternatives.

In truth, nuns controlled an astounding variety of institutions: orphanages; schools that were elementary, secondary, and industrial; teacher education colleges; university residences; hospitals; Magdalene asylums; and mother-and-baby homes. In Cork's north side stood the enormous Good Shepherd Convent. The Victorian red brick edifice, now in ruins, housed the city's Magdalene asylum. At the far end of the city the quasi-rural district of Mahon was the location of Bessborough, a mother-and-baby home operated by the Sisters of the Sacred Hearts of Jesus and Mary. Both of these institutions were spoken of in hushed terms; what went on behind their walls was not a matter of public discourse.

Beginning in the 1990s, Ireland began to awaken from its *grande noirceur* under the heel of the Catholic Church. A series of scandals— one of which brought down the government— buttressed by investigations by journalists, academics, and public inquiries exposed both a pedophile priest problem and rampant abuse in Church-run institutions. The old taboos that placed religious personnel, both male and

Preface

female, above criticism were undermined as former inmates of orphanages and industrial schools spoke of the horrors and humiliations they had been forced to endure while in "care." Magdalene asylums and mother-and-baby homes were special cases in that they existed for the incarceration of females only—"wayward" and "fallen" women—and were run by nuns who specialized in the work. The revelations in these cases sparked a scandal that resonated around the world.[1]

In May 2018 a referendum removed the constitutional ban on abortion. It followed in the wake of earlier reforms that had legalized birth control, divorce, and same-sex marriage and was a defining moment in the country's transformation.[2] The old Catholic Ireland in which I had been raised, inward-looking and suspicious of modernity, was gone or just about.

The legacy of the past lingers in places. The country still has Catholic historians who pen the praises of nuns and their "contributions" to society.[3] They are firmly on the wrong side of history and few take them seriously. They have been bypassed by a new generation of secular scholars who don't hesitate to investigate the dark side of the convent system.[4] Understanding Irish society and how it has evolved over the past half-century or so is impossible without reference to religious orders and the mechanisms of control exercised by the Church. It's a topic that has never been far from my interests.

In my research on Canada's policy towards its Indigenous peoples, nuns again made an appearance. They did most of the teaching in the residential schools operated by the Catholic Church. Radical cultural assimilation was the agenda of these schools. As the schools came under the critical scrutiny of secular scholars, they were recognized as the darkest chapter in Canadian history.[5] The heroic missionary bringing true religion to idolatrous heathens has disappeared from the national narrative.

During 2014 I chanced upon a litigation case making its way through the justice system of Montana, not far from where I was living at the time in southern Alberta. Former students at the Ursuline Academy on the Flathead Reservation were suing the Ursuline Sisters for sexual and physical abuse. I began to follow the case since it combined a number of my research interests, and I even planned to attend the court hearing in person. An out-of-court settlement disrupted my plan, but I decided nonetheless to write an account of it. It didn't take long before I found myself engaged in a much larger project that was completely untouched: the sexual predator nun.

Preface

As the many dimensions of the research opened up, I realized that the stories I was discovering completely contradicted the existing official histories of American nuns. No surprise here since the overwhelming majority of the literature on the subject is the work of Catholic scholars. The writings of these scholars tend to take the form of great nun biographies or heroic institution-building narratives or a blend of both. And Catholic historians form an exclusive club of mutual support and self-congratulation. They gather together every three years at the Conference on the History of Women Religious, sponsored by the University of Notre Dame's Cushwa Center for the Study of American Catholicism. Nuns are prominent among the participants presenting papers that "celebrate," "commemorate," "remember," or "document" the achievements of their own congregations. The problem with these kinds of histories, whether the work of nuns or lay Catholic scholars, is that they blend together myths, miracles, and distortions of evidence to craft pleasing and affirmative narratives that assiduously screen out uncomfortable episodes from the past. What are their typical sins of omission?

Lay sisters. These were a class of servant nuns who came to religious life without the education or resources of choir sisters. Their lives of endless drudgery in the kitchen and laundry just don't fit with the great nun image. Their existence is usually ignored or only mentioned briefly in passing.[6]

Magdalene asylums. They comprised a gulag of convents for the incarceration of "bad girls" and "fallen women" run usually, but not exclusively, by the Sisters of the Good Shepherd. Few Catholic historians want to touch them even though they existed in just about every state of the union.[7] Note: They were not just an Irish phenomenon.

Slavery. At least eight religious sisterhoods owned slaves and exploited their labor in the antebellum South. Philippine Duchesne, who led the Society of the Sacred Heart to frontier Missouri in 1818 and is now a saint, was a slave owner.[8] You will find few references to any of this in the official histories.

Sexual predators. The sexual predator nun is the ultimate taboo. Of all the subjects that make Catholic historians uncomfortable, this one is in a special category. Even the most passing reference to it is a bridge that is never crossed. In fact, you will seek in vain to find any discussion of sexuality in the literature. It is assumed that when novice nuns took their vows their sexuality was eliminated. Eunuchs for the sake of the kingdom of heaven?

Preface

When survivors of nun sexual exploitation file lawsuits against predators and their congregations, they want more than anything to have their stories placed on record and the Church and its agencies held accountable. The sanitized narratives of Catholic historians will never serve those purposes. This book may begin to do so.

A few words of explanation are in order respecting the structure and logic of the book. It begins with a chapter that surveys the Church's sexual predator problem, the main focus being on priests. The principal theme here is the struggle for justice by survivors of abuse and the countermeasures taken by the bishops to protect the Church's assets and reputation. The episcopal strategies are instructive since they allow for comparison with the responses of religious sisterhoods when faced with criminals in their ranks.

This is followed by a chapter on the vow of chastity and how novice nuns were prepared for it. A grasp of how congregations dealt with human sexuality in the novitiate is in order so that we may make some sense of deviance in the convent.

The next three chapters examine sexual abuse in a diversity of institutional settings: convent novitiates, orphanages, and boarding schools on Native American reservations. In each chapter the problem is approached through a sample of three case studies selected as reasonably representative of the goings-on in these settings.

Chapter 6, which deals with Catholic schools, is also structured around case studies, 18 in all. It is well to remember that the vast majority of American nuns were employed as teachers in these schools and a much larger sample is therefore required to provide an adequate survey of the abuse problem.

The final chapter tells of the depredations of the only two nuns, both of them serial predators, who were prosecuted in the criminal justice system. An *idée fixe* that links these chapters together is the quest of nun abuse survivors for accountability from the convent system and the obstacles thrown in their path.

1

Syllabus of Errors

The Church and Its Sexual Predators

> The files of a Bishop concerning his priests are altogether private; their forced acquisition by civil authority would be an intolerable attack upon the free exercise of religion in the United States....[1]
> —Congregation for the Clergy to Manuel Moreno, archbishop of Tucson, Arizona, 1984

In 1972, the recently ordained Father Gilbert Gauthe was assigned to the parish in Broussard, Louisiana. His supervisor, Bishop Gerard Frey of Lafayette, was soon made aware that Gauthe was sexually abusing boys in the town. And so began the bishop's practice of moving the errant priest to other parishes as complaints from parents reached his ears. It worked until 1984, when a group of parents filed lawsuits against the diocese. Most of the plaintiffs were prepared to settle out of court—the Church's preferred strategy to avoid scandal—but one family refused the hush money. Glenn and Fey Gastal were determined to expose the priest's depredations and hired an aggressive lawyer, J. Minos Simon, to pursue criminal charges against Gauthe. The priest pleaded guilty and received a 10-year jail sentence. The phenomenon of the pedophile priest was now in the public domain.[2]

The Gauthe case was a scandalous tale that shocked American Catholics who had been taught from the earliest age to revere men of the cloth. While there appeared to be something novel about it, it was nothing of the sort. The Church had been grappling with the problem of clerical predators since its earliest centuries. A few examples will suffice. A decree of the Council of Elvira, 306 CE, prohibited priests from sexually abusing children—a prohibition that would hardly have been necessary were it something that never happened. And Peter Damien, a monk who became cardinal bishop of Ostia, denounced clerics who sodomized young boys in his *Liber Gomorrhianus* (*Book of Gomorrah*), which appeared in 1051. At times, the abuse reached the highest echelons in the Church. The infatuation of Pope Julius III (1550–1555) with Innocenzo, a 15-year-old street beggar he rescued in Parma, was well known at the time.[3]

It was relatively easy to contain the taint of scandal associated with wayward priests over the centuries in preponderantly Catholic countries where church and state worked in mutual harmony. But the rise of secularism and anti-clericalism in modern times put the Church on the defensive. France's *laïcité* law of December 1905 comes to mind as well as the revolution in Portugal that began in 1910. The traditional privileges of the clergy were stripped away in both instances.[4] The crimes of priests and monks were welcome propaganda for anti-clericals, and it became all the more imperative for the Church to shroud them in secrecy.

One of the privileges claimed by the Church was a form of self-governance respecting the discipline of its religious personnel. It preferred that errant clergy face judgment not in the secular justice system but in the Church's own procedures as set forth in canon law. Decrees and proclamations of popes and Church councils over the centuries formed the basis of canon law, and the miscellaneous documentation was consolidated into one coherent code in 1917 (and revised in 1983).[5]

Secrecy was at the heart of the canonical judicial system. Scandal that might undermine the Church's moral authority and bring joy to its enemies had to be avoided. Accordingly, canon law required dioceses to maintain secret files on clerical misconduct. Secrecy was also required in procedures addressing the misconduct. A combination of counseling, prayer, and penance or what was called "pastoral methods" that aimed to correct the behavior was the most common approach. In effect, misconduct by a priest was considered a sin rather than a crime. It was rare for a priest to be laicized or returned to the secular state. Excommunication, the ultimate sanction, was reserved mainly for heresy.[6]

The secrecy was compounded by the decree *Crimen Sollicitationis* issued by Pope Pius XI in 1922. The decree, sent confidentially to bishops across the world, forbade them from reporting priestly sexual misconduct to secular authorities. The misconduct was specified as: homosexuality, bestiality, soliciting sex in the confessional, and sexual assault of children. A bishop who broke what was called the "secret of the Holy Office" could face excommunication. Pope Paul VI's instruction of February 1974, *Secreta Continere*, updated *Crimen Sollicitationis* with minor modifications. The secret now became known as the

1. Syllabus of Errors

"pontifical secret." Its very existence was also a secret; the Vatican did not publicly acknowledge it until 2001.[7] It was the Church's version of *omertà*, the mafia code of silence, and there was a distinctly underworld reasoning to it: a bishop informing the police that a priest had sexually assaulted a child, for example, earned a far greater sanction than the assault itself.

Bishop Frey's behavior in the Gauthe case is better understood in light of the Vatican's confidentiality directives. The prelate was not just trying to prevent scandal or protect diocesan assets; he was also acting strictly in accordance with the pontifical secret.

The Gauthe case was the first of many revelations of clerical child abuse and attempted cover-ups. The publicity surrounding it encouraged more victims to come forward with their stories. Much of the initial publicity was the work of journalist Jason Berry, who covered the story of Father Gauthe in a May 1985 newspaper article.[8] He continued to write extensively about predatory priests during the decades that followed. A new generation of litigation lawyers appeared at this time too, ready to challenge the Church on behalf of sexual abuse victims. Jeff Anderson of St. Paul, Minnesota, was the most prominent among them. Both Berry and Anderson were vilified by Church apologists as sworn enemies and liars, and they both appeared on Geraldo Rivera's television show in November 1988 when the topic was "The Church's Sexual Watergate." The show featured several victims of abusive priests who spoke explicitly of their experiences.[9] A year earlier, the Survivors Network of those Abused by Priests, known by its acronym, SNAP, had been established in Chicago as an advocacy group supporting those seeking justice from the Church. With organized advocacy, lawyers, and journalists in print and broadcast media on their side, the momentum was with the victims/survivors.

When bishops received complaints about priestly crimes, their first instinct was to offer compensation in return for confidentiality. In the event of recourse to the law, whether civil or criminal, they often resorted to aggressive tactics such as investigating plaintiffs' sexual history in order to discredit them.[10] Whenever possible, they sheltered their priests behind statutes of limitations respecting the crimes. The statutes varied from state to state, but in a general sense they allowed victims but a short time frame from the date of the crime in which to bring charges against their assailants. In dealing with the generality of the revelations, the bishops promised reform and future transparency. They also tried to minimize the extent of the problem, attributing it to the proverbial "few bad apples" while arguing that priests were no worse than laymen when it came to child abuse.[11]

How did survivors and their supporters contend with legal obstacles and Church tactics? There was a helpful breakthrough in 1988 that was unrelated to problem clerics. In that year, Patti Barton, a 34-year-old homemaker from Everett, Washington, who had been sexually molested by her father during her childhood, successfully lobbied the state legislature to modify the statute of limitations in a manner that allowed victims of such crimes to take legal action for up to three years after they had discovered an injury resulting from the abuse.[12] This was the "delayed discovery of injury" argument. With each passing year the volume of clinical studies documenting the phenomenon of "traumatic amnesia" mounted, overwhelming attempts to discredit it. By 1992 statute of limitation laws in almost one third of states nationwide had been modified to accommodate delayed discovery.[13]

It was a major setback for the Church, whose dioceses now faced a growing barrage of lawsuits. By 1993 more than 400 priests had been accused in either civil or criminal proceedings. Lawyers for survivors found that they could force dioceses to disclose their secret files on errant priests through the legal process known as discovery. It was another blow to the Church since the files frequently revealed that bishops had been covering up crime.[14]

This was all unfolding during the 26-year pontificate of John Paul II. Acclaimed by his admirers as one of history's great popes, he did hold a few records: He visited more countries and canonized more saints than any of his predecessors. Strictly conservative on social and sexual issues, he was an ardent anti-communist and worked to undermine the political regime under which he had once lived in his native Poland. The most egregious failure of his reign was his ineptitude and inaction in dealing with the Church's sexual abuse problem in spite of what Jason Berry called "clear evidence of a criminal underground in the priesthood." The story most often cited as evidence of this failure was his unflinching support for Father Marcial Maciel Degollado, the Mexican priest and notorious sexual predator who founded the Legionaries of Christ, a conservative religious order. The pope was so impressed with Maciel's fundraising, his seminaries filled with short-haired young men training for the priesthood, and his virulent anti-communism, that he turned a blind eye to his criminality.[15]

John Paul visited America in 1993 and briefly addressed the sexual abuse problem at an international youth conference in Denver in

1. Syllabus of Errors

August. He expressed regret at the scandal, while condemning the media sensationalism surrounding it. He blamed it all on modern permissiveness, or what he called the "moral evil which flows from personal choices."[16] In his view, the scandal that was damaging the Church was the real problem. Not a word of concern was uttered for the thousands of children and adolescents who had been traumatized by sexual predator priests.

The indifference of the pope and the American bishops meant that the scandal continued to accelerate and weaken the Church. The case that attracted the most publicity to date burst on the national scene in 2002 when investigative journalists with the *Boston Globe* exposed the depth of the problem in their own locality. According to the *Globe*, the archdiocese of Boston had quietly settled sexual assault claims against at least 70 priests over the previous decade. In the most notorious case, Father John Geoghan was alleged to have assaulted more than 130 children over several decades while his supervisors moved him about rather than reporting him to the civil authorities. Cardinal Bernard F. Law, archbishop of Boston, was described by the *Globe* as the "central figure in a scandal of criminal abuse, denial, payoff and cover-up that resonates around the world." Law, who was on close terms with Pope John Paul II and the two Bush presidents, was forced to resign in December 2002 and was spirited away to a comfortable sinecure in the Vatican.[17]

Thrown once again on the defensive, the bishops sensed that some sort of action was required. In June 2002 they held their annual national conference in Dallas, Texas, with 285 in attendance. They spent several days listening to victims of predator priests, and many were defensive respecting their failure to act when problems had been reported to them. They resolved to do better and concluded their conference by adopting a Charter for the Protection of Children and Young People. Known as the Dallas Charter, it committed the bishops to

- the immediate suspension of an accused priest,
- the reporting of all allegations to civil authorities,
- cooperation with investigations,
- providing full reports on priests transferred to new parishes, and
- conducting background checks on all priests working with children.[18]

It looked promising at first glance, but the bishops were quickly reminded by the Vatican that reporting to civil authorities violated the pontifical secret. Discussions with the Congregation for the Doctrine of the Faith ensued, and on December 8 a particular exemption for the United States was agreed to: the bishops would be obliged to report priestly sex crimes to the secular justice system—but only where local law required them to do so.[19] There is no evidence that such reporting ever took place. Shortly after adopting the Dallas Charter, the bishops established a review board to monitor its operations. The first two chairs of the board, a former governor and a judge (both laypeople), soon resigned, noting that the practices of cover-up and obfuscation were still the norm.[20]

Two years after the Dallas Charter, an event took place that illustrated both the financial stress the abuse crisis was inflicting on the Church and a novel survival strategy that appealed to bishops and religious orders. In July 2004 the archdiocese of Portland became the first Catholic institution to seek protection under Chapter 11 bankruptcy law. The archdiocese was in a financial mess. To date it had parted with $53 million to settle more than 100 abuse cases. Twenty-two of those cases involved allegations against Father Maurice Grammond (died 2002) and had been settled out of court. But one of Grammond's victims, James Devereaux, would not settle. He wanted his day in court and was seeking compensation to the tune of $130 million. On the eve of jury selection, the archdiocese filed for bankruptcy protection, bringing the proceedings to a halt. It was now up to a federal judge to decide the level of compensation that would enable the archdiocese to avoid insolvency. The disadvantage of the strategy was that archdiocesan finances would be subject to court supervision and public scrutiny. The advantage lay in the probability of a smaller financial penalty than that which a civil court might award. Moreover, there would be no discovery process requiring the disclosure of sensitive documentation from secret files.[21]

In April 2005 Pope John Paul II died. During his 26 years at the helm he had mentioned the sex abuse scandal in public only about a dozen times even though it was the worst crisis to afflict the Church since the Reformation. He always insisted that Church teachings and practices were in no way responsible; the blame lay entirely with a materialistic and hedonistic world. Nor did he see the merit of punishing errant clerics. For example, when Cardinal Hans Hermann Groër, archbishop of Vienna, resigned in 1995 following accusations of sexually propositioning seminarians, there were no sanctions. The pope said nothing about Groër, whom he had personally selected for office.[22]

1. *Syllabus of Errors*

The Polish pope was succeeded by a German one—Cardinal Joseph Ratzinger—who took the name Benedict XVI. Benedict was the ultimate Vatican insider and enforcer who had served as prefect of the Congregation for the Doctrine of the Faith since 1981. The Congregation had been known as the Inquisition until 1904 and was responsible for rooting out religious beliefs and practices that did not accord with Church orthodoxy. It had been handed the sex abuse file in 2001 from the Congregation for the Clergy, which had done little about it. Benedict was of the same conservative bent as his predecessor. His theology was influenced by the ideas of Saint Augustine and viewed sexual desire as shameful. He blamed the abuse crisis on the sexual revolution of the 1960s, the proliferation of pornography, the reforms of the Second Vatican Council, and the banishment of God from society. His instinct on the scandal was to cover it up.[23]

One of Pope Benedict's initiatives seemed to suggest a greater commitment to openness. In 2010 he issued a *Motu Proprio* ordering bishops to report clerical sex crimes to civil authorities, but only where local laws required it. It was the same concession that had been made to the American bishops in 2002 and was now universal. What appeared to be a weakening of the pontifical secret was really an exercise in public relations. Laws requiring disclosure of crimes—or "misprision of felony" in legal jargon—were usually imprecise.[24] There is little evidence of a bishop voluntarily turning in his priests at a police station or being prosecuted for failure to do so. In March 2019 a French court convicted Cardinal Philippe Barbarin of failing to report a priest's sex crimes, but his six-month suspended sentence was overturned on appeal the following year.[25]

Benedict's *Motu Propio* did not dilute the code of silence. In some ways, it actually strengthened it by extending the original list of sex crimes protected by it. Bishops were now forbidden to report priests who possessed child pornography or who had had sex with persons who "habitually lack the use of reason."[26] The pornography provision was likely a response to the arrest at Ottawa International Airport in September 2009 of Raymond Lahey, bishop of Antigonish, Nova Scotia. Customs officials, acting on a tip, found thousands of pornographic images on the bishop's laptop, many of them of young boys in bondage positions employing Catholic paraphernalia.[27]

Bishop Lahey was not the first prelate to resign following revelations of sexual misconduct. Nor was he the last. In April 2010 Roger Vangheluwe, the long-serving bishop of Bruges, Belgium, stepped aside upon admitting that he had abused a boy back in the 1980s.[28] In February 2013, the pope announced that he had accepted the resignation of Cardinal Keith O'Brien, archbishop of St. Andrews-Edinburgh, Scotland, because of inappropriate sexual activity.[29] Canada, Belgium, Scotland ... the expanding international scope of the abuse scandal was too obvious to ignore. It was no longer possible to claim, as Pope John Paul II had once done, that it was a distinctly American problem.

Not only was the scandal spreading around the globe, but new mechanisms to confront it were coming into play that alarmed the Church. One of these was the public inquiry—often initiated because of popular outrage at revelations and evidence of cover-up. For example, the Commission to Inquire into Child Abuse (Ryan Commission) was established by the Irish government in 1999 following media reports about abuse in Church-run institutions. Reporting in 2009, the commission exposed brutality and depravity towards thousands of children in industrial schools and orphanages operated by 18 religious orders.[30] Another example was the Truth and Reconciliation Commission set up by the Canadian federal government in 2008 to investigate abuse in the system of residential schools that had been deployed to assimilate Native children. About half of the schools had been managed by Catholic religious orders.[31] A third example was the Royal Commission into Institutional Responses to Child Sexual Abuse announced by the Australian government in 2012.[32]

Public inquiries were worrisome. They allowed for the interrogation of Church personnel and the surrender of secret files. Moreover, they created a secure milieu in which survivors of abuse could tell their stories. And the potential for enormous financial settlements was never far from view. The inquiries signaled that the Church was under siege from an encroaching secularism, and it was happening in countries such as the Republic of Ireland, where, only a few short years earlier, it had been revered and feared.

It is not difficult to understand why the pope was dismayed by it all. He was even losing control of things right in the Vatican. Ettore Gotti Tedeschi, an experienced banker who had been appointed by Benedict as president of the Institute for Works of Religion (the Vatican bank) in 2009, was ousted by the board of directors in May 2012 for alleged incompetence. He claimed that he had been investigating corruption and money laundering in the troubled bank and had run afoul of insiders.[33] In the same month Benedict's butler, Paulo Gabriele, was arrested for leaking a large quantity of confidential documents to an Italian

1. Syllabus of Errors

journalist. The documents revealed that the Curia—the Vatican civil service—had become a cesspool of factional infighting that was undermining the pope.[34]

It is probable that the tsunami of crises overwhelming the Church contributed to what next transpired. On February 11, 2013, Benedict, speaking in Latin, announced his abdication, citing his advanced age (he was 85) and deteriorating strength as the reasons. The effective date of his departure was February 28. It was the first papal abdication in almost 600 years. The survivors of clergy sex abuse were quick to label him an unloved figure who would not be missed. David Clohessy, a director of the Survivors Network of those Abused by Priests (SNAP), had this to say: "He knows more about clergy sex crimes and cover-ups than anyone else in the Church, yet he had done precious little to protect children."[35]

Habemus papam. On the evening of March 13, 2013, white smoke and the sounding of bells at the Vatican signaled the election of a new pope. Cardinal Jorge Bergoglio, archbishop of Buenos Aires, was the chosen one. The first Jesuit and first non–European to be elected to the position, his adopted name, Francis, after St. Francis of Assisi, was also a first and suggested a more modest persona than that of his predecessors. His spurning of the flamboyant regalia and extravagances of most princes of the Church reinforced this impression. Moreover, his stated commitment to rooting out corruption in the Curia and his idea that the Church should serve the poor aroused the suspicions of conservatives, as did his interventions in environmental and political matters.[36]

How would Francis deal with the sex abuse scandal that had plagued his predecessors? A number of developments in the United States would put him to the test. First, a review of the state of the scandal in that country during the early years of Francis's papacy is in order. Between 1950 and 2015 American bishops received allegations of sexual abuse by 6,528 priests under their supervision. The allegations involved 17,651 victims. Nineteen bishops were personally accused of abuse. Two-thirds of the bishops tried to cover up the abuse by moving the predators to other locations. One consequence of the allegations was that 325 priests were defrocked or laicized. Little is known about the others. Perhaps they were dead, in prison, or returned to ministry. More than 3,000 civil lawsuits were filed against dioceses and religious orders between 1984 and 2009, and over $3 billion was awarded in compensation settlements. The compensation payments meant that three

Predatory Nuns

religious orders and 15 dioceses/archdioceses had filed for bankruptcy protection.[37]

Much worse was to come. The year of 2018 would not be a good year for the Church in America with news emerging of more sexual depredations and systematic cover-ups. One of the revelations concerned a prominent member of the hierarchy. Theodore McCarrick's ecclesiastical career was a success by any measure. Ordained to the priesthood in 1958, he went on to become bishop of Metuchen in 1981, and archbishop of Newark in 1986, both appointments in the state of New Jersey. A popular media personality, an avid collector of honorary degrees, and a successful fundraiser, he was close to Pope John Paul II, whose favorite causes he supported financially. In 2001 the pope raised him to the College of Cardinals and named him archbishop of Washington, a post he held until reaching the retirement age of 75 in 2006. In Washington he was considered an influential power broker and, upon retiring, took on a new role as a special Vatican emissary. In January 2008, he was one of the speakers at a session on faith and modernization at the World Economic Forum in Davos, Switzerland.

Those who had worked with McCarrick over the years were well aware of his secret life. By the mid–1990s the Church in New Jersey was receiving reports about his sexual behavior with seminarians. Beginning in 2005, the diocese of Metuchen and the archdiocese of Newark were paying hush money to former seminarians who had lodged complaints against him. It turned out that the prelate's problems had a much longer history. On June 20, 2018, a review board of the archdiocese of New York disclosed that in 1971 and 1972 he had sexually abused an altar boy at St. Patrick's Cathedral.

On July 27, Pope Francis removed McCarrick from his ministry and sentenced him to a life of prayer and penance in seclusion. In February 2019, the errant cleric was laicized. In November 2020, the Vatican made an unusual move: it released a 447-page report on McCarrick's history of abuse. The report showed that he had molested at least 17 teenagers/young men over the years, some of them repeatedly, often ingratiating himself with their families as he did so. Generous with gifts to his victims, he lured them to his beach house on the Jersey shore, where the liquor flowed freely. At times, Uncle Ted, as he liked to be called, made little attempt at discretion, openly flaunting his relationships with seminarians. Relying on his friends in high places upon whom he had lavished cash "donations," he believed he was untouchable. When Pope John Paul II elevated him to the College of Cardinals

1. *Syllabus of Errors*

and appointed him archbishop of Washington, he did so in spite of clear warnings about his sexual predilections from Cardinal John O'Connor of New York. The report on McCarrick cast further doubts on the Vatican's decision to fast-track the Polish pope to sainthood. Canonized in 2014, Pope John Paul II and his legacy will be forever tarnished by his terrible judgment and myopic ineptitude in dealing with the sex abuse scandal.[38]

Less than two months after the fall of McCarrick, the Church in America faced another damning revelation. In mid–August 2018, Josh Shapiro, the attorney general for Pennsylvania, released a 1,400-page grand jury report on predator priests in six of the state's dioceses. During an 18-month investigation, the grand jury had reviewed more than two million documents, many of them from secret Church files. In scathing language and disturbing detail, the report identified more than 300 priests who had sexually abused more than 1,000 boys and girls since the 1940s. According to Shapiro, there had been a "sophisticated cover-up" by the Church during these decades. In the words of the report: "Several diocesan administrators, including the bishops, often dissuaded victims from reporting abuse to police, pressured law enforcement to terminate or avoid an investigation or conducted their own deficient, biased investigation without reporting crimes against children to the proper authorities.... The main thing was not to help children, but to avoid scandal."[39]

Cardinal Donald Wuerl, who had been bishop of Pittsburgh between 1988 and 2006 and was now archbishop of Washington, was identified in the report as one of the leaders who had covered up the abuse. Initially, he tried to defend his actions, but soon offered to resign from the archbishopric. In accepting the resignation, Pope Francis praised Wuerl's "nobility" and allowed him to retain his cardinal's hat and his position on the Congregation for Bishops, giving him a role in choosing future members of the American hierarchy.[40]

The survivors of abuse in Pennsylvania were understandably disappointed at the lack of accountability. And all the more so since the statute of limitations protected most of the predators from either criminal prosecution or civil litigation. And the report, in spite of its detail, had one glaring omission: it only examined the records of diocesan priests, while members of religious orders, male and female, were not even considered. Some survivors had hoped that the federal Department of Justice would launch a Racketeer Influenced and Corrupt Organizations Act (RICO) investigation of the Catholic Church. It never happened.[41]

Predatory Nuns

The Pennsylvania report, in spite of its shortcomings, brought a number of tangible results. On October 17, 2018, two priests identified in it, David Paulsen and James Sweeney, pleaded guilty to criminal charges. The report itself, and the fact that other states were considering similar inquiries, prompted many dioceses across the country to make a noteworthy gesture of accountability: They began to publish on their websites the names of religious personnel credibly accused of sex crimes against children. The diocese of Tucson, Arizona, had been the first to do this in 2002, but others had been slow to follow. In the aftermath of the Pennsylvania report, however, there was a surge of such disclosures. By January 2020, there were 178 lists on public view from both dioceses and religious orders. The lists were uneven in what they disclosed, as survivors of abuse were quick to point out. Some provided detailed information about the predators and their work assignments; others simply provided names. Members of religious orders were included in some cases, but frequently only diocesan priests made the list.[42]

Not all of the posted lists had appeared voluntarily. At times they were products of negotiated settlements that arose from lawsuits. For example, in April 2015 the diocese of Helena, Montana, in resolving a number of lawsuits brought against it by abuse survivors, agreed to publish a list of predators on its website for "a period of not less than ten years." The list featured 21 diocesan priests and 17 priests and brothers belonging to religious orders, mainly the Jesuits. In addition, 27 nuns were also named as sexual predators, 21 of whom were Ursuline Sisters.[43] The numbers did not garner much publicity, but for those who did notice, the abuse scandal was taking on a new dimension: nuns were sexual predators too and could no longer be ignored. It would take a few more years before the media picked up on it.

Archbishop Timothy Dolan of New York was one of the prelates who balked at publishing a predator list. His pretext was that the names were already in the public domain.[44] In October 2016 he had established the Independent Reconciliation and Compensation Program, which he touted as his way of seeking "reconciliation with those who have been harmed and feel alienated from the Church." The idea was to compensate survivors of abuse on financial terms that the archdiocese could control and without the uncertainty of court-ordered settlements. In accepting the deal, survivors agreed to release the archdiocese from further responsibility for their injuries. Dolan encouraged other dioceses in New York to establish similar programs, and they did so. There was a lot more to it than "healing" and "closure." The archbishop was aware

1. Syllabus of Errors

that survivors and their advocates—Child USA and SNAP, for example—were pressing the state legislature to enact a temporary suspension of the statute of limitations on sexual crimes against minors that, if implemented, could bring a deluge of litigation. The Church's lobbyists in Albany were able to point to the compensation program as proof that the problem was being addressed and that suspending the statute was unnecessary.[45]

Beginning in 2011, the various dioceses in New York State had begun to spend money lobbying politicians in the state legislature in order to prevent modifications to the statute of limitations. A specialized unit known as the Catholic Conference Policy Group was tasked with employing the most powerful lobbying firms in the state to this end. Before the decade was out, lobbying had cost the Church almost three million dollars.[46]

In attempting to protect the status quo, the Church was defending a very restrictive statute of limitations that required both civil and criminal cases to be filed before a victim reached the age of 23, while civil suits against institutions were cut off at age 21. As long as Republicans controlled the state senate, nothing changed. But in the elections of November 2018, Democrats took control of both houses of the state legislature and new legislation became possible. The Child Victims Act, signed into law in January 2019, opened a 12-month "lookback window"—later extended to 24 months—during which victims of sexual assault could file civil suits against their assailants regardless of when the crime had been committed. And when the "window" closed, victims would still be able to file civil suits until the age of 55.[47]

New York was not alone. At least 15 states were already in the process of enacting similar legislation. According to one estimate, the changes in the states of California, New Jersey, and New York alone contained the potential of 5,000 lawsuits against the Church and compensation payments exceeding the four billion dollars it had already parted with since the 1980s.[48]

When New York's lookback window opened on August 14, 2019, a flood of lawsuits appeared, mainly directed at the Catholic Church, but not exclusively so. The Boy Scouts of America, miscellaneous sports coaches, and the other usual suspects were also targeted. On the first day alone there were 400 suits against the Church, by December more than 1,000. Less than a month after the window opened, the diocese of Rochester, facing claims estimated at $500 million, filed for bankruptcy protection. Others followed: Buffalo in February 2020, Syracuse in June

Predatory Nuns

2020, and Rockville Centre in October 2020. Bishop John O. Barres of Rockville Centre explained the bankruptcy move as a means of protecting the Church's "spiritual, charitable and educational missions." Jeff Anderson, the attorney representing some of the plaintiffs in the diocese, called it "strategic, cowardly and wholly self-serving."[49]

It became common practice for law firms representing plaintiffs to release to the public the names of those they were suing. In June 2020, a list of accused was released in the diocese of Albany. Of the 20 identified on the list, 13 were priests and seven were nuns. Of the latter, four were Sisters of St. Joseph and three were Sisters of Mercy. The Sisters of Mercy had been in Albany for many decades, where they operated an extensive network of schools. When Walter and Katherine Graber moved to the area in the early 1920s, they sent their children to be educated by the Sisters. It was a very large family, even by Catholic standards, with 15 children in all. Four of the girls, Anne, Martha, Agnes, and Kay, became Sisters of Mercy as they came of age—a great triumph from the Church's point of view. The triumph was illusionary. Agnes Graber, known in religion as Sister Mercedes, was among the three Sisters of Mercy named on the list of 20 mentioned above. Deceased in 1997, she was accused of the sexual abuse of a minor while teaching at Mercy High School in Albany between 1978 and 1981. There was something of interest too about the Sisters of St. Joseph on the accused list. Three of them, Sisters Giovanna Marie, Marionella Graham, and Rosara Anne, were alleged to have sexually abused minors at St. Joseph's parish school in Green Island between 1961 and 1965. The godless public school, just a couple of blocks away, would surely have been a safer place for children than the nuns' school with three alleged pedophiles on staff.[50]

As states other than New York opened lookback windows, lists of accused religious personnel proliferated. Priests dominated the lists, but nun predators were also identified. The states in question were California, Kentucky, New Jersey, and North Carolina. Washington, D.C., and the Pacific territory of Guam were also included. The Vermont and Guam "windows" were opened permanently.[51] Guam provided a disturbing example of convent crime. In March 2019, a man identified as ABC filed a lawsuit in the local district court against the Sisters of Mercy. He alleged that, in 1958, when he was 12 years old and enrolled in Santa Barbara Catholic School in Dededo, a nun turned him into her sex slave. Two or three times a week she would rendezvous with him outside her sleeping quarters where she "plied her sexual art." The abuse, which he

1. Syllabus of Errors

endured for two years, impaired his ability to concentrate on his studies. Some months later, an amended lawsuit identified the abuser as Sister Camalin. Another nun, Sister Andrea, was also accused of abusing him when he passed into Grade 7. Both Sisters of Mercy were deceased at the time.[52]

The existence of sexual predator nuns had been known for some years—at least as far back as 1992. As already indicated, they had largely avoided publicity while predator priests grabbed the headlines. In time the survivors of abuse by nuns became organized and received the backing of SNAP. One of their strategies was to demand a clear policy respecting the prevention of abuse from the Leadership Conference of Women Religious (LCWR), the national body representing the vast majority of religious sisterhoods. When the LCWR refused to adopt something akin to the Dallas Charter of the American bishops, flawed though it was, there was disappointment. In August 2004, when the Leadership Conference was holding its annual meeting in Fort Worth, Texas, SNAP requested that a group of survivors be allowed 30 minutes to address the delegates. The request was refused. The refusal became an annual event, and every year survivors gathered outside the meeting in protest. The chain of correspondence from the LCWR to SNAP was filled with palaver about the nuns' commitment to protecting children—but there was nothing except stonewalling when it came to action.[53]

And the stories of abusive nuns continued to surface. In 2007 Sister Patricia Mary Anne of Portland, Oregon, was accused of sexually abusing a boy at least 100 times over a two-year period beginning in 1964. And Sister Genevieve Marie of McMinnville, also in Oregon, was accused of cruelty to and "harmful offensive touching" of a boy and girl in the mid- to late 1950s. Both of the accused were Sisters of St. Francis. Portland attorney Kelly Clark, who was representing the survivors in these cases, said: "I have met more resistance these days from religious orders involving nuns, more denial, than I have from any archdiocese or any religious order involving priests."[54]

With the evidence of convent crimes mounting, the LCWR's refusal to even acknowledge the problem made them seem increasingly irrelevant and out of touch. On August 15, 2019, a day after New York opened its lookback window, Sharlet Wagner, the Holy Cross Sister who was president of the Leadership Conference, finally addressed the issue at the organization's annual assembly in Scottsdale, Arizona. Speaking to an audience of almost 700, she said: "It is a source of deep pain for us that, in some instances, our own sisters have been perpetrators of the abuse. This is a truth that we must not attempt to avoid." She added that they should reject cover-ups and secrecy and should ensure that abusers were held responsible.

Members of SNAP, who were picketing the assembly as was their custom, found it unconvincing. They pointed out that the bishops were publishing lists of sexual predators on diocesan websites and had allowed survivors of abuse to address their assemblies—while the nuns had done nothing of the sort. Mary Dispenza, one of SNAP's directors and herself a former nun, was unimpressed and explained: "We are convinced that there are hundreds of nuns and ex-nuns who have hurt innocent kids or vulnerable adults and may still be violating others because they're unsupervised, 'under the radar,' and have experienced no consequences for their destructive actions."[55]

The LCWR did advise its constituent congregations to take allegations of abuse seriously and to provide support for survivors. Beyond that, it was not prepared to act. Its lack of legal authority over its members was the excuse made.[56] When it came to protecting children from sexual abuse, the Leadership Conference had little to offer in terms of leadership.

Conclusion

As it broke into the public domain in the 1980s, the sexual predator priest problem quickly evolved into the Catholic Church's greatest challenge since Martin Luther's defiance in 1517. In America the scandal was marked by a struggle of multiple decades between abuse survivors seeking accountability and justice, and a Church determined to protect its assets, reputation, and what it called its "mission." The bishops employed a number of defensive strategies: shuffling predators from place to place, paying hush money to secure confidentiality, enforcing codes of silence, seeking bankruptcy protection to limit financial losses, and hiding behind statutes of limitations while lobbying to prevent their suspension or liberalization. The Church emerged badly scarred from the battle. Public trust was impaired, and it had lost more than $4 billion in compensation payments. Moreover, countless priests were in jail and several bishops, archbishops, and cardinals had been forced to resign in disgrace for either covering up crimes against children or for participating personally in them.

The scandal and its attendant publicity distracted from a parallel

1. Syllabus of Errors

problem that went largely overlooked until recent years—that of predator nuns. As statutes of limitations respecting child sexual assault were either loosened or suspended, a deluge of abuse allegations appeared that forced convent crime from the shadows. Leaders of religious sisterhoods were uncomfortable even acknowledging the problem. And when they did so it was in language that minimized its true extent. All the more reason for it to command our attention.

2

Foolish Virgins

Novice Nuns and the Vow of Chastity

> In a word, if you desire to possess the purity which becomes the spouse of Jesus, you must cut off all dangerous occasions: you must cherish a holy ignorance of all that is opposed to chastity, and abstain from reading whatever has the slightest tendency to sully the soul.[1]
> —St. Alfonso di Liguori,
> *The True Spouse of Jesus Christ*

Founded in 1840s England by American convert Cornelia Connolly, the religious order known as the Sisters of the Holy Child Jesus had 17 convent schools in that country by the 1960s and many more overseas. In 1962 18-year-old Karen Armstrong, a graduate of one of those schools, entered the order's novitiate in Tripton, Buckinghamshire. Following her training she was sent to study English at St. Anne's College, Oxford. The world of books and literature both intrigued and perplexed the young nun, especially when she encountered descriptions of lovemaking. Let her explain:

> Yes, body fitted body, men and women groaned and panted, but what exactly were they doing? My knowledge of the male body was confined solely to dimly remembered and modestly fig-leaved pictures in art appreciation lessons at school. I hadn't a clue how this alien body worked sexually, and without this all-important information I realized that my understanding of sex was centrally incomplete. In fact, now that I came to think about it, my knowledge of my own body was rudimentary.... How had I come to make a vow of chastity with such a vague idea of what I was renouncing?[2]

That Armstrong was puzzled, if not annoyed, by her own ignorance of the human body and its reproductive functions should not surprise. The Church's exaltation of the celibate state over the married and its

2. Foolish Virgins

ambivalence about sexuality in general meant that those who entered religious life were often left in the dark respecting the body and its natural desires, except of course for dire warnings about sins of the flesh. Which leads to the questions: What did American novice nuns know or learn about sexuality as they prepared to take the vow of chastity? And how did their state of awareness or unawareness prepare them for the social interaction with seculars that their professional work required? We shall begin with some history.

Chastity has always been the most defining characteristic of nuns. It allegedly places them on a higher moral plain than ordinary women, and especially those who are "defiled" by men. The Christian idea that chastity is a necessary condition of the truly virtuous life can be traced to the cult of the Blessed Virgin, and in particular to the belief that Mary was a virgin both before and after the birth of Jesus.[3] As this idea found acceptance in the early Church, it became possible to argue, as Saint Augustine did, that all sexual activity—even in marriage for the purposes of procreation—was somehow tainted with sin.[4] The moral superiority of chastity was reinforced in biographical accounts of early Christian female martyrs. These stories followed a predictable pattern: beautiful Christian woman takes a vow of chastity, rebuffs the advances of a pagan male authority figure, and is horribly tortured and killed while preserving her virginity. Most of these stories were purely fictional, but they do indicate a tradition of consecrated virginity in the Church long before monasticism emerged as an institutional form.[5]

There was no shortage of endorsements of the superiority of virginity to sexual activity in the works of Church fathers and doctors over the centuries. The clearest modern pronouncement on the matter came from Pius XII in his 1954 encyclical, *Sacra Virginitas*. The pope described virginity as "the angelic virtue," citing Saint Cyprian, who had claimed that the preservation of chastity made you equal to "the angels of God."[6] Saint Methodius and Saint Gregory were also quoted approvingly in declaring virginity the equivalent of martyrdom. The reasoning was that virginity was a difficult virtue requiring "a constant vigilance and struggle to contain and dominate rebellious movements of body and soul, a flight from the importunings of this world, a struggle to conquer the wiles of Satan."[7]

Remaining a virgin was not, however, necessarily virtuous in itself. Motivation for doing so was important. It was no good if virginity were chosen in order to "shun the burdens of marriage" or because you wanted to "proudly flaunt your physical integrity."[8] Virginity became virtuous, it was said, only when accompanied by the deliberate act of consecrating it to God in a religious vow. And the consecration had to be until death; it wouldn't do if it were simply a temporary commitment, which had been the case with ancient Rome's vestal virgins, for example.[9]

The origins of monasticism are usually attributed to Pachomius, who gathered a group of ascetically minded men together in an abandoned village on the Nile around 320 CE. His sister established a parallel community of women on the other side of the river. Pachomius devised a simple set of rules to guide both communities in their daily routines of prayer, work, and study. Female monasticism, then, made its appearance at the same time as its male equivalent.[10]

Pachomius's rules were adapted and refined by later saintly figures—Basil of Caesaria, Augustine of Hippo, Benedict of Nursia—as they designed governance structures for monasteries and convents. While there were differences in the details of the various rules, some concepts remained constant: absolute obedience to the abbot or abbess, strict schedules of work and prayer, property held in common, chastity and its accouterments, modesty in dress, and restricted contact with the outside world and with the opposite sex in particular.[11]

Limiting contact with the world was known as "enclosure" or "cloister." It meant staying inside the monastic compound and keeping visitors out. Enclosure was much stricter in female monasticism than in its male counterpart, chastity being the major concern. It was assumed that women were frivolous and weak by nature and more easily beguiled by Satan—an idea linked to the story of Eve, who was led astray by a smooth-talking serpent. The preservation of chastity was fundamental to the logic of the convent. From the earliest days women religious or nuns were considered spouses of Christ whose bodies were off limits to ordinary mortals. Caesarius of Arles, who founded a convent in the sixth century, described nuns as "consecrated virgins, souls vowed to God, who await the coming of the Lord with lighted lamps and a tranquil conscience."[12]

The rule on modest dress was a further safeguard for chastity. By the sixth century religious women wore distinctive if plain clothing that covered the body almost completely and that included a veil on the head. Showing hair had sexual connotations, and it had to be kept from view. Being dressed in the habit for the first time—taking the veil—became a ritualized beginning of a nun's new life in Christ. And the uniformity of habits symbolized a loss of individuality and a commitment to the community and its goals.[13] The ritual of veiling was followed later by the taking of the three vows of poverty, chastity, and obedience—in effect, making a solemn commitment to following the rules or constitutions in their essentials.

While the original model of monasticism was based on the idea of retreat from the world and its wickedness, a new model emerged in the context of the Counter-Reformation of the 1500s. Congregations of women religious such as the Ursulines were active rather than contemplative and undertook useful functions such as educating girls—functions that required a bit more contact with the world.[14]

As the Catholic Church established itself in America, active congregations began to play a critical role in establishing, directing, and staffing its network of institutions—schools, hospitals, orphanages, and the like. The Catholic school system—private, fee-paying, and in direct competition with public schools—would never have achieved its impressive growth without the free labor of countless teaching sisters. Further expansion following the Second World War to accommodate the baby-boom generation meant that the need for more nuns to staff classrooms became urgent. The need was met by systematic and often aggressive recruitment of girls considered suitable for the religious life.[15]

Aggressive recruitment was problematic since it frequently encountered objections from the parents of the girls targeted as convent material. Catholic families who sought social advancement to the middle class tended to be wary of careers in religion. They sensed that their daughters would be happier pursuing their education, embarking on professional careers, and/or marrying well. And they felt that a girl should only enter the convent when she could make mature judgment, had experience of the world, and was familiar with the "facts of life."[16]

The "facts of life" objection can be readily understood since a young woman taking a vow of chastity should presumably have some understanding of what she was renouncing. The objection was a difficult one for the recruiters since the Church was adamant in its opposition to sex education. In *Divini Illius Magistri* (1929) Pope Pius XI had denounced sex education as a "reckless" and "perilous" premise advanced by those who refused "to recognize the innate weakness of humanity." His successor, Pius XII, was equally opposed to instruction on reproduction in schools, but urged Christian parents "carefully and tactfully to lift the veil of the truth, to the degree that appears necessary" while preserving in their children "their natural and particular instinct of shame whereby Providence wills to restrain them from being too easily misled by their passions."[17] The "Pope of Purity," as some of his admirers called him, also objected to instructional manuals on sexuality, even if they were intended for couples about to be married, on the grounds that such literature "greatly exaggerate[d] the importance and scope of the sexual element in life."[18]

The recruiters were well aware that the vast majority of parents were uncomfortable in lifting "the veil of the truth" themselves but somehow wanted their daughters to be fully aware of the implications of chastity before embracing it for life. Fathers Jude Senieur and Godfrey Poage, the two most prominent advocates of aggressive recruitment, were quick to assure such parents that their children would not enter religion in ignorance but would become "acquainted with the facts of life and the true meaning of sex-life" during their novitiate. Their children would be innocent, said Senieur, but it would be "an informed innocence that makes their decision not only an intelligent one, but a very meritorious choice."[19] Poage, in addressing his fellow recruiters, had this advice: "All you need to do is point out how in the seminary or convent their youngsters will get the whole truth about human love and sex—but from God's viewpoint. The only thing they don't get is a sordid or prejudiced approach. All seminarians or novices are better informed before their vows than most couples on the verge of matrimony."[20] It is difficult to fathom exactly what was meant by "the true meaning of sex-life" or "God's viewpoint" on it. It is not unreasonable to assume, however, that these assertions were at least misleading, if not a total misrepresentation of what was really going on. There is little evidence that either novices or nuns were well informed about sexuality, and considerable evidence to the contrary.

The typical candidate for the religious life was a product of the Catholic school system and entered the convent straight from that experience. During the post-war years, she was often a high school graduate, but this was not always so. These teenagers, usually no more than 18 years old, first entered as postulants. The postulancy, the first official stage of religious formation, derived its name from the Latin verb *postulare*, meaning "to ask." In effect, a postulant was asking a congregation to admit her to its ranks upon judging her suitability over the six to 12 months of the program. But she was also deciding if a life in religion was what she wanted for herself. Once both parties were satisfied with the suitability question, the candidate became a novice and found herself in a program that lasted a minimum of one year—the canonical

2. Foolish Virgins

year—and perhaps a second one—the apostolic year—depending on the congregation.[21]

The canonical year of the novitiate was conducted in complete isolation from the outside world—not even contact with family was permitted. Novices followed a strict routine designed to transform them into an obedient and desexualized workforce prepared to staff the Church's institutions without remuneration. The desexualization began early. On reception day, a novice entered the chapel and went through a wedding ceremony in which Jesus was the bridegroom. She was then led away to have her hair sheared off and to be clothed in her religious habit. The habit itself, uncomfortable and impractical, served to disguise her body shape beneath layers of heavy fabric. Free movement now became difficult. Athletic activity—if you don't count croquet—was now impossible, and dancing was out of the question. Patricia O'Donnell, who entered the Adrian Dominicans in 1963, remembered the experience vividly: "The parts of my body that enabled me to attract a man as well as have children were no longer important, and everything about my new habit reinforced this weakened status of my womanhood."[22]

The radical resocialization that was at the heart of the novitiate required the internalization of a deportment and decorum that were peculiar to the convent. A novice, in learning to behave like a nun, was becoming, in Midge Turk's memorable phrase, "one of those serene gliding creatures."[23] Posture was important. A nun stood erect and never slouched or leaned against a wall. When sitting down she did not cross her legs. Her hands were kept hidden from view beneath voluminous garments—unless deployed usefully in some way. And she never stretched in the presence of others. Moving about was subject to similar strictures. A nun walked but never ran. She walked purposefully but without haste. She made as little noise as possible while doing so, and kept her eyes cast downwards. "Custody of the eyes" was an essential and hard-won skill; there could be no looking around, no smiles or nods of recognition for a friend, and no humming or whistling. Father Charles J. Mullaly explained it this way: "Custody of the eyes curbs worldly curiosity and is a sign of the humility that goes with the Religious state. It should be easy for a Sister to guard her eyes. She is unlike the woman of the world whose eyes ever seek new sights and new objects to feed a frivolous soul sated with the things of earth. A Sister will only see what will lift her thoughts to God."[24] The story was often told of Saint Clare's resolve never to fix her gaze on the face of a man. One day during Mass, however, she lifted her eyes to see the consecrated host and found herself looking at the priest's face, an episode that disturbed her greatly.[25]

The manner of personal communication was also regulated. A nun spoke in subdued tones and only when necessary. Casual and spontaneous remarks were out of the question. She did not gesticulate with her hands or crack jokes. She did not look people in the eye or become familiar.[26] Every task was approached with careful deliberation and in accordance with age-old customs. At least two convents even had protocols for eating bananas; they could not be eaten "the monkey way."[27]

Novices followed a strict schedule of prayer, physical labor, and study to prepare them for profession day, when they would take the vows of poverty, chastity, and obedience. The behaviors required in the "evangelical counsels" were not to be embraced only after the vows were taken; rather they needed years of practice to ensure that the commitments were not entered into lightly. The novitiate was much more than preparation for the vows; it was a carefully monitored practice of them. There was no question of a "last fling" before profession day. It was claimed that in living according to the vows, a nun was imitating the life of Christ and removing impediments to serving him without reserve. Father Felix Kirsch explained it like this: "The vows represent the voluntary giving up of the objects of human desires, and hence remove the three chief obstacles that stand in the way of the perfect reign of love and virtue in our hearts. These obstacles are the greed of gold, the lust of sensual pleasures, and the inordinate attachment to our own will and our own opinion."[28] We shall focus on the vow of chastity.

According to the brief descriptions we have of the life of Jesus, he remained chaste or uninvolved physically with anyone. Father Bernard Mullahy put it this way: "Christ was chaste; born of a Virgin, He lived a life of the most radiant virginity the world has ever seen. It is the desire to imitate the radiance of this purity that draws the religious to make a vow of perpetual chastity."[29] The vow meant that all sensual or sexual intimacy with someone of the opposite or of the same sex, or with yourself, was forbidden. One former nun described it as being "pretty much dead from the neck down."[30] One of the concerns prompting parents to oppose their daughters' vocations was the fear that they might not understand what they were giving up when taking the vow of chastity. Was this concern legitimate?

In Marie Gass's interviews with 73 ex-nuns, 55 answered the question respecting their prior knowledge of sex upon entering the convent. Of those respondents, 13 confessed to complete ignorance.[31] Of the 42

2. Foolish Virgins

who claimed to be informed, many admitted to being vague on details. Fran Fisher's interviews with 49 former nuns revealed that very few in the sample had "informed sexual knowledge" when they began their postulancies and novitiates. Many admitted to being scared of sexuality because it was unknown and mysterious.[32]

There is further evidence from the autobiographies of former nuns. Deborah Larsen, who entered the Sisters of Charity of the Blessed Virgin Mary in Dubuque, Iowa, in 1960, upon observing two of her fellow novices gazing at one another, noted: "Most of us barely knew how men and women made love, much less—and we didn't want to think about it—women and women."[33] Susan Bassler, who became a novice with the Ursulines on Long Island, New York, in 1960, knew nothing about sex, having been sheltered from anything vulgar or erotic during her youth. Here are her words: "I hadn't had a serious boyfriend or a passionate kiss. I didn't consider myself abnormal, because I knew others who were living the same way. I didn't even hear the word 'masturbation' until I was in college. It was alluded to, of course. But I didn't do it. I was saving myself."[34]

Some novices were informed about human sexuality, but often what they knew was not particularly helpful. When Orice Klaas was 12 and entering puberty, her mother gave in to her persistent questions and disclosed the basic facts of conception and birth to her, describing sex as a necessary evil for the purposes of procreation. Klaas was horrified at what she learned and resolved never to marry. She never masturbated and, in 1958, at age 15, she entered the Benedictine convent at Mount Angel, Oregon. At the time, she resolved to ignore her body "from the waist down."[35]

Teresa Price entered the Ursuline novitiate in Glennon Heights, Crystal City, Missouri, in July 1955, when she was 17 years of age. She had received no formal sex education at the Catholic school she attended in Idaho, except for harangues by the local priest about the dangers of getting too close to boys. Even so, she did learn about baby making in the "dirty talk" of her peers in the rough logging town of her youth. She was convinced, however, that some of her fellow Ursuline novices did not have that basic knowledge.[36]

If many or even most novices were "innocents" respecting sexuality, what did they learn about it before making the commitment to chastity? Larsen and her fellow novices with the Sisters of Charity of the Blessed Virgin Mary were given a book that explained what she called "the hydraulics of sex," with explicit references to penis, vagina, and penetration. In discussing the book, the novice mistress admitted that sex was "very pleasurable," but since she had never actually experienced it herself, she added that "it would be hard to understand the particulars of the gratification." Furthermore, she had discussed the subject with a married laywoman who had assured her that she "didn't much enjoy sex and that it was something of a nuisance." With this insight at her disposal, Larsen reasoned that the vow of chastity would not be such a hardship after all.[37]

Nancy Sodeman's experience was similar when she was a novice with the Missionary Sisters of the Holy Rosary in Bryn Mawr, Pennsylvania, in 1962. In a private interview shortly before profession day, the novice mistress explained the basics of "the marital act" so that she would understand the sacrifice entailed in the vow. In describing the interactions of penis and vagina, Mother Benedict assured Sodeman that the act was "not very enjoyable" and often painful for the woman, while the man received great pleasure.[38]

A native of Oklahoma, Joyce Vandever joined the Sisters Adorers of the Most Precious Blood in Kansas in 1959, when she was 18. Her novice mistress, Sister Mary, informed her charges that they needed to know what they were relinquishing before taking the vow of chastity. She then proceeded to explain the "mechanics" of intercourse while reading solemnly from her notes. She admitted that sex was "very pleasurable"—going red-faced as she did so. Vandever had been unclear of the details of sex and reproduction until Sister Mary's explanation, which had been unusually frank and honest in the context. She reflected on giving up marriage, sex, and babies and was prepared to accept it, saying to herself, "All for thee, Jesus."[39]

Far too often, the explanations were vague and perplexing to novices who may have been unclear about what it was they were being asked to renounce. Sister Lorraine, novice mistress with the Benedictines at Mount Angel, Oregon, in the late 1950s, told her charges that celibacy was the renunciation of married love, not because it was evil, but because the religious state was superior. Details were not forthcoming. "The vow of chastity," she began, "frees us from having a husband and from being obliged to bear children." Then came a fairly typical warning: "You must avoid every temptation that would lead you to expressing the desires of the flesh. Strengthen your devotion to Jesus, your future bridegroom, and love every member of the community with a chaste heart. This will keep you pure and holy in the eyes of God."[40]

2. Foolish Virgins

When Mary Zenchoff joined the Sisters of the Third Order of St. Dominic in New York in 1952, she was 18 years old. She admitted that she and her fellow novices "barely knew" their own bodies. When it came to instruction on the vow of chastity and what it entailed, novice mistress Mother Josepha was not very helpful. She only provided "a few red-faced explanations" that were not any better than the vague admonitions Zenchoff had received from another nun when in Grade 7. The young novice was, however, prepared to remain ignorant on the matter, which she rationalized as follows: "I knew I wasn't getting married, so why give a class in calculus to students who needed to learn only the multiplication tables."[41]

By her own account, Marion Kenneally was a naïve and easily manipulated 18-year-old when she entered the novitiate of the Holy Union Sisters in Fall River, Massachusetts, in 1952. The instructions she received on the vow of chastity from novice mistress Mother Consolata were typically vague. Mother Consolata never once mentioned sexual desire but emphasized that through the vow, sisters would be able to "sublimate" their need for human attachments. Kenneally never questioned what she learned or didn't learn; she was in love with the illusion of being a bride of Christ.[42]

Fifty teenage girls who had just graduated from school joined the novitiate of the Sisters of St. Joseph of Carondelet in St. Paul, Minnesota, in 1963. In studying the constitutions of the congregation, they learned of their obligation to "abstain from every interior and exterior act opposed to chastity and contrary to the sixth and ninth commandments of God." They were urged to impose controls on their thoughts and passions and to practice mortification. And they were warned about conversations with seculars, especially those of the opposite sex. Marge Rogers Barrett, one of the novices in this cohort, found it all very confusing. She was unsure how the interest she had once had in boys was now supposed to be replaced with a general love of all humankind. "Sublimation" was the word used to describe the process, but no details were provided. If she learned anything from the instruction it was to be cautious around men and wary of friendship with women.[43]

It was Father John E. Moffat, a well-known Jesuit retreat master, who provided instruction on the vow of chastity for the novices at the Ursuline convent in Crystal City, Missouri, in October 1957. He used as his text Pope Pius XII's encyclical, *Sacra Virginitas* (1954). The novices learned that consecrated virgins were privileged mortals selected

Predatory Nuns

by God himself to transcend corrupt human nature. Physical pleasure, therefore, was for lesser beings; truly holy people would never debase themselves with it. Teresa Price, who was in the audience, found it all very unsatisfactory. Here's what she had to say:

> The reality of never having a loving physical relationship with a man, of never giving birth to a child, or holding a newborn infant to nurse was never explicitly spoken nor pondered. The all-too-human aspect of feminine hormones coursing through our developing bodies exposing physical and psychological desires was glossed over as "rebellious movements of the body and soul," and as sinister "wiles of the devil" that we must struggle to overcome.[44]

The record of novitiate programs in preparing their young women for an informed commitment to chastity was at best mixed, and there were far too many cases in which novices were kept completely in the dark. Margaret Lynch was already a junior professed nun with the Sisters of Charity of St. Elizabeth in Convent Station, New Jersey, in the mid–1950s when she learned how human reproduction worked. Her spiritual director, Sister Caritas, arranged to have a sister who was a registered nurse lecture the juniors on the subject in order to combat ignorance. Lynch learned much from these lectures, and, judging by the questions from her fellow juniors, ignorance about sexuality was widespread. Some thought that kissing could cause pregnancy.[45] It is well to remember that these junior professed nuns had already taken the vow of chastity.

Rose Gordy entered Mount Mercy College in Oakland, Pennsylvania, in 1957, when she was 18 years old. When she took her vows as a Sister of Mercy three years later, she was still confused about sexuality and reproduction: "I never quite grasped what I had given up by my vow of Chastity. My pre-convent sex education and subsequent sexual experiences had been so slight. My only understanding of celibacy was as an up-in-the-clouds concept."[46]

A contemporary religious writer, Father John McGoey, readily acknowledged the problem of sexual ignorance among "most religious." Here are his words:

> There is no reasonable excuse for withholding full knowledge of sex from those making the vow of chastity. Yet most religious do not have this knowledge. Any court of the land would consider it illegal to sell something to a client ignorant of what he was getting, with as little knowledge about it as the average religious has about the material of her vow. Lack of sufficient knowledge invalidates the ordinary contract. Yet through ignorance or

2. Foolish Virgins

narrowness, due knowledge is even withheld from many taking the vow of chastity.[47]

In his book *Sister's Vow of Chastity* (1965), Father Philip E. Dion, lecturer at the Seminary of Our Lady of Angels, Albany, New York, shared McGoey's views: "Yet such ignorance in regard to the renunciation demanded by the vow of chastity has been known to exist and, moreover, to lead to mental torture, scrupulosity, needless discouragement—and often to temptations to abandon a life that has come to appear to be well-nigh impossible of observance." He knew of those who equated ignorance with innocence, observing that in some convents excellent chapters on chastity had "literally been torn out of spiritual reading books" before being made available to sisters. Before taking her vows, he added, a novice had not only a right, but a duty to understand what she was renouncing, and those instructing her could not assume that she had such knowledge or that her knowledge was accurate. In order to remedy the problem, he then proceeded to describe the process of human reproduction in detail, including sexual arousal, penetration, and so forth, all of which was presented as part of God's wonderful plan of creation:

> God devised the climax of the beautiful act of human generation to be reached when, after the organs of both husband and wife have been prepared by nature, the male organ of the husband penetrates the vagina of the wife. Beyond being merely a physical source of extremely pleasurable sensations, this union is likewise a moment of supreme spiritual joy to the partners in marriage.

Dion then went on to describe pregnancy and childbirth, and the pain of the latter experience, which he also attributed to God as punishment for the sin of Eve and which was accordingly visited on all her descendants.[48]

McGoey and Dion were right. Ignorance of human sexuality was a problem in the convent and in particular in the context of the formation of novices. But the problem was much bigger than that in the broader ranks of celibate women and men. In fact, it reached to the very highest level of the hierarchy. Consider the following description of sexual intercourse between a married man and his wife by Karol Wojtyła, later Pope John Paul II—a passage almost laughable in its absurdity and which could be interpreted as a justification for rape:

> It is in the very nature of the act that the man plays the active role and takes the initiative, while the woman is a comparatively passive partner, whose

function it is to accept and to experience. For the purposes of the sexual act it is enough for her to be passive and unresisting, so much so that it may even take place without her volition while she is in a state in which she has no awareness at all of what is happening—for instance while she is asleep, or unconscious.[49]

The view of McGoey and Dion that novices ought to be informed about sex was not widely shared, however. Many of their contemporaries held to the idea that ignorance was the best antidote to the problem. Father Paulo Provera, for example, conceded that curiosity about "natural processes of which one is ignorant" was not in itself sinful, but attempting to satisfy that curiosity could lead to "a lot of trouble." "In general," he advised, "it is dangerous to read books on the subject, for this can be a way of indulging in fancies of the imagination; many begin their perversion in this way."[50]

Perversion may seem like a strong term, but it was used as a generic descriptor for two phenomena that novice mistresses and spiritual advisors believed were poor indicators of success in chastity: particular friendships and solitary vice. Father James Alberione, in a book of advice for mothers superior, warned them to be vigilant of "abnormal sexual attraction towards persons of the same sex" among candidates for the religious life since it was "very difficult to correct this tendency when it is accentuated."[51] And in a collection of conferences for religious, Father Frederick Hoeger reminded his readers that the Devil did not abandon his efforts to stimulate the sexual instinct among those who had dedicated themselves to "spiritual motherhood." In fact, sometimes Satan even tried to "sidetrack it into abnormal outlets."[52]

Among the Sisters of Providence, St. Mary-of-the-Woods, Indiana, novices were obliged to draw up lists of the people with whom they had spent time during recreation. The novice mistress examined the lists to see if any patterns of frequent association were developing.[53] Mother Mary Hubert Manion, mistress with the Sisters, Servants of the Immaculate Heart of Mary (Monroe, Michigan) between 1938 and 1956, kept a close eye on novices who got on well with one another lest the influence of Satan be detected. Her rule governing the number of people socializing together was "seldom one, never two, always three or more."[54]

Prohibitions on two people spending time together were commonplace in novitiates. Sister Lorraine, novice mistress with the Benedictines in Mount Angel, Oregon, in the late 1950s, warned that twosomes could degenerate into "particular friendships." Such friendships, she

2. Foolish Virgins

explained, could encourage the development of "inordinate attachments," obsession and jealousy that threatened the vow of chastity. The vague language in which these dangers was couched puzzled Orice Klaas until a fellow novice explained that the nuns feared they might become homosexuals: "Homosexuals—you know—when two women do it with one another." These words perplexed and terrified Klaas. Awake at night, she wondered how two women would even "do it." On a subsequent occasion, Sister Lorraine pulled out a letter that had purportedly been intercepted between two former members of the community and read out parts of it. The writer wrote of her longing for her lover and proposed another tryst at their "secret spot behind the Grotto." Klaas was now more confused and shocked than before and wondered if she could ever even have a friend. Chastity seemed "impossibly difficult."[55]

Placing impediments in the way of finding a willing partner was helpful, but there was still the problem of what you could do when you were all alone. Some writers considered masturbation a problem of such magnitude that it constituted a virtual rejection of Christ's call. Here is Father Alberione: "The solitary sin, too, is not easily corrected, yet after a sufficient test, persons once guilty of it can be admitted to religious life. But a long test and sure proof is required; at times, it is necessary to wait three years and even more to make sure there are no more falls."[56]

Since the combined postulancy and novitiate typically lasted for almost three years, there was lots of time for "a long test and sure proof." Father Felix Kirsch was equally adamant on this point. He advised an extensive period of probation to ensure that "the habit of mortal sin" was really conquered, especially in cases where there were "overpowering outbursts of nature."[57] Father Paul Philippe, a well-known theologian and retreat master, acknowledged that his fellow male experts on the subject could not agree on the actual length of the "sufficiently protracted period of complete victory" without a "fall" that a novice was supposed to demonstrate before being admitted to her vows. There was little hope, he surmised, for those who sinned "by themselves with frenzy." But if a novice showed determination to conquer her habit by making small and constant sacrifices, he believed that she should be given a chance, even if it meant, at the discretion of the mistress, extending the novitiate by six months to ensure total "victory."

But how would the novice mistress know of such delicate matters? Father Philippe suggested that if a mistress gained the complete confidence of her novices, disclosure would be forthcoming. A novice who kept her habit of solitary pleasure a secret, however, would have to admit it in confession since it was a mortal sin and a ticket to damnation. The confessor would therefore know all and would advise her to reveal her habit to the mistress. In the event that she refused, the confessor could compel her to inform the mistress that he opposed her admission to the vows and the right decision would then be taken.[58]

It is well to remember that in 1975 the Church reiterated its age-old condemnation of masturbation. *Persona Humana: Declaration on Certain Questions Concerning Sexual Ethics*, a document from the Congregation for the Doctrine of the Faith issued in response to an alleged increase in "the corruption of morals" and the "unbridled exaltation of sex," made it clear that extramarital sex and homosexual activity were in violation of Church doctrine and its "authentic interpretation of natural law." So too was masturbation, which was described as "an intrinsically and seriously disordered act."[59]

How should the novice combat temptations against chastity? According to Alberione, erotic fantasies should be "banished at once" without thinking about them. "It is in this flight that safety lies," he advised. "The Blessed Virgin is to be invoked and then the mind is to be turned to other things."[60] Hoeger suggested keeping busy, noting that very few religious had much time to spare in any case. He also championed a bit of pain: "Planned mortification, with purity in view, is almost a necessity for the preservation of chastity."[61] René Biot and Pierre Galimard, French doctors who advised the Church on medical matters connected to the religious life, agreed: "It may be opportune with certain subjects to advise corporal penances, and a voluntary privation—even a few strokes of the discipline is often good training."[62] And Father Hubert van Zeller, in a 1957 book of advice for monks and nuns, had this to say: "To prevent ourselves from pampering the body we have to chastise it. If we do not chastise it, it will, with its constant demand to be pampered, chastise us. Even when we weaken, listening to our lower nature, we get no peace; our higher nature reproaches us."[63] Writing a few years later, Father John E. Moffatt advised nuns, young and old, against softness, sloth, idle dreaming, and "overindulgence in delicacies," adding: "The occasional sting of mortification is a *sine qua non* to maintain the soul in a wholesome, healthy state to meet and repulse the assaults made by the foe upon the angelic virtue."[64] Father Philip Dion advised nuns to not be surprised if attraction to the opposite sex appeared occasionally, especially were they to meet a handsome man.

2. Foolish Virgins

Inadvertent sexual arousal, he said, was not sinful in itself, as long as it was not prolonged or deliberate. He, too, championed mortification as long as it was in accordance with community rules and had the approval of a spiritual director.[65]

Mortification, or self-inflicted pain, was not unknown among congregations at the time, although it began to fall into disuse in the 1960s. As a novice with the Sisters of the Immaculate Heart of Mary in Hollywood, California, in 1949, Midge Turk received early instruction from her mistress, Mother Regina, on how to make flagellation whips from Venetian blind cords. She and her fellow novices were told only to use the whips on their bare backs, legs, and buttocks in private and at a specified hour on Wednesday and Friday afternoons. They were not supposed to draw blood.[66] The Ursulines of Long Island, New York, had a similar practice when Susan Bassler entered their novitiate in 1960. One of the first recreational activities for the novices was the fashioning of personal whips with five strands from knotted twine. The strands represented the "five holy wounds of Jesus." At bedtime on Fridays, these young women, at a given signal, lifted their nightgowns and lashed themselves while reciting the Lord's Prayer.[67] The Sisters of St. Joseph issued whips to their novices both in Baltimore and Cleveland to be used on their bare flesh as the occasion warranted. The practice made sense to Mary Jane Masterson since it allowed her to make reparation for her own sins and for those of others.[68]

There was a long tradition of self-imposed physical suffering in Catholic monasticism, and many prominent theologians and doctors of the Church advocated such practices to suppress the annoyance of sensual feelings. An oft-repeated story was that of Saint Benedict, who threw himself naked into a growth of nettles and thorns in order to subdue the flesh.[69] In a more recent example, Josémaría Escrivá de Balaguer (1902–1975), the Spanish priest who founded Opus Dei, combatted weaknesses of the flesh by regular self-flagellation with a cat-o'-nine-tails, smearing his bathroom with blood as he did so.[70]

Novitiate training took place under the watchful gaze of the mistress of novices, one of whose tasks was to weed out anyone considered unsuitable for the constraints of convent life. Only those who had adjusted well to the radical resocialization were allowed to proceed to the vows of obedience, poverty, and chastity and enter the ranks of junior professed sisters. It was presumed they were ready to obey without questioning, willing to work without pay, and had renounced their sexuality.

Conclusion

Chastity and its preservation were central to the purpose and function of monasticism. Partial removal from a wicked world; a strict regime of work, prayer, discipline, and surveillance; and a solemn vow to reject the pleasures of the flesh were supposed to secure for nuns a virgin-like purity unsullied by either the touch or gaze of a man or woman. The structures of constraint and control recognized that chastity was the most difficult of the evangelical counsels. And for that reason, it received far more attention than the vows of obedience and poverty during the period of novitiate formation.

Even so, there was a great ambivalence in novitiates with respect to the nature and content of instruction on chastity, and especially when it came to sex education. It is well to remember that the overwhelming majority of novices were products of Catholic schools and were often innocents with only a vague understanding—and sometimes none at all—of how the human species reproduced itself. But much depended on the novitiate they entered. Some programs provided specifics of "the marital act," some limited themselves to red-faced euphemisms, and there were those that had nothing to offer beyond dire warnings against demonic temptations. The lack of consistency in what was provided mirrored disagreements on the matter among clerical writers who advised the convent system. There were those who argued that the vow of chastity was worthless if you didn't know what you were forsaking in taking it, while others felt that innocence was virtuous in itself and the best antidote to fleshly desires.

Even when novices took their vows and entered the ranks of professed sisters, chastity remained a challenge. Prayer, work, rituals of penitence, warnings about the wiles of Satan, and a heavy dose of Saint Alfonso's "holy ignorance" were never enough to obliterate the desire for human intimacy. As we shall see, particular friendships were not unknown within the convent and could at times take an abusive form in situations entailing imbalances of power. A much greater problem arose when psychologically and socially immature nuns were placed in charge of young people and where their authority as people of God went unquestioned. Chastity may have been at the heart of the convent system, but when it faltered, it became its greatest peril.

3

A Laying On of Hands
Older Nuns and Younger Ones

> In the case of Sisters, the combination of celibacy, intimate and communal living arrangements, and an historical lack of openness with regard to sexual identity and sexuality may create an environment that encourages invitations to sexual activity by some women.[1]
> —Chibnall, Wolf, and Duckro, 1998

Donatus of Besançon (594–660), a bishop in what is now eastern France, was the author of a monastic rule for nuns. Concerned at the possibility of physical intimacy or sensuality, he decreed that, ideally, nuns should sleep alone and fully clothed.[2] The fears of this Dark Ages cleric continued to haunt female monasticism over the centuries. Would a group of women confined together behind convent walls and largely cut off from the world and the men in it turn to themselves in the search for intimacy? Or would they do so anyway as their first preference? Would their vow of chastity and spiritual marriage to Jesus be enough to ward off the wiles of Satan who despised their way of life and strove to undermine it by preying on the weakness of the flesh?

"Particular friendships" was the peculiar euphemism employed in convents to describe same-sex relationships between nuns. Novices received many a dire warning throughout their training respecting the moral hazards inherent in getting too friendly with any "particular" member of the community. The specifics of the danger were rarely spelled out, much to the perplexity of those new to convent life. The vigilance of the novice mistress and strict rules governing social interaction were supposed to safeguard the situation. It is worth noting here one other structural arrangement that was most likely put in place for the same purpose.

In most convent compounds the novitiate building was separate from that which housed the professed nuns. Social contact between professed nuns and postulants or novices was limited. While they all shared the same chapel and refectory, they were placed in different sections to restrict interaction. It was never explained to those who went through the novitiate why this segregation was necessary, but it did not stop them from speculating. During her postulancy with the Sisters of St. Joseph (Cleveland) in the late 1940s, Mary Jane Masterson surmised that the still-worldly habits of those who had yet to take their vows might disturb those who had already done so. The bad influence could work in reverse too, she thought. If professed nuns showed any dissatisfaction with the religious life, might it not discourage postulants and novices from pursuing their vocations?[3] Marta Danylewycz, in her study of two congregations in nineteenth-century Québec, described the isolation of nuns-in-training as a measure to shelter them "from the negative influences of some of the less exemplary professed members of the community."[4]

But the mutual isolation was not absolute, and "negative influences" could at times prevail. Patricia Marks joined the Religious Sisters Filippini novitiate in Morristown, New Jersey, in 1959, only to discover—and she refused to believe it at first—that one of the professed nuns was having "a very, very intense sexual relationship" with one of her fellow novices. The nun and the novice left shortly afterwards.[5] Michelle Callahan entered the Sisters of the Immaculate Heart of Mary in Los Angeles in 1966. While still a postulant she had sexual affairs with Sister Paul Emmanuelle, a professed nun, and Sister Dominic Anne, a novice. At the time the order was reshaping its practices in accordance with Second Vatican Council expectations, and the looser rules permitted greater social interaction across convent ranks. Her contemporary and close friend Jeanne Córdova was also attracted to women—in particular the beautiful and elegant novice Sister Antonia Marie (a pseudonym)—but never acted on her inclinations until she had left religious life at the end of the postulancy.[6]

Same-sex relationships also existed within specific convent ranks—sometimes leading to departures, sometimes not. The Sisters of the Immaculate Heart of Mary expelled 11 of the 1948 novitiate class after a few weeks for a number of reasons, including particular friendships, some of them genuinely sexual, some too close for comfort.[7] During Mary Gilligan's novitiate with the Sisters of Providence, St. Mary-of-the-Woods, Indiana, in the mid–1960s, two of her companions struck up a particular friendship that they refused to relinquish in spite of gossip and surveillance. They were both asked to withdraw.[8]

3. A Laying On of Hands

Sister Paul Emmanuelle, IHM, who had initiated a same-sex relationship with postulant Michelle Callahan, explained that there were four kinds of gay nuns: "Those who are and do; those who are and don't; those who are, do, and deny it; and those who confined themselves to emotional romance and hand-holding."[9] The complexity of these relationships within the confines of convent culture was brought into public view with the publication in 1985 of *Lesbian Nuns: Breaking Silence*, an anthology edited by Nancy Manahan and Rosemary Keefe Curb that documented the experiences of 50 former nuns. Banned in Boston and denounced by the Catholic Church, it received national attention because of shrewd marketing by the publishers and co-editors.[10]

These stories and struggles are interesting in themselves and especially so as illustrations of the Church's confused teachings of sexuality. But they do not give us a full picture of particular friendship rule-breaking in convents. The only survey that addresses the issue is that of Halstead and Halstead in the mid–1970s, and the 75 respondents were ex-nuns. A survey of those who stayed in religious life might have given different results. In any case, the researchers established that 21 percent of those completing the questionnaire had had homosexual encounters while in the convent.[11]

But what if some were unwilling participants? Chibnall, Wolf, and Duckro's 1998 study of the unwelcome sexual experiences of nuns is instructive here and all the more so since it surveyed women still in religious life rather than those who had already left. Twenty-five hundred questionnaires were distributed and 1,164 returned (46 percent). At the time, the total number of nuns in the country had declined from a high of 180,000 in 1965 to around 89,000. The subjects were in active rather than in contemplative congregations. They were preponderantly Caucasian and either were or had been involved in teaching. All states were represented. The study found that, while priests were the principal source of harassment, "more than one Sister in ten" reported experiencing "unwanted sexual attention within the community of Sisters." Those initiating the sexual encounters tended to be older nuns in positions of authority such as mentor, novice mistress, or mother superior.[12]

The imbalance of power in these cases raises the possibility of exploitation. Were there instances of sexual abuse in which younger nuns acquiesced against their wills to their superiors' demands for fear of reprisal? The answer to this question will be found in a number of case studies. It is well to remember that sexual predator nuns in positions of power are not unknown in the history of female monasticism.

Predatory Nuns

Before turning to the North American examples, a brief digression to review two European cases will provide historical perspective.

In 1613 Benedetta Carlini, a 23-year-old nun in the Theatine Convent of the Mother of God in Pescia, the Grand Duchy of Tuscany, began to experience mystical visions. The visions being sometimes frightening, the young Sister Bartolomea Crivelli was asked to share her cell. In time Sister Benedetta was accepted as a true mystic and received the stigmata or holy wounds of Jesus. In 1619 she was elected abbess. But some Church officials remained skeptical. Fake mystics were not uncommon and, besides, visions, even if genuine, might be demonic in origin. In 1622 the newly appointed papal nuncio in the duchy sent a number of clerics to examine Benedetta and her claims. The testimony of Sister Bartolomea, her cellmate, shocked the investigators. The young nun provided graphic descriptions of sexual activities between the two of them, including mutual masturbation, the forceful kissing of genitals, and intercourse: "And she would stir on top of her so that both of them corrupted themselves." All of this was initiated by Benedetta, who claimed that it was not her but her guardian angel, Splenditello, who was responsible. Bartolomea had always felt guilty about the sinful nature of the encounters but acquiesced for fear of the formidable abbess. When questioned by the investigators, Benedetta denied all knowledge of sex but evidently was not very convincing. Saint Teresa of Avila, herself given to mystical raptures, had recommended life imprisonment for nuns guilty of the "sin of sensuality," and that was Sister Benedetta's fate. She died in 1661 having spent more than three decades imprisoned in the convent.[13]

Childless, twice widowed, and in poor health, German aristocrat Katharina von Hohenzollern-Sigmaringen moved to Rome in 1858 where she entered the convent of Sant'Ambrogio. At first, she was impressed with her novice mistress, Sister Maria Luisa (born Maria Ridolfi)—beautiful, charming, and only 27 years old at the time. But her suspicions were aroused when she learned that Maria Luisa experienced frequent visions, received letters from the Virgin Mary that appeared in a locked casket, made prophesies, performed exorcisms, and invited novices to share her cell at night. Shortly after she challenged the novice mistress about her practices and claims, Katharina fell ill and believed she was being poisoned. Rescued from the convent by a German archbishop whom she knew, she wrote a report on the convent goings-on that resulted in an inquiry by the Roman Inquisition. Dominican friar Vincenzo Sallua, who conducted the inquiry between December 1859

3. A Laying On of Hands

and February 1862, was horrified at what he found. Although the nuns of the Regulated Third Order of Holy Saint Francis resident in Sant'Ambrogio were supposed to live lives of strict enclosure and austerity, it was revealed that Maria Luisa had established a lax set of rules based on her visions and heavenly letters and that her authority went unquestioned. Moreover, when the mistress invited novices to her cell, she claimed her vagina contained a liquid of great purifying and sanctifying power that she wished to share with them by entwining their naked bodies together. During Maria Luisa's own interrogation, she confessed to the entire litany of allegations against her—feigned holiness, "female sodomy," poisonings, and the like. She was sentenced to 18 years of monastic imprisonment. Although released when the Kingdom of Italy annexed the last remnants of the Papal States in 1870, things did not go well for her. Mentally and physically damaged, she spent time in an asylum, fell into destitution, and died in obscurity. The Regulated Third Order, to which she had belonged, was dissolved following the inquiry that led to her downfall.[14]

The Church's discomfort with sexuality and its obsession with secrecy meant that these two stories remained hidden in the archives for centuries. Only the diligence of two outstanding historians, Judith Brown of Stanford University and Hubert Wolf of the University of Münster, brought them to light in recent decades. The stories followed a similar trajectory: ambitious young nuns laid claim to supernatural gifts in order to advance to positions of power in their convents. Once in power, the supernatural was again invoked to facilitate and justify sexual depredations. The austere regimentation that defined convent culture was ruptured by an explosive convergence of mysticism, fleshly desire, domination, and submission. Could anything of this sort take place in modern America? Yes, but shorn of the mysticism and exoticism. Three case studies shall be presented by way of illustration.

Sister Gloria Czarniewicz, Sisters of the Holy Family of Nazareth

The religious order known as the Sisters of the Holy Family of Nazareth was founded in Rome in 1875 by Polish aristocrat Mary Frances Siedliska. Its purpose was to operate schools, hospitals, and orphanages while seeking "reparation for the outrages committed ... against the Divine Majesty by continual prayer for the needs of the Church and

Predatory Nuns

the Sovereign Pontiff." In 1885 Mother Siedliska led an entourage of 11 of her nuns to Chicago, where they opened parish schools for the Polish immigrant community. The order subsequently expanded its operations in the U.S. until it formed itself into three provinces or administrative regions. And all the while it retained its ethnic identity—recruiting new members mainly, although not exclusively, from among Polish-American women.[15]

One of those so recruited was born Victoria Czarniewicz in 1927, the third child of Polish immigrants. In her youth she attended St. Stanislaus Kostka Elementary School and the well-regarded Girls' High School in her native Brooklyn, New York. She worked as a bookkeeper for five years after graduation and then, in December 1950, became a postulant with the Sisters of the Holy Family of Nazareth at their novitiate in Torresdale, Pennsylvania. Upon taking her vows, Sister Gloria, as she was now known, worked in various capacities for the order but principally as a high school business teacher. Her passions included collecting paraphernalia based on Snoopy, Charlie Brown's pet beagle in the Peanuts comic strip, and baking, potato pancakes and Linzer tarts being her specialties.[16]

Jean Patricia Henninger was 20 years old when she took her vows with the Sisters of the Holy Family of Nazareth. Shortly afterwards, during the summer of 1968, she was assigned to work at St. Christopher Ottilie children's services in the village of Sea Cliff, Long Island, New York. Sister Gloria Czarniewicz was mother superior at the convent. Beginning in September that year, a serious problem arose between the two nuns. One evening Czarniewicz allegedly came to Henninger's bedroom when she was asleep, lay on top of her, and initiated sexual fondling. When Henninger resisted, she was told that nothing had happened and that there was no point in attempting to report it since nobody would take the word of one so recently in religious life against that of a mother superior. The sexual abuse continued from time to time until February 1969 when Czarniewicz was transferred elsewhere. Fearful that she would be expelled from religious life, Henninger did not report the problem to the congregation's provincial superior.

In 1987 she was sent to teach at Mercy High School in Riverbend, New York. Upon arrival at her new posting, she was dismayed to discover that Czarniewicz was not only on staff, but also resident in the same convent. Depressed, she sought out a counselor to whom she revealed the abuse for the first time. Later, she disclosed her experience to the provincial superior, who responded with indifference. "We

3. A Laying On of Hands

all slip from time to time," was the superior's only comment. Realizing that no action would be taken against her abuser, she applied for and was granted an indult of exclaustration, or leave of absence from the congregation.

In July 1994, Henninger's case became public knowledge when she filed a civil lawsuit seeking damages of $3.75 million for severe psychological trauma from the Sisters of the Holy Family of Nazareth. The dioceses of Rockville Centre and Brooklyn, which were responsible for St. Christopher Ottilie, were also named in the suit. Her lawyer, Michael Montesano, was aware that the statute of limitations on crimes such as this had expired several decades previously, but he argued that it should be measured from the time she took her leave of absence in 1989. Prior to then, he said, she had been powerless to act since she had been a member of the order and under its supervision. In November, the case was dismissed in the state supreme court. In his decision, Justice Alfred S. Robbins said: "New York law does not recognize psychological trauma or repression as justification for avoiding the statute of limitations." Sister Janice Kobierowski, the provincial superior of the Sisters at Monroe, Connecticut, refused to comment on the case or its outcome.[17]

Were there any repercussions for Sister Gloria Czarniewicz as a consequence of the revelations? It seems not. She continued her teaching career until 1997, when she retired at the age of 70. For a number of years she worked in the finance department of a children's service in New York before moving in 2005 to the Immaculate Heart of Mary Convent in Monroe, Connecticut. Confined to a wheelchair in her later years, she filled the days with word searches and jigsaw puzzles. In reflecting upon her life before her death on August 20, 2016, she said: "My religious life was strengthened by my increasing trust in the Lord and supported and influenced by my devotion to the Holy Spirit and the Blessed Virgin Mary. My devotion to our Mother Foundress, Blessed Mary of Jesus the Good Shepherd developed and became more intense as the years passed by. In His will is our peace."[18]

Sister Mary Finn, Sisters, Home Visitors of Mary

The congregation known as the Sisters, Home Visitors of Mary, was founded in Detroit, Michigan, in 1949 at the initiative of Cardinal Edward Mooney, the local archbishop. Its mandate was somewhat

Predatory Nuns

unusual: "Its special work is home visiting and the recruiting of lapsed Catholics and prospective converts, principally among Negroes."[19] At the time African Americans were moving to the city in substantial numbers, and the sisters hoped to attach some of them to the Church. The Home Visitors remained a relatively obscure congregation and, with the exception of a small mission to Nigeria, never expanded beyond the state boundaries.

Frank Finn of County Tyrone, Ireland, settled in Detroit, where he worked as a streetcar motorman and married Mary O'Hara, a Chicago native. The first daughter of this working-class family, Mary Catherine Finn, was born in 1934. A natural athlete, she was an avid baseball and basketball player during her high school days. In 1952, at age 18, she entered the novitiate of the Home Visitors. Finn studied sociology and theology at Marquette University and Duquesne University and rose quickly to prominence in her small congregation. She became well known in Detroit's Catholic community as a lecturer and retreat director and loved her evenings with young people at the Catholic Information Center on Oakland Avenue. In 1969 she joined the faculty of the Sacred Heart Seminary as an assistant professor of theology, which involved her in the education of future priests. At the same time she was also mistress of novices for her own congregation.[20]

As the 1970s began, Finn had two novices under her charge in her community, Theresa Camden and a young woman whom we will call Olivia since she wishes to remain anonymous. On the pretext that they needed to experience nature, Finn would take her novices on weekend retreats to a cottage in the countryside owned by the nuns. Here, as the three of them lay down together, she explained that the physical closeness was a necessary part of their "deep and wholesome spiritual relationship." In 1972 the two novices were expelled from the Home Visitors without explanation. Camden, who admits to having been very naive at the time, spent years discussing their experiences with Olivia as they attempted to understand it. They also enrolled in therapy sessions. It turned out that Olivia's encounters with Finn had been more explicitly sexual than Camden's, but here too the clearly inappropriate behavior took its emotional toll.

During the mid–1990s, the two former novices, accompanied by a friend, met with Sister Barbara Dakoske, head of the Home Visitors. Camden explained that she was not seeking compensation but just wanted to ensure that Finn was held accountable. She was concerned that the predator was still working with young people. Sister Barbara

3. A Laying On of Hands

produced a money order for the sum of $20,000, which she presented to Olivia along with a non-disclosure agreement. The money was to pay for the therapy sessions. Camden was convinced that nothing would be done to restrict Finn, whom she believed was too well connected with the local Church establishment. The nun was part of the "good old boys club" and was untouchable.[21]

Camden was right. During the 1970s Finn both worked and lived at the Sacred Heart Seminary. Once again, her behavior became a source of concern. She was known to wander at night into the part of the building housing the seminarians, where she would encounter them emerging partly dressed from the showers. One former seminarian said that she saw herself as "everyone's mom" but that there were clear boundary issues: "She was very emotionally manipulative of people, very passive aggressive." She had a reputation for being "handsy" among seminarians, and her extended hugs and physical contact were considered inappropriate. Several complaints were made about her behavior but they went nowhere. She had a cult following among some faculty members who regarded her as saintly and above reproach. As Camden had observed, she was untouchable.[22] But not forever.

Frustrated at the Church's inaction, Camden decided to go public with her story, and it appeared in *Deadline Detroit*, a local news outlet, on January 17, 2019. Sacred Heart Seminary immediately announced Finn's resignation as assistant professor of theology and posted her letter of resignation on its website: "More than 50 years ago, I misused my position of authority as a director of novices in the Home Visitors of Mary (HVM) Order, engaging in inappropriate conduct with two adult novices. I regret that behavior, have repented of my actions, and sincerely apologize for the harm I have caused. Please know of my great love for our Eucharistic Jesus, our Church, the Home Visitors and the Sacred Heart Seminary Community." Allen H. Vigneron, archbishop of Detroit, who had been rector of Sacred Heart Seminary in the mid–1990s, admitted: "I was given partial details about Sister Mary's inappropriate conduct that had occurred in the early 1970s. At the time, I thought that the matter had been resolved."[23] On January 4, 2021, at the age of 86, Sister Mary Finn "passed to her eternal reward with the Lord and the dominion of Saints."[24]

Theresa Camden despises everything Catholic and only enters a church today for weddings and funerals. She admits to finding it a struggle even on those occasions because of the dishonesty of the Church and its readiness to protect sexual predators.[25]

Predatory Nuns

Sister Jeanne Wilfort, Sisters of the Holy Cross

The Congregation of the Holy Cross is a religious order of priests and brothers established in Le Mans, France, in 1837 by Father Basile Moreau. The idea was to repopulate French parishes with religious personnel after the losses incurred during the Revolution. In 1841 Moreau founded a religious sisterhood to be part of this work: the Marianites of the Holy Cross. In 1847 four of the sisters were sent to Montréal in response to a request by the local bishop, Ignace Bourget, where they established a Canadian province of the order. Following the American Civil War the Marianites began to establish schools in New England towns where French Canadians were settling in order to work in the textile mills. In 1883, because of communication problems, the Canadian province separated from the French motherhouse to form a new religious order. Now known as the Sisters of the Holy Cross (*Les Soeurs de Sainte-Croix*), by 1900 they had foundations in Massachusetts, New Hampshire, and Vermont while maintaining close ties with the motherhouse in Saint-Laurent, Québec.[26]

Manchester is a city of a little over 100,000 people in southern New Hampshire. It was here, in December 1951, that Jane McDonald was born. Raised in a dysfunctional Catholic family, she experienced sexual, physical, and emotional abuse during her early years. School, on the other hand, was more to her liking; it was a much safer place. Immaculata High School, an all-girls institution run by the Sisters of the Holy Cross, was where she spent her adolescence.[27] Those who remembered her from that time described her as "fun-loving" and not at all the type you would expect to join a convent. But then, in her senior year, she returned from a religious retreat a changed person and announced her intention to become a nun.[28] In 1972, at the age of 20, she entered the novitiate of the Sisters of the Holy Cross in Franklin, New Hampshire, and continued her training at the congregation's convents in Albany, New York, and Groton, Connecticut.[29]

As McDonald worked her way through the various stages of formation, the Sisters were grappling with the changes arising from the Second Vatican Council. It meant searching for new forms of monasticism that allowed for engagement with the world rather than withdrawal from it. It was an enormous challenge for all congregations, accompanied as it was by significant desertions from religious life. One consequence was that the staffing of schools and other Catholic institutions dependent on the labors of nuns became increasingly unsustainable.[30]

3. *A Laying On of Hands*

The Sisters of the Holy Cross who did not abandon their vows wanted greater individual freedom and a rejection of the pre–Vatican II world of rules and submission. They wanted to explore careers other than school teaching and to seek out new "spiritualities." In this context the ideas of Father André Rochais fit perfectly. In fact, many congregations, and not just Holy Cross, were turning to the French priest for guidance in reconstituting religious community life. Rochais had been influenced by the ideas of Carl Rogers, the American humanistic psychologist whose encounter groups had been popular during the 1960s as a means of self-discovery and the realization of human potential. The priest, too, wanted human development in the sense that Rogers understood it, but added a component about a renewed relationship with God. In other words, it was a Catholic spin on what was essentially a secular-humanist idea. His movement was known in English as Personality and Human Relations, but it went by its French acronym, PRH (*Personalité et relations humaines*).[31]

During the summer of 1975 the New England Province of the Sisters of the Holy Cross invited Sister Jeanne Wilfort to conduct a workshop on PRH for their members at the novitiate and retreat center in Franklin. About 40 years old at the time, Wilfort was superior of the Western Canada Province of the order. She came across as the personification of the post-conciliar modern nun who had shed the habit and gave presentations in her bare feet. Moreover, she claimed to specialize in "affectivity," or the art of expressing affection. She was the guru of love. Very cool. Hip. Groovy.[32]

McDonald was in attendance and became intrigued. And when Wilfort encouraged sisters who were having difficulty with community life to join her in western Canada, she signed on. The impressionable young novice travelled in September 1975 to Edmonton, Alberta, where she spent a year under the superior's guidance. Afterwards, she returned to New Hampshire for two more years of study at Holy Cross colleges. And all the while Wilfort stayed in touch providing further guidance on PRH techniques—including encouragement to get physically close to other women to overcome discomfort with touching. McDonald began to see the older nun as a mentor—an influential spiritual guide. And when the mentor invited her to join a new ministry she was establishing in Manitoba, she didn't hesitate, returning to the Canadian West in May 1978.

The new ministry was located in Lorette, a small prairie town east of Winnipeg. There is nothing remarkable about the place except for its location about 10 kilometers south of the Trans-Canada Highway at a location considered to be the longitudinal center of the country. In other words, if you were driving from St. John's, Newfoundland, to Victoria, British Columbia, you would be halfway there as you passed by Lorette. The ministry was known as *Maison de croissance,* or Home for Growth, and consisted of about five Holy Cross sisters and one Oblate priest, Father Raymond Beauregard. One thing was clear: this was Wilfort's project, and she was completely in charge. Here she conducted PRH workshops attended by nuns from several different religious orders, with priests and members of the laity also taking part. Sister Jeanne Dusseault was superior general of the Holy Cross Sisters in Canada at the time and on her several visits to the *Maison* showed her complete confidence in the ministry.

But Wilfort was beginning to diverge from the mainstream PRH movement. Developing her own theories and therapies, she took the view that everyone somehow was wounded and in need of healing, even if completely unaware of it. Professionally qualified therapists were useless, she believed, because God had no place in their practice. They were unable to heal the "whole person."

When McDonald arrived in Lorette, she was very much under the spell of Wilfort and her ideas. The older nun impressed on her the special character of the *Maison de croissance* community and the need for confidentiality respecting its practices. Communication with outsiders was discouraged. This should have been a warning signal. On a number of occasions Wilfort and her second-in-command, Sister Claire Marquis, came to McDonald's bedroom and lay on the bed with her, one on either side. They just wanted to surround her with love, they explained. Although everyone remained clothed, the behavior might have been regarded as odd, to say the least. Then Wilfort began to hold private counseling sessions with her new recruit at which McDonald disclosed the abusive scenes from her childhood and her emotional struggles ever since. The vulnerability of her client laid bare, Wilfort claimed that she could heal the hurt by becoming a good mother to her.

According to McDonald, one night Wilfort entered her bedroom uninvited, undressed herself and slipped beneath the covers. She urged the younger nun to undress as well, and this was done, except for her panties. Proclaiming herself the good mother, she invited McDonald to suck her breasts in order to acquire her spiritual goodness. Again, her victim complied and after several more evenings of similar goings-on, agreed to remove her panties. At that point, Wilfort pulled the younger

3. *A Laying On of Hands*

nun on top of her, groping her all over, including her vagina, and all the while explaining that it was part of God's healing.

McDonald had been uncomfortable with the naked trysts ever since the first night of Wilfort's advances but had gone along with it. The palaver about God and spirituality convinced her, at least in part, that it really was a form of therapy. But she became increasingly dubious as the sexual nature of the encounters became more pronounced. And yet she felt that she needed to comply since she had been trained to obey and the predator was her religious superior. As the early months of 1979 rolled by, her resolve to resist strengthened. One night she simply refused Wilfort's demands. The older nun, unaccustomed to having her "love" rejected, flew into a rage. From then onwards McDonald was made to feel like a pariah at the *Maison*; her superior snubbed her and excluded her from community events.

McDonald left Lorette in 1980 and went for a year of study at the Holy Cross motherhouse in Saint-Laurent, Québec. At the end of this time she was ordered to return to Manitoba and complied, with understandable misgivings. While she loved the Canadian West, she was fearful of Wilfort's wrath. She settled in Winnipeg and spent a number of years as a cook with the Salvation Army mission in the city center. Working with society's less fortunate was very much to her liking, and she aspired to become a professional social worker. It was a reasonable ambition since Holy Cross nuns of her generation were being sent to university in accordance with their wishes. Not only was she denied the opportunity to advance her education, but she noticed a growing coldness towards her in the religious community. She blamed it all on Wilfort's baneful influence. In the meantime *Maisons de Croissance* were expanding until they were at least seven in number in and around Winnipeg. Knowing what she did, McDonald viewed the growth with concern; she believed that the *Maisons* were a cult within the Holy Cross order.[33]

In May 1987 she rented a storefront at 676 Main Street, in Winnipeg's most down-and-out neighborhood. She transformed it into a drop-in center for the unemployed, drug addicts, and prostitutes who lived nearby. Although officially part of the Holy Cross mission in the city, the Sisters refused financial support. McDonald simply raised the money herself. Our Place/Chez Nous, as she named her center, allowed her to operate independently of Wilfort and the order. She lived in a shabby apartment upstairs with a bedroom window overlooking an alley lined with garbage cans. For her work with the poor she became known

Predatory Nuns

as "Winnipeg's Mother Teresa," and in July 2002 she was among those honored with a "people who make a difference Canada Day award."[34]

As the 1990s drew to a close, a number of Holy Cross Sisters loyal to Wilfort began to meddle in the operations of Our Place/Chez Nous. It was a source of stress for McDonald, who felt helpless to put a stop to it. In the spring of 1999 she determined that the best course of action was to disclose what had happened to her in Lorette to Sister Liette Finnerty, superior general of the order in Saint-Laurent, Québec, and to Sister Lucienne Landry, regional superior in Edmonton. The superiors responded guardedly, and McDonald sensed that they either did not believe her or were refusing to do so because of the implications. Needing more evidence, she approached three other nuns whom she believed had been subjected to Wilfort's "therapies" in the *Maisons*. When the nuns confirmed the similarities of their experiences, she passed their names on to Finnerty and Landry, but it seemed to make no difference.[35]

Residents of Winnipeg take winter seriously, and with good reason. The corner of Portage and Main streets, not far from McDonald's apartment, is known both as the crossroads of Canada and the country's coldest intersection when the wind blows—which is all too often. And let's not forget the swirling snow. These are conditions that are life threatening to the unwary. New Year's Day 2000 came in at a chilling -36 degrees Celsius. It was to be a particularly chilling year for the nun, and for reasons unrelated to the brutal climate of the city where she had made her home. In January, while receiving spiritual counseling from Father Dominic Kerbrat, she disclosed her experiences with Wilfort. The priest identified the behavior as sexual abuse, confirming what she had believed for some time. Then, that very month, there was distressing news: she was diagnosed with aggressive breast cancer. Chemotherapy sessions beginning in February left her exhausted, nauseated, and subject to regular infections. She had a radical mastectomy in July, followed by radiation.

Throughout these challenging months, McDonald remained in contact with Sister Finnerty, the superior general, who advised her to focus on the battle with cancer and to trust her in dealing with the sexual abuse. Her communications with Sister Landry were more discouraging. Landry insisted that Wilfort had healing and spiritual gifts and that her therapies, which she had learned in Québec, were beneficial. And, in one remarkably dismissive comment, she told McDonald that she could return to the United States if she were that unhappy.

3. A Laying On of Hands

By December McDonald had been through the worst of the battle with cancer and was feeling much better. Frustrated at the attitude of the Holy Cross superiors, she took her concerns to the recently appointed archbishop of Winnipeg, James Weisberger. In recounting what had transpired in Lorette, she described the *Maisons de Croissance* as a cult and provided the names of the others who had been abused by Wilfort. The prelate appeared to be sympathetic and expressed his own misgivings about the *Maisons*. Later, in March 2001, he informed her that the Congregation for the Religious in Rome had appointed Sister Marguerite Letourneau, former superior of the Sisters of Charity of Montréal (Grey Nuns), to inquire into the matter. It is not known if Letourneau completed her inquiry or what became of it if she did. That one nun would be asked to investigate the activities of another did not inspire confidence. It had all the appearances of a classic cover-up—a ruse by the Church to buy more time while a potentially embarrassing situation was buried.[36]

As all of this transpired, McDonald was feeling depressed and in a state of virtual despair. She sought professional help from Cynthia Jordan, a psychologist, and Vicki Frankel, a counselor. The therapy confirmed that Wilfort had caused her significant harm. But it also helped, and by the fall of 2001 she was feeling better and was determined to set things right in her life. She resolved to leave religious life and seek compensation for the abuse.

In November she told her story to Tony Dalmyn, a litigation lawyer, who agreed to take her case. In December she applied for an indult of secularization or official release from her religious vows. In March 2002 a letter arrived from the Congregation for the Religious granting the indult, which was not in effect until signed. This she refused to do until matters were resolved with the Sisters of the Holy Cross.

On May 10, 2002, Tony Dalmyn filed a lawsuit on her behalf against Wilfort and the Sisters of the Holy Cross seeking financial compensation for "sexual, physical and emotional abuse" at the *Maison de croissance* in Lorette between 1978 and 1979. An apology and the removal of Wilfort from religious life were also demanded as part of the settlement. Things did not proceed smoothly. Lawyers for the Sisters insisted on lengthy depositions and cross-examinations knowing, as they did, that McDonald's continuing poor health would not allow her to sit through them. More than a year after the initial filing, they still had not responded with documents denying the allegations. The plaintiff was convinced that her order would rather see her dead than allow its dark secrets to be exposed to public view. Dalmyn, himself a practicing Catholic, was appalled at the confrontational approach. He sensed that the Sisters were stonewalling and were treating his client as a whistleblower who had betrayed them.[37]

Meanwhile, McDonald remained a virtual prisoner in her shabby apartment. Her cancer had returned after a period of remission, and chemotherapy was again taking its toll: hair loss, nausea, chronic pain, and lethargy. She could do little beyond household chores, and even these were a challenge. On better days she looked in on the project that had been her life for many years—Our Place/Chez Nous—which still operated on the ground floor. Her years of labor with the Holy Cross order had yielded nothing in the way of benefits or pension. Money was scarce, and she was often reliant on the assistance of friends. Her disillusionment with the organization that she had been part of for most of her life was complete. "The moral conscience of the congregation has died," she noted. "There has to be one Sister of the Holy Cross out there who still has a conscience and is still willing to act morally on this." That moral sister never stepped forward.[38] On July 29, 2003, Sister Jane McDonald died, a victim of the cancer that had been with her on and off since January 2000. She was 51 years old.[39]

What happened to Sister Jeanne Wilfort? It was reported that she left Manitoba when McDonald's court case hit the newsstands—even the national newspaper, *The Globe and Mail*, picked up the story. Religious orders invariably protect their members and have the resources to spirit them away in the event of potential scandal. Following Wilfort's departure, it appears that the *Maisons de Croissance* folded. At the end of May 2019 the Maison-de-la-Providence Retreat Center in Ottawa hosted the 38th annual conference of the Holy Cross History Association—a gathering of elderly nuns, brothers, and priests at which papers are presented congratulating themselves on their past achievements. Catholic history has a suspect reputation among serious scholars, and when the history of nuns is written by nuns themselves, a new low is reached. Wilfort resurfaced at the conference having reinvented herself as a historian of her religious order. Her presentation, *"Les Soeurs de Sainte-Croix de l'Ouest Canadien, fêtent leur centenaire en 2020,"* was a celebration of the work of the sisters in western Canada over the previous century. In typical nun's history fashion, she praised the sisters' tireless devotion and willingness to endure hardships as they built and staffed schools in various parts of Alberta and British Columbia. Not a word was said about the *Maisons de Croissance*. The New Age experiment that had tarnished the order's reputation had been conveniently shuffled off into the shadows.[40]

A few more remarks are required to conclude this story. The newsletter recording the details of the Holy Cross History Conference of 2019 identifies Wilfort by name, provides a summary of her presentation, and even features a photograph of her—portly, frumpy, and nothing like the barefoot guru who had once lured young nuns to her convent sex cult in Manitoba. But there is an anomaly in her case. Several hundred papers have been presented at this conference since its inception in 1982. They are all listed on the Holy Cross History Association website. For the 2019 conference Wilfort's name is not placed opposite the title of her presentation. She is simply "A Canadian Sister," the only presenter since 1982 to remain anonymous. Make of this what you will.[41]

Conclusion

Young women who were either in training to become nuns or were already in the early years of profession were sometimes the objects of sexual attention by older nuns, and especially those in positions of authority. Chibnall, Wolf, and Duckro's study pegged the incidence of this phenomenon at around 10 percent. The experiences of Jean Patricia Henninger, Theresa Camden, and Jane McDonald show us that the sexual attention could take the form of sexual assault: as unwanted groping, or as a lengthy grooming dressed up in the language of spiritual healing that led to sexual activity.

When confronted with complaints about the behavior, the superiors of the religious orders in question responded unsympathetically. A remark such as "We all slip from time to time" was not helpful. In fact, it implied that sexual misconduct by the accused nuns, and perhaps by others, was not unknown in the community and was tolerated. And when the religious superiors resorted to legal maneuvers and obfuscation to avoid compensation—as they did in two of the cases discussed—it showed a complete indifference to the victims and the harm done to them. The whistleblowers were given the pariah treatment, and the system closed ranks in support of the predators. The problem of sexual assault in religious life was not addressed. It was simply covered up.

4

Sorrowful Mysteries
Orphanages

> We were beaten into submission psychologically and physically. Who was going to believe children over the Catholic nuns who devoted their lives in service to orphans? We lived in terror of and absolute rule of these nuns. They were the ultimate authority and we were only children.[1]
> —June Maloney, former resident of St. Colman's Home for Boys and Girls

Orphanages don't have the best reputation as places in which to spend your youth. Charles Dickens is often blamed for this, but the realities of institutional "care" were often much worse than the Victorian novelist had observed or imagined. For many of those sent to orphanages run by Catholic nuns, it was indeed the worst of times. Nor did it seem to matter in which country the institution was located. Public inquiries in Australia, Canada, Ireland, and Scotland have revealed some of the horrors inflicted on children in convent orphanages. Catholic sisterhoods were also heavily involved in running orphanages in America. Three case studies will illustrate the problematic nature of this enterprise. But first, a brief diversion will throw some light on the childcare record of two of the religious orders involved in these cases in their countries of origin.

With the assistance of Bishop Ignace Bourget, Madame Emilie Tavernier (Gamelin), a pious widow, founded the Sisters of Charity of Providence in Montréal in 1843. The new religious order embarked on an ambitious program of institution building—schools, hospitals, asylums, and orphanages. Mount Providence, in Montréal, was one of the orphanages. By the 1950s, the Canadian federal government was providing daily subsidies of $1.25 for orphans, but $2.75 for psychiatric patients. It occurred to the Sisters that it would be greatly to their

4. Sorrowful Mysteries

financial advantage to reclassify their orphans as mental patients, and that's what happened at Mount Providence in 1955. A similar move was made by six other religious orders that ran orphanages in the province of Québec. In all, more than 20,000 orphans were so reclassified with the active collaboration of the provincial government of the authoritarian Premier Maurice Duplessis, who allowed total domination of education and social services by the Catholic Church and whose time in office (1936–39; 1944–59) was known as *la grande norceur* (the great darkness). The treatment of the children now labeled mentally deficient immediately deteriorated. Education came to an end, and incidents of physical and sexual abuse became noticeably more pronounced with disastrous effects on their well-being. It took many decades of agitation and legal action before the government of Québec was prepared to acknowledge the wrong done to *les orphelins de Duplessis.* In 2001 it apologized and provided survivors with individual compensation of $10,000 and $1,000 for each year spent in an institution. The Catholic Church refused to apologize or contribute to the compensation. A spokesperson for the religious orders dismissed the affair as "very much sensationalized."[2]

The religious order known as the Sisters of the Presentation of the Blessed Virgin Mary was founded in Cork, Ireland, in 1775 by Nano Nagle, a wealthy middle-class woman. The major work of the order was educating girls, and particularly those born into poverty, "in the principles of religion and Christian piety." The Sisters were successful in expanding their operations, not just in Ireland, but throughout the Irish diaspora. They operated two industrial schools in County Tipperary, St. Francis's in Cashel and St. Bernard's in Dundrum; the latter was relocated to Fethard at a subsequent date. The Commission to Inquire into Child Abuse—popularly known as the Ryan Commission—that reported in 2009 identified rampant physical, emotional, and sexual abuse in the country's industrial schools and orphanages, a list that included St. Francis's and St. Bernard's. Sister Claude Meagher, a spokesperson for the Presentation Sisters, admitted to the commissioners the possibility of suffering—"We feel that people would have suffered there, they may have suffered..."—but would not go beyond this vague acknowledgment. Even so, the Sisters agreed to contribute five million euros to the compensation fund established by the Commission—an admission in itself of wrongdoing. Moreover, one of them, Sister Elizabeth Maxwell, played a leading role on the negotiating team representing the 18 male and female religious orders responsible for the institutions that sought to minimize the damage they might face as a consequence of inquiry. In 2002, for example, long before the Commission released its report, they pressured the Irish government to accept a ridiculously low financial liability on their part and to grant immunity from prosecution to their members irrespective of their crimes against children.[3]

We shall meet the Sisters of Charity of Providence and the Sisters of the Presentation of the Blessed Virgin Mary once again in America.

St. Vincent-St. Thomas Orphanage, Louisville, Kentucky: Sisters of Charity of Nazareth

In 1773, legendary frontiersman Daniel Boone led a party of settlers through the Cumberland Gap to lands west of the Appalachians. The intrusion into their territory was resisted by the Shawnee, leading to what became known as Lord Dunmore's War. Following defeat at the Battle of Point Pleasant in October 1774, the Shawnee conceded their claim to the lands south of the Ohio River. Settlers from the coastal states now flooded in unimpeded. When part of those lands became the state of Kentucky in 1792, most Native Americans had been driven farther west.[4] It was another ugly chapter in America's history of—in today's parlance—ethnic cleansing.

By the new century, there were more than a thousand Catholic families among the settlers in the state, and the Church sought to provide them with educational and other services through its own institutions. In 1813, 19-year-old Catherine Spalding and two other women volunteered for this work and formed the nucleus of a new religious congregation—the Sisters of Charity of Nazareth.[5]

The Sisters began to establish Catholic schools where demand warranted. In 1832, they opened St. Vincent Orphanage for girls in Louisville, the fastest-growing urban center with a thriving slave market due to its position on the Ohio River. The Sisters themselves owned slaves and used them in constructing their first institutions, including St. Vincent's. They also employed slave labor on the farms that produced food for their various operations.[6] In 1850, they took charge of St. Thomas Orphanage for boys that opened in Bardstown. After more than a century, the two orphanages were combined into one in 1952. The new coeducational entity, known as St. Vincent-St. Thomas Orphanage, was located in Anchorage, a wealthy suburb of Louisville. In operation until

4. Sorrowful Mysteries

1983, it was the property of the archdiocese of Louisville and was managed by the Sisters.[7] But little was known of its sinister side until 21 years had passed since its closure.

A brief digression will provide some background on a pivotal figure in the scandal that was to emerge in the summer of 2004. Herman J. Lammers was born in 1907 and grew up in Louisville. Following ordination to the priesthood in 1932, he worked in a number of Kentucky parishes. He acquired a fleeting moment of fame when he administered the last rites to Rainey Bethea, a young African American who was hanged in Owensboro in August 1936. It was the last public execution in the United States. In 1939, the archdiocese of Louisville appointed Father Lammers director of its Catholic charities and resident chaplain at St. Thomas Orphanage. When St. Thomas merged with St. Vincent in 1952, he continued as chaplain. Upon his death in 1983, he was praised for his work with refugees and victims of disaster, and for his leadership in combatting abortion.[8]

The dark side of St. Vincent-St. Thomas first saw the light in 2004 when a lawsuit was filed in Jefferson Circuit Court on July 15 on behalf of six women and one man who had spent part of their youth in the institution. The suit alleged sexual abuse, mainly, although not exclusively, by Father Lammers. One of the plaintiffs, Helen Edwards, claimed that the chaplain had made her pregnant leading later to a miscarriage. The victims had complained to the Sisters at the time of the abuse, but the response had been either disbelief or punishment. The suit therefore accused the Sisters of having been aware of the abuse, and of failing to stop it or report it to the law enforcement authorities. Compensation and punitive damages were sought.[9]

The plaintiffs were represented by attorney William McMurry, who had secured a settlement of $25.7 million from the archdiocese of Louisville the previous year on behalf of 243 victims of sexual predator priests. As the months went by, more former inmates of the orphanage came forward with allegations of abuse, and McMurry added their names to the lawsuit. By the summer of 2005 the plaintiffs were 50 in number, most of them alleging abuse by Father Lammers in a pattern that was compellingly consistent. Deborah Ferguson, for example, said that she was not only assaulted by the chaplain, but also witnessed him raping a young girl. When she reported the incident to the mother superior, she was called a liar and was locked in a closet.[10]

Kim Michele Richardson and her older sisters Caity, Pamela, and Gayla were sent to St. Vincent-St. Thomas in 1960 when the State of

Predatory Nuns

Kentucky declared their mother, Diane, an unfit parent. Kim was an infant at the time and literally grew up in the orphanage. One night, when she was around seven years old (birthdays were neither noted nor celebrated at the institution), a nun whom she had never seen before awakened her and led her to Father Lammers's private quarters. She was already scared of the priest, who usually stank of pipe tobacco and booze, and with good reason. Father Lammers began to ply the youngster with wine before commencing the sexual abuse.[11]

But that was not the entire story. From the very beginning, some of the Sisters, too, were accused of sexual assault. By the time the list of plaintiffs was complete, no fewer than 13 Sisters of Charity of Nazareth had been named as abusers. Several of them were said to have had multiple victims. Sister Mary Ann Powers, for example, had five allegations against her, while Sister Mary Camilla Donoghue had four. Sister Joseph Michael, a manly-looking nun, also had four victims, including Kim Richardson's older sister, Caity. Most of the abusers targeted females only, but for at least two of them, the gender of the victim was not a consideration. Sisters Madeline de Paul Galatine and Anthony Louise Pereira not only allegedly assaulted Patricia and Elizabeth Hill, but also their brother, Clifford. Moreover, Clifford claimed that the two nuns had forced him to perform sexual acts with other boys for their amusement. Sister Stanislaus Kotska Willet, superior of the orphanage from 1940 to 1944, was also among the accused.[12] Small wonder, then, that complaints about Father Lammers or the Sisters fell on deaf ears. There was really nobody who would have listened to the victims or acted on their behalf.

In addition to the sexual assaults, many of the plaintiffs complained of harsh treatment at the hands of the Sisters. Punishments that were cited included beatings, confinement in dark closets without food, being thrown down the stairs, being forced to crawl on hands and knees for hours, force-feeding to the point of gagging, and being made to stand naked in front of others. The abuse in its various forms was alleged to have taken place from the 1940s to the 1970s.[13]

Sister Charlie was a large nun with hard eyes, tight lips, and an unpleasant smell about her that lingered in the air even after she moved elsewhere. No one had ever seen her smile. She was in charge of the dormitory where Kim Richardson spent her earliest years and kept the girl in a state of perpetual fear. Kim recalled that when she was about three years of age Sister Charlie dunked her head in a toilet bowl upon finding some soiling in her underwear. On another occasion, the nun stripped

4. Sorrowful Mysteries

her naked and flailed her with a wooden paddle on the legs, buttocks, and genitals. And when Kim had the misfortune to vomit, Sister Charlie pushed her face into it. Some of the other nuns were not much better in the matter of violence. Sister Anthony, in charge of another dormitory, was bad-tempered and sadistic and lashed out at the children with little provocation. Sister Deloris Marie, who supervised the cafeteria, was of a similar disposition. Few escaped the frequent blows from her beefy hands.[14]

Sister Susan Gatz, head of the Western Province of the Sisters of Charity of Nazareth, in responding to the accusations, said that the Sisters found it all "heartbreaking." They were struggling, she said, to reconcile the claims of the plaintiffs with their own positive memories of those accused, most of whom were dead. She added that they had no written record of any of the complaints.[15] The latter statement was probably the truth. St. Vincent-St. Thomas and the Sisters who ran it had functioned in a culture of denial for decades, and there was no good reason to document their misdeeds in print.

A major obstacle facing the lawsuits was Kentucky's criminal statute of limitations law. In the case of sexual offences with a minor, the law required action to be initiated within five years of the victim reaching 18 years of age. Attorney McMurry argued in his suit that the Sisters had concealed criminal activity and therefore the statute of limitations should not apply. He had employed that line of reasoning in his suit against the archdiocese of Louisville, but its validity had not been tested at the time because an out-of-court settlement had been reached.[16]

During the summer of 2005 McMurry proposed combining the individual components of the lawsuit into a class-action suit. It seemed to make sense since there were similar claims of injury against a common accused—the Sisters. He believed that such a measure would lead to a speedier resolution for his clients than if the suits were adjudicated by a dozen or more judges. But the Sisters opposed such a move, and their objections were sustained in a ruling by Judge Denise Clayton on September 28. Elizabeth Mandel, attorney for the Sisters, announced at the time that she planned to file motions of dismissal on all charges since the statute of limitations on the alleged crimes had long since expired. She added that her clients had no interest in a settlement; they continued to maintain that they had done no wrong.[17]

It looked as if the Sisters were prepared to fight it out. But a year later they had thought better of such a course and entered negotiations towards a settlement. In a final mediation on July 27, 2006, an agreement was reached. The Sisters were to provide $1.5 million in compensation to the plaintiffs, but they would not be required to acknowledge any wrongdoing. Even so, they could not brush away the tales of abuse that had been widely reported in the local media for the best part of two years. In issuing a statement that sought to mitigate the damage to their reputation, they were less than convincing: "After much prayer and discernment, we have entered into an agreement.... We have made this decision based on a number of reasons, most importantly a desire to bring about closure and healing for all involved in the lawsuit.... We want to emphasize that we believe in the goodness of the sisters and former members who were accused, most of whom are long dead."[18]

On July 26, 2015, a bronze statue of Catherine Spalding was unveiled outside the Cathedral of the Assumption in Louisville. Mother Spalding was depicted striding forward carrying an orphan child in her left arm while a second walked beside her clutching her dress. Sister Susan Gatz, in speaking for the Sisters of Charity of Nazareth, had this to say: "I can imagine that Catherine is delighted to be back on the streets of Louisville where she found so much need and so many collaborators ... and to be portrayed with her beloved orphans must give her great joy."[19] The irony cannot have been lost on the 50 former orphans whose lives were scarred by the horrors they had endured in Mother Spalding's favorite institution.

St. Joseph's Orphanage, Burlington, Vermont: Sisters of Charity of Providence

French Canadian migration to the New England states began in the 1830s, first in response to the political turmoil known as the Patriot Rebellions of 1837 and 1838, and later as a consequence of economic need and opportunity. The transition to commercial agriculture in what became the province of Québec in 1867 created a class of landless laborers that industrializing Montréal could not absorb. Meanwhile, New England's industrial sector, especially its cotton and woolen mills, was beginning to thrive. French Canadian men, women, and children found employment in the mills, and they tended to gather in their own ghettoes known as *les petits Canadas* on the fringes of the mill towns. Here, they resisted assimilation with their own churches, parish schools, newspapers, and festivals.[20]

Burlington, Vermont, only 150 kilometers south of Montréal along

4. Sorrowful Mysteries

the Champlain Valley, was an early destination for the migrants. St. Joseph's—built in 1852—was the first French Canadian parish church in the U.S. with its own French-speaking priest. And the nuns, whose work in staffing Catholic institutions was essential, were not far behind. The Sisters of Charity of Providence were among the early arrivals, opening an orphanage, also called St. Joseph's, in 1854. The original building at Pearl and South Prospect streets was replaced in 1883 by a four-story red brick edifice on North Avenue with little to commend it as a piece of architecture. At the celebrations marking the 100th anniversary of its foundation, the bishop of Burlington, Edward F. Ryan, praised the Sisters, who were still preponderantly from Québec, for their devoted self-sacrifice, noting that they not only provided for the children's physical needs, but also "cared for the souls of these little ones so dear to Christ by giving them the advantages of a Catholic home and a truly Catholic training." St. Joseph's closed its doors in 1974 when new practices respecting children who were orphaned or neglected became the norm. During its 120-year existence the orphanage housed an estimated 13,000 people for part of their young lives.[21]

Clifton Lawrence Balazs was born in February 1948 in New York State. In May 1951, when he was barely three years old, he was sent to live in St. Joseph's. Although his time at the orphanage was not long, a number of traumatic events during these years continued to haunt him in the decades that followed. Most notable was an incident in which a nun, whose name he could not recall, allegedly dragged him into a small room and forced him to have oral sexual contact with her. She also fondled him roughly, cutting his testicles as she did so. Fortunately for him, in May 1953 he was adopted by the Barquin family of Barre, Vermont, and escaped the abusive environment.[22]

Now with a new name, Joseph R. Barquin, he spent the rest of his youth in a supportive family environment. Those close to him called him Joey. In adulthood he moved to Florida, where he made a living as a diver. Throughout these years he said nothing of his experiences at St. Joseph's. That changed when he married in 1991. He found sex difficult, and his wife, herself a therapist, urged him to seek help and suggested that the Church should pay for it. With this in mind, Barquin returned to Vermont, where the diocese of Burlington agreed to pick up the costs for 13 therapy sessions. But his therapist told him that he would need at least two years of treatment, perhaps more.[23]

Realizing that recourse to the law was now his best path forward, Barquin found a sympathetic ear in Philip White, a Montpelier attorney specializing in child abuse cases. On June 7, 1993, White lodged a complaint with the U.S. District Court, seeking $50,000 in damages from the diocese of Burlington, Vermont Catholic Charities, St. Joseph's Orphan Asylum, and "Sister Jane Doe" for physical, psychological, and sexual abuse to his client.[24]

Barquin and his lawyer were well aware that his claim to have been sexually molested by a nun would be greeted with disbelief and that the Church would fight the case with its best legal arsenal. With this in mind, they arranged a televised press conference at which Barquin told his story in the hope that other former orphans would come forward to share their experiences. They did so, and in droves. A support group called the Survivors of St. Joseph's Orphanage and Friends quickly formed and swelled to more than 80 members. In commenting on their emotionally charged meetings, Barquin noted how messed up the survivors' lives were, adding: "I'm like the guy in the dark cave who lit the first match."[25]

The diocese of Burlington and Vermont Catholic Charities determined that it would be best to seek dismissal of Barquin's case. They were granted a hearing at the U.S. District Court, Vermont, on November 10, 1993. Invoking the statute of limitations was their first tactic. State law required those seeking damages for injuries resulting from "childhood sexual abuse" to take action within "six years of the act alleged to have caused the injury or condition, or six years from the time the victim discovered that the injury or condition was caused by that act." The defendants claimed that since the alleged abuse had occurred more than 40 years previously, it was reasonable to assume that the plaintiff should have discovered the cause of his injury before 1992. Presiding judge Fred I. Parker did not agree. He accepted Barquin's assertion that he had acted with due diligence on the matter and had only discovered the cause of his injuries the year before.

The defendants' second ground for dismissal was that they had not had access to records or witnesses that would have allowed for a proper defense and had therefore been denied due process. Again, Parker disagreed. He pointed out that they had not demonstrated the unavailability of records or witnesses, but rather that it would have been difficult to locate them. There was no violation of due process.

The final argument put forward by the defendants was constitutional in nature. They claimed that because St. Joseph's was in its essence a religious institution, it was protected under the First Amendment's

4. Sorrowful Mysteries

guarantee on freedom of religion. Caring for orphans was part of the religious activities of the nuns and was therefore protected from state interference. In rejecting this claim, Judge Parker said that operating an orphanage involved both purely religious activities and purely secular ones, such as, in the latter instance, driving a bus. It had not been demonstrated to him that Sister Jane Doe's actions in reference to the plaintiff had been purely religious in nature.[26]

The Church was clearly alarmed at its failure to dismiss the case, the publicity generated by the survivors' group, and the possibility of dozens of other lawsuits being filed against it. William O'Brien, attorney for the diocese, said that Bishop Kenneth Angell was willing to assist the survivors "without making any admission of liability." Preserving the institution's assets appeared, unsurprisingly, to be the main concern: "We want to see whether reasonable accommodations can be made, but we won't give away the farm." When Sally Miller, one of the survivors, visited the bishop in his office early in 1994, she found him unsympathetic. Angell said that he, too, had been abused during his youth but just got over it. He did not understand why others could not do the same. He followed this dismissive remark with what seemed to be an explanation for what had happened at the orphanage, which may have contained an element of truth: "Well, these were nuns that were just frustrated ladies and they didn't know how to handle children. They hadn't had children of their own."[27]

The bishop's hesitancy in dealing with what was now a growing scandal may have been due to his awareness that the diocese has no insurance to cover potential claims. In his pastoral letter circulated on the weekend of February 3–4, 1996, he expressed sorrow that Church personnel had harmed anyone and offered a vague apology. Ever cautious with words—and probably on legal advice—he never mentioned St. Joseph's. And then he acted. The former orphans were offered a settlement of $5,000 each in return for an agreement not to sue the Church. Although the exact figure is not known, more than 60 are believed to have accepted the deal.[28]

During the months that followed, Sam Hemingway, a reporter with the *Burlington Free Press*, interviewed 40 of those who had settled in order to learn of their experiences at St. Joseph's. Thirty-three of the former orphans recalled being physically abused by the nuns. Twenty-three complained of sexual abuse, with the abusers about evenly divided between nuns and male personnel. Nine recalled being forced to eat their own vomit. Three said that they had witnessed a nun singe the fingertips of a girl accused of stealing. And seven spoke of complaining to the nuns and priests of their ill treatment only to be ignored or punished.[29]

At the time of the $5,000 settlement, Philip White decided for personal health reasons that he could no longer represent those seeking justice from the Church. Barquin and those who had refused to settle were now represented by Florida attorney Robert Widman, who was shocked at the stories of abuse recounted by the former orphans.[30]

Barquin's suit against the Church was scheduled for trial in October 1996, but on July 12, after two days of negotiation, an out-of-court settlement was agreed to. While a confidentiality clause prevented disclosure of the financial terms, Barquin described them as "significant" and was clearly pleased with the outcome. There were still former orphans, however, who had not accepted the earlier $5,000 settlement offer and who were determined to pursue their claims against the Church. With Barquin's exit they had lost an articulate leader for their cause, and some even felt a sense of betrayal.[31]

By October 1996 there were 14 cases pending against the Church in the Vermont courts, and others would follow. Of the 14 plaintiffs, four men and four women claimed to have been sexually abused by the nuns during their time at St. Joseph's. They also alleged physical and emotional abuse. In the six remaining cases, the complaints were of brutal and humiliating treatment.[32]

Sally Dale, who evidently spent more of her youth in the orphanage than any of the other plaintiffs, had many a tale of horror to tell at her deposition in November 1996. She showed scars from the various brutalities inflicted on her by the nuns, as, for instance, when Sister Blanche pressed a hot iron on her hands. She told of how she had been forced to masturbate a nun in the nun's bedroom. And she described how, around 1944, she had seen a nun throw a boy to his death from a fourth-floor window. Another nun, who was escorting her through the grounds at the time, had hustled her away and, when she protested, accused her of imagining things.[33]

It is possible that the defenestration resulted from a threat that had gone awry. Robert Cadorette, who was also in St. Joseph's in the early 1940s, recalled how Sister Claire had once tried to push him out a window, but that he had managed to hold on. She then threatened him with the same punishment were he ever "bad" again. Cadorette also provided a list of other scary nuns: Sister Leontine, Sister Magdeline of the Redeemer, and Sister Pauline Germaine. And he claimed that Brother

4. Sorrowful Mysteries

Gelineau and Father Robert Devoy had attempted, but not succeeded, in assaulting him sexually.[34]

Physical threats were only one part of Sister Claire's arsenal. Donna Savard, who had spent 1958 to 1964 at St. Joseph's, complained of repeated sexual abuse by the nun. Moreover, she recalled harsh physical punishments, such as being beaten with paddles and having her legs forced against hot pipes. Insults and threats of damnation came easily to the sisters. Savard was told that her parents' divorce condemned all of them to hell. A similar remark was directed at Linda Fenton, whom the nuns said was of bad blood—a devil child.[35]

In his deposition, Cadorette had identified a small list of nuns with terrifying reputations. As Widman gathered evidence and filed cases on behalf of his clients, the list grew to include the following: Sisters Albert, Dominic, James Mary, Jane of the Rosary, Louis Hector, and Priscille. Fathers Edward Foster and Michael Madden joined the list of priests with criminal propensities.[36]

They sowed fear, and reaped a harvest in abundance. Being in a constant state of fear was Donald Shuttle's most enduring memory of his years in the orphanage. Debbie Hazen recalled how frightened she was when locked in a trunk as punishment. As Widman observed the similarities in the experiences of his clients, he felt it best to combine them into one class-action suit. Such a procedure would at once save time and money and would increase the probability of success in the courts with many stories corroborating one another. It was not to be. In the spring of 1998 a judge ruled out a class-action suit; the cases would have to proceed individually. To compound matters, he rejected Widman's demand that the Church make available the evidence submitted some years earlier by Philip White's clients who had settled for $5,000.[37]

Discouraged by this setback, some plaintiffs abandoned their suits. Those who pressed on found themselves facing an unsympathetic judiciary. In August 1998 Judge J. Garvan Murtha dismissed six of the cases brought before him, including those of Sally Dale, Donna Savard, and Donald Shuttle. His reasoning was that the statute of limitations had long since expired and that the defendants could not be held liable for abuses they had not been aware of. The defense lawyers crowed with satisfaction. John Gravel, representing Vermont Catholic Charities, had this to say: "We deny any such abuse ever took place." William O'Brien, for the diocese of Burlington, added: "The most important part of this is that the judge found no evidence whatsoever that my client was on notice of any abusive situation at all."[38]

Widman had argued before the court that abuse at St. Joseph's had been so rampant that those in charge could not possibly have been unaware of it. Believing in the merit of this assertion and that a consolidated case was still possible, he decided to appeal the decision. In the spring of 1999, having weighed up the risks entailed in an appeal, the Church proposed a settlement. Widman advised his clients to accept, and they did. The financial details remained confidential. One plaintiff considered it paltry and insufficient to buy a used car; another later revealed that he had received $10,000.[39]

The St. Joseph's Orphanage scandal appeared to be at an end. But a few short years later the Church's duplicity in dealing with the victims was revealed. In the early 2000s Vermont's attorney general was investigating the problem of pedophile priests in the Burlington diocese and was encountering nothing but obstruction and delay. Bishop Angell, in spite of his declared commitment to transparency and cooperation, was reluctant to release the personnel files of the accused priests under his jurisdiction. And when the files were eventually released, it was discovered that five of the eight chaplains who had worked in St. Joseph's between 1935 and its closure in 1974 had been sex abusers. Among those so named were two who had been identified by the former orphans as predators: Fathers Robert Devoy and Michael Madden.[40] Had this information been available when the orphanage cases were before the courts, it would have been impossible for the Church to mount a defense based on blanket denial.

St. Colman's Home for Boys and Girls, Watervliet, New York: Sisters of the Presentation of the Blessed Virgin Mary

The city of Watervliet can be found on the west bank of the Hudson River, about 13 kilometers north of New York's state capital, Albany. During the nineteenth century it had few claims to fame or infamy, except perhaps as the home of a large bell foundry, church bells being in great demand at the time. And then the Irish nuns turned up. In 1881, when Watervliet was still known as West Troy, the Sisters of the Presentation of the Blessed Virgin opened an orphanage on Haswell Road. The Sisters named their institution after Saint Colman, a popular saint in their native County Cork. During the course of its long history, St. Colman's Home for Boys and Girls served, in the words of the Sisters, as a "haven of security for more than 8,000 little ones."[41]

4. Sorrowful Mysteries

As its name indicates, the orphanage was open to children of both genders. Family unity, however, was not the point. Since the boys were kept separate from the girls in just about every respect, brothers and sisters could not communicate with one another—a source of much stress. And when the boys reached the ages of 11–12, or just before puberty kicked in, they were removed from St. Colman's and sent to La Salle School in Albany, an orphanage under the direction of the Brothers of the Christian Schools—a religious order of French origins with its own troubled history.[42]

With its strict schedules and rigid behavioral codes, St. Colman's functioned very much like a convent. The nuns simply sought to impose the strictures of monastic life on the young people submitted to their care. The children rose at 5 a.m., washed themselves, attended Mass, ate breakfast, completed chores, attended classes, and so forth, all according to an unbending and unchanging timetable. The nuns could not conceive of another way of living; there was no question of adapting monasticism to the needs of young children. And those who could not meet the expectations, especially instant obedience, faced harsh and humiliating punishments.[43]

There were four children in the Maloney family. Willie, the only boy, was the eldest, and the girls, in descending order of age, were Grace, Susanne, and June. In the summer of 1957, when Susanne was six, their mother had a nervous breakdown and their father deposited them in St. Colman's. It was the beginning of a long and difficult experience. And especially so for Susanne, who was inclined to be independent and outspoken; people like her were not appreciated in convent culture. There was one nun in particular who targeted her early on for special treatment: the much-feared Sister Regina. Crushing the girl's spirit became this nun's obsession.[44]

Elaine Ann Losee was born in Brooklyn, New York, in 1932. Received into the Sisters of the Presentation in 1951, she became known in religion as Sister Mary Regina and took her first vows in 1953. A year or two of kindergarten teaching followed before she was assigned to St. Colman's, where she spent the remainder of her career. She would have been 25 when the Maloney children arrived in 1957.[45]

On the very first day, the trouble began. June, who was six at the time, began to miss her mother and started to cry. If she was expecting sympathy or understanding, she was sorely mistaken. Sister Regina appeared out of the blue, slapped the girl's face, and told her to shut up. Susanne jumped to her little sister's defense, pleading for an end to the violence. But as she did so, she tugged at Regina's veil, which came loose exposing a bald head. The nun exploded in rage, hitting Susanne so hard she fell to the ground where she received a kick that broke her ribs. It was the first of many such encounters.[46]

The Maloney girls were not the only victims of the ill-tempered Sister Regina. Peter R. Gerace, who was placed in St. Colman's in 1959 when he was five, recalled her kicking his younger sister, Mary Ellen, on the side, an assault requiring hospitalization. Judy Gregory, who entered in 1969 aged eight, said she was beaten by the nun on her bare buttocks. Here's what she had to say about Sister Regina: "She was evil. She would say 'look into my eyes,' and her eyes were like glass looking right through you. You had a feeling she was not right."[47]

Leona (Winney) Adams, who was sent to St. Colman's with her two brothers in the late 1940s when her parents divorced, remembered the place as a "hell hole" and a "torture chamber." Only seven years old at the time of admission, she was often a victim of nun brutality, identifying Sister Loretta as particularly violent. One beating she received at the hands of Loretta stood out in her memory. The pretext: she had simply asked to spend time with her four-year-old brother whom she saw crying at the other side of the playground.[48]

Susanne Maloney also noted the cruelty of Sister Loretta. As observed earlier, boys were removed from St. Colman's before puberty could take hold. But nobody was told where they were going or why. Among the girls, rumors and speculation abounded. One story had them being taken to the mountains to be released in the wilderness to fend for themselves; another had them being drowned in the Hudson River. One day Susanne noticed her brother, Willie, among a group of boys lining up for their departure. She instantly rushed across the playground to hug him and warn him to make a run for it. But Sister Loretta was quickly on the spot prying them apart. The nun dragged her away for the inevitable beating—on the bare buttocks with a brush handle. She didn't see Willie for another six years.[49]

Sisters Cecilia, Christopher, Eucharia, and Rose were also on the list of nuns feared for their tempers and outbursts of violence. Peter Gerace, for example, recounted how Sister Rose, a very fat nun, once stomped on Peter Buchanan's leg while he was sitting on the ground and broke it. And Susanne Maloney told of how the 300-pound Sister Annunciata knocked her down in the dormitory, sat on her, and banged her head on the floor.[50]

Nano Nagle, founder of the Presentation Sisters, is acclaimed by

4. Sorrowful Mysteries

her admirers as a pioneer Catholic educator who took a special interest in the poor. According to a website maintained by the Sisters, their learning communities allegedly "strive to ensure that the dignity of persons is respected in a happy safe environment where they can learn and grow."[51] Classroom instruction to Grade 6 was provided at St. Colman's; it was anything but a "happy safe environment."

When Susanne Maloney entered the orphanage, she found herself in the Grade 3 classroom of the dreaded Sister Loretta, whose foul breath made her even more terrifying when up close. Whenever a student struggled to answer a question, the nun's response was not guidance, but a beating. One student, Louise Sharpe, just happened to be left-handed, a condition that drew the special ire of the teacher. A sharp crack of a cane on the knuckles of her left hand quickly followed whenever she attempted to grasp a pen or pencil in the manner that came most naturally to her. In Loretta's words, she was "the devil's child." The remark should not surprise; there was a long-standing belief in the Catholic Church that the devil was left-handed.[52] In Grade 5 the violence aimed not just to hurt, but to humiliate. Students answering questions incorrectly were obliged to stand against the wall while waiting to receive a beating on the bare buttocks in front of the entire class. By Grade 7 the boys had since left for La Salle School and the girls were sent to Watervliet Junior/Senior High School while still living at St. Colman's. The orphans quickly discovered that they were academically behind those who had benefited from public elementary schooling. The pedagogy of fear and intimidation as practiced by the Sisters of the Presentation was exposed in all its failings.[53]

The Sisters' penchant for beating children on the bare buttocks has been noted a number of times. And some of them seemed to take a prurient interest in the naked bodies of girls experiencing puberty. When Leona Adams was 12 she became increasingly aware of her developing body. The awareness made her more and more uneasy when the nuns stared at her and her companions as they entered and exited the showers in a state of undress—the voyeurism noted in other orphanages as well.[54]

In some instances, the interest in girls' bodies took the form of sexual sadism. One morning, as Susanne Maloney was lining up for the showers, Sister Regina noticed that she was wearing a training bra given to her by an aunt. The nun flew into her habitual rage, ripped off the girl's slip, bra, and panties, and pushed her into the shower. She then produced a bottle of Lysol and a bar of brown soap, rubbing a mixture of them all over the 12-year-old's body and, forcibly, into her vagina. The sexual assault was accompanied by a warning never again to flaunt her body. Later, when Susanne was raped in the boiler room by the maintenance man, there was no sympathy. Instead, she received the violent Lysol treatment from Regina once again. Her two sisters, June and Grace, also claimed to have been digitally raped by the same nun when going through puberty.[55]

There was no point in complaining. Besides, to whom would you complain? Parents and relatives did visit from time to time, and the nuns issued dire warnings beforehand should anything negative be said to them. Just in case, a nun was always present during the visits and ready to intervene at the slightest hint of unhappiness. Visitors only saw nuns who behaved as if they were sweet and caring. It was all a sham. The striking contrast between public image and private reality could also be seen when the state's inspectors turned up. Tablecloths and the good china appeared, and the children were served meatloaf, green peas, mashed potatoes, and even dessert. The next day, it was back to the regular, unvarying diet in which thick, barely palatable oatmeal dominated.[56]

Childhood at St. Colman's was a time of fear accentuated by an awareness that both escape and resistance were out of the question. Peter Gerace remembered it this way: "The atmosphere was electric with fear and trembling. The constant dread of being hit or beaten was a distinct possibility as I witnessed many such acts of violence inflicted upon tiny and helpless lives."[57]

During the mid–1960s their father removed the Maloney girls from St. Colman's and took them to live with him in the house he shared with his new girlfriend. Susanne finished high school, went to work in New York, and got married. Following a divorce, she married again in 1984. Her new husband, Scott Robertson, was an engineer, and they moved to Washington State when he found work with Boeing. Now known as Susanne Robertson, she was able to put the nightmare of St. Colman's behind her, at least for a few years.[58]

There were six children in the Bonneau family. In 1947, when their mother was hospitalized following a breakdown, the three youngest, Dannie, Ernie, and Gilbert, were placed in St. Colman's by their father. Gilbert, the youngest, was only two at the time. In September 1953, Dannie and Ernie were approaching puberty and were sent, according to custom, to La Salle School in Albany. Gilbert, now eight years old, was alone and terrified. Within two months he was dead. At the

4. Sorrowful Mysteries

time the family accepted the official explanation that he had died of an infection. But as the years passed, they grew suspicious, especially after receiving a phone call from a former orphan who claimed that she had seen Gilbert being badly beaten by a nun shortly before his death.[59]

In the fall of 1995 Bill and Ernie Bonneau launched a campaign in the newspapers around Watervliet seeking information about Gilbert's death. The campaign was controversial in a community where the Presentation Sisters had their defenders. But it did prompt others to go public with their own tales of abuse at the orphanage. The nuns themselves vigorously denied the allegations. Mother Virginia, who had spent more than 50 years at St. Colman's, dismissed them as the imaginings of troubled children who had grown into troubled adults.[60] When the controversy reached Susanne Robertson's ears in Washington State, she decided to add her voice to what was being said. She reported an incident at St. Colman's in 1963 when she had witnessed Sister Regina kicking Mark Langdale on the ground. A few days later, the nun informed her that Mark had died of a ruptured appendix.[61]

The Albany County district attorney's office now had two mysterious deaths to investigate. By February 1996 it had a third case on its hands: the death of six-year-old Andrew Rada at St. Colman's in 1943. The investigation was inconclusive, but the Bonneau family was convinced that the Catholic Church had been impeding the process or bringing influence to bear behind the scenes to prevent a result unfavorable to its interests. St. Colman's was now a school for autistic and emotionally challenged children. The nuns were still there, but in greatly diminished numbers and advancing in age. Sister Regina, for instance, remained at the institution until her death in 2012 at the age of 80.[62]

Susanne Robertson continued her campaign to publicize what had happened to her and others at St. Colman's. In 2002, she published a book about her experiences, *The Throw Away Child*. Assisted by a cadre of former orphans, the campaign became part of a larger movement to revise New York's strict statute of limitations respecting the abuse of children. Success came in February 2019 when Governor Andrew Cuomo signed the Child Victims Act creating a 12-month window of opportunity for victims to sue their abusers. On August 14, the date that opened the window of opportunity, Susanne Robertson and her sisters, June and Grace, filed claims of sexual abuse against the Sisters of the Presentation. At the time of writing, their cases have yet to go to court.[63]

Conclusion

The most enduring memory of those who spent part of their youth in the convent orphanages examined here was fear—being in a state of almost constant fear. It's not difficult to understand why. Insults, humiliating punishments, physical violence, and sexual assault were so commonplace as to be part of institutional culture. That nuns, who had vowed themselves to lives of chastity, would use children for sexual satisfaction is particularly noteworthy. The entire range of abusive behavior was on display here: voyeurism, fondling, simulated sex, oral sex, digital penetration, and intercourse. Beatings on the bare buttocks—sexual sadism—was all too frequent. Both girls and boys were sexually assaulted by priests and other male personnel at the orphanages—behavior that the nuns in charge ignored when it was brought to their attention.

When, years later, former orphans brought civil suits against their abusers, the Church reacted with denial and legal obstructionism. And even when the courts ruled in favor of the plaintiffs and awarded compensation, the dioceses and religious orders refused to acknowledge the terrible wrongs for which they had been responsible.

Why were there such horrors in these places? It is only possible to speculate on the answer. It may well be that operating orphanages was a low priority for religious orders and that they were not staffed with the best personnel. Placing nuns with brutal and sexually deviant inclinations in these settings may have made sense if it meant that their depredations were less likely to become a source of public scandal. After all, visiting relatives and state inspectors were served up a carefully orchestrated masquerade of happiness and well-being that camouflaged the harsh realities.

And matters may have been aggravated by the disdain shown by the nuns for the children placed in their care. The children were not necessarily orphans in the normally understood meaning of the term: children whose parents had died. Some were assigned to the institutions by the courts when their parents were judged negligent or incompetent. Others arrived after a divorce or other family difficulty. And some had been born out of wedlock. The nuns were quite aware of these circumstances and were ready to pass judgment on the parents for their failure to create ideal Catholic families. And they appear to have assumed that the children too were flawed. This idea of bad blood had a long history in the Judeo-Christian tradition and is usually traced to a statement

4. Sorrowful Mysteries

repeated a number of times in the Bible respecting the Lord "punishing children to the third and fourth generation for their fathers' wickedness" (Exodus 20:5; Exodus 34:7; Numbers 14:18).

Clear explanations for the cruelty and perversity of the nuns remain elusive. Perhaps it is best to end by repeating a quotation from Bishop Kenneth Angell of Burlington that may have revealed more than he intended: "Well, these were nuns that were just frustrated ladies and they didn't know how to handle children. They hadn't had children of their own."

5

Weaknesses of the Flesh

Missions to Native Americans

> The child molesters would come and go as the Church rotated them among the Indian missions. We children stood by each other as best we could, but for a child, it was a disturbing, sickening place to be. I have often wondered where did the nuns and priests learn those things.[1]
> —Sherwyn Zephier, former student,
> St. Paul's Mission School, Yankton
> Sioux Reservation, South Dakota

Having secured its independence from Britain in 1783, the United States embarked on a policy of expansion that in time brought it to the Pacific coast and beyond. There were substantial land purchases from Spain, France, and Russia along the way, as well as a war of annexation with Mexico. And all the while Anglo-American settlers were pushing westward into the new territories that were home to Native Americans whose objections to the newcomers required resolution. At times negotiated treaties led to the peaceful surrender of Native lands, but there were also forced confiscations and relocations. And there was resistance, especially in the years following the Civil War as settlers, gold seekers, big game hunters, and railway builders moved into the Great Plains west of the Mississippi. Here the Apache, Arapaho, Cheyenne, Comanche, and Sioux peoples, among others, took up arms to defend their traditional lands and way of life. In spite of their heroism, they were no match for the U.S. Army with its superior weaponry and ruthless, scorched-earth tactics. By 1880 what were called the "Indian wars" were over and Native Americans were adjusting to the unfamiliar tedium of reservation life.[2]

The reservation system was viewed by Washington as a temporary arrangement until such time as Native Americans had been fully assimilated into the cultural norms of the Anglo-American state. And the

5. Weaknesses of the Flesh

key to the desired transformation was the education or re-education of the younger generation. Carlisle Indian Industrial School, founded in Pennsylvania in 1879 by military veteran Richard Henry Pratt, became the prototype embraced by the federal Bureau of Indian Affairs in providing education on reservations. The institution's strict discipline was focused on eradicating all vestiges of Native identity in its students—names, language, dress, beliefs, cultural practices. And since it was a boarding school, all student contact with parents and other members of their communities was severed lest their influence persist. In addition to schools directed by the bureau, there were also some that were subcontracted to Christian missionary bodies, both Catholic and Protestant. The assumption was that missionary zeal in combatting "paganism" would accelerate conversion to Christianity, which was considered an essential component of assimilation.[3]

The typical Catholic mission to Native Americans was led by an order of missionary priests, such as the Jesuits. The priests usually engaged the services of a religious sisterhood, which was assigned most of the teaching and everyday care in the boarding school. We shall examine three case studies of this type of arrangement and how students experienced it.

South Dakota

There is a modest stone monument at Wounded Knee Creek on the Pine Ridge Reservation, South Dakota, where, on December 29, 1890, an estimated 300 largely unarmed Lakota (western Sioux) men, women, and children were massacred by soldiers of the U.S. Seventh Cavalry. A number of cavalrymen received Congressional Medals of Honor for their role in the atrocity. The Black Hills lie about 120 kilometers to the northwest and are the location of Custer State Park, the largest in the state. The park is named after George Armstrong Custer, a former commander of the Seventh Cavalry who, more than two decades earlier, had been responsible for another massacre. In November 1868, Custer and his troops killed more than 100 peaceful Cheyenne men, women, and children at their reservation village on the Washita River (present-day Oklahoma). But his depredations during the "Indian wars" came to

Predatory Nuns

a violent end at Little Bighorn River in June 1875 when he and more than 200 of his men were wiped out by a force of Arapaho, Lakota, and Northern Cheyenne. Honoring such a man in this way is an insult and provocation to Native Americans. Attempts to rename the park after Crazy Horse or Sitting Bull, among the leaders of the victorious forces at Little Bighorn, have met with no success.[4]

These legacies of the past alert us to South Dakota's history of difficult relations between Native and settler. In the stories that unfold below, we will be able to discern if time has healed the difficulties.

In July 2002, Gary Frischer, a Los Angeles litigation consultant, received a phone call from Sherwyn Zephier, a South Dakota Native American, who described the systematic abuse that he and many others known to him had experienced during their childhood at Catholic boarding schools in the state. Horrified at what he heard, Frischer spent several months in South Dakota where he, Zephier, and Zephier's sister, Adele, visited reservations and gathered evidence from former boarding school students. By April 2003, he had enough information to file a class-action lawsuit against the federal government. The plaintiffs sought $25 billion in damages from the government, which had been responsible for the schools even though it had farmed out the business of running them to Catholic missionaries.

The principal argument of the suit was that Washington had failed to honor one of its obligations under the Treaty of Fort Laramie, 1868, signed at the end of Red Cloud's War. In Article 1 of the treaty, the government pledged to arrest and punish "bad men among the whites" who committed crimes against the Indians and to compensate those who were wronged. The bad white men in this instance were abusive missionaries, and the category was presumed to include bad white women. Three schools that had employed such individuals were identified: Holy Rosary on the Pine Ridge Reservation, St. Francis on the Rosebud Reservation, and St. Paul's on the Yankton Reservation.

The suit, which began with a few former students, soon had hundreds of participants. By Frischer's estimate, there may have been up to 10,000 victims of abuse throughout the state. He saw the suit not just as an opportunity to address a great wrong, but also as an instrument to educate Native Americans on their rights as citizens. He was also planning to file additional lawsuits against the Catholic dioceses and religious orders that had handled the direct management of the schools.[5]

In 2004 the U.S. Court of Federal Claims in Washington dismissed the lawsuit.[6] The former students now decided to pursue their claims in

5. Weaknesses of the Flesh

state court alleging that the religious bodies that ran the schools had been negligent in the hiring and supervision of staff and had consequently failed to protect them from abuse.

St. Paul's Mission School

As white settlers encroached on their traditional territory between the Sioux and Missouri rivers, the Yankton (Ihanktonwan) Sioux signed a treaty in 1858 in which, in return for relinquishing aboriginal title to their domains, they secured annuities, services, and a reservation of over 400,000 acres bordering the Missouri in what is now eastern South Dakota. Their chief, Struck by the Ree, favored peace with the whites and kept his people out of the Minnesota uprising four years later.[7]

From the time of his arrival in 1917 to his death in 1948, the Benedictine priest Sylvester Eisenman was the guiding force in the St. Paul Catholic Mission on the reservation. Missionaries tend to take a dim view of the beliefs and cultural practices of those they seek to evangelize, and Eisenman was no different from the norm. Describing the Yankton Sioux as "animal-like," he declared their minds to be "selfish, baby-like, and not ready to make sacrifices." Their dances he described as "horrible bodily contortions and diabolical grimaces" that demanded suppression. For his mission to be a success he wanted a boarding school to shield the younger generation from traditional ways.[8]

In 1922, hoping to engage teaching sisters for his school, Eisenman visited Katharine Drexel, the Philadelphia banking heiress who was devoting her personal fortune to Catholic missionary work. In 1891 Drexel had established a new religious order, the Sisters of the Blessed Sacrament for Indians and Colored People. In doing so, she decided that her nuns would be exclusively white and that the "Indians and Colored People" for whom they operated schools would not be permitted to join the order. She agreed to send three of her nuns to Yankton, where they formed the nucleus of the teaching staff of St. Paul's Mission School. In 1935, in response to requests from some of their former students to enter religious life, Drexel and Eisenman decided to create an affiliate religious community—the Oblate Sisters of the Blessed Sacrament. Membership in the Oblate Sisters was open exclusively to Native Americans, and they did most of the physical labor around the missions. Boarding schools required many hands to do the cooking, cleaning, laundry, and gardening, and the Oblate Sisters fit the bill. In effect, they were a racially segregated body of lay sisters.[9]

The distinction between lay and choir sisters in religious orders requires a brief explanation. Nuns who worked in professional roles such as teaching and nursing were known as "choir sisters," were educated, and came from families with the means to provide them with dowries. So that choir sisters might be able to focus their energies exclusively on their professional work, many religious orders featured a second category of women religious: lay or coadjutrix sisters. Lay sisters came from families of modest means and were usually limited in their education. They were, in effect, servant nuns, and they worked in convent kitchens, laundries, and gardens. At St. Paul's, therefore, the Sisters of the Blessed Sacrament did the classroom instruction while the Oblate Sisters performed the more menial tasks.[10]

As the lawsuits directed at those who staffed St. Paul's were being assembled, former students began to speak publicly of their experiences there. Sherwyn Zephier, who had attended between 1963 and 1975, had this to say about the place: "The school was essentially a prison. With every door locked and total control of the children.... The windows were covered with bars or chain-link grates and the campus had barbed wire around the church itself." Such bleak surroundings were well suited to the institutional culture of violence and abuse created and sustained by the nuns and priests. Zephier was convinced that their hostility to Native ways was at the root of much of it: "That's where the Church confused a lot of our people, conditioning them to think the traditional way of prayer was evil, the devil's way. And if you didn't believe them, they'd beat you."[11]

Physical violence was pervasive. For Zephier his time at St. Paul's was "twelve years of punishment and torture." He recalled regular beatings with leather straps and a piece of wood called the "board of education." During showers the boys could see how bruised each one of them was. Nobody was immune to the brutality. "The beatings were so frequent," he said, "we adapted to the pain and got used to living that way." Sandy Wade told of how a nun used to grab her brother, Frank, by the ears and cheeks, leaving them red and bruised.[12]

Girls did not escape the violence. Zephier's sister, Adele, remembered with horror a particular nun who used to pick her up by the hair, shake her, and lock her in a closet for hours. Christine Horn said she was thrown down a three-story laundry chute for speaking the Dakota language.[13]

5. Weaknesses of the Flesh

Being in a constant state of fear was engrained in the memories of former students. Sherwyn Zephier summed it up in these words: "The nuns were as vicious as the priests—real brutes.... At night they'd pretend they'd left us, then stand in the dark corners of the dorm room, eerie in their hooded robes."[14]

There was sexual abuse as well, by both nuns and priests. Zephier recalled the occasion in which he peered through a keyhole and saw a nun sexually assaulting an older male student who happened to be his cousin. His contemporary, Mike Archambeau, witnessed the repeated molestation of a classmate by a nun. Adele Zephier was assaulted by a priest, as was Sandy Wade's brother, Frank. At the time none of them complained of the abuse. They were ashamed of what had happened to them and distrusted the judicial system. Those who told their parents were greeted with disbelief.[15]

The mission system came to an end at the conclusion of the 1975 school year when St. Paul's passed to tribal council control and was renamed Marty Indian School. At the commencement ceremony that summer, medicine man Pete Catches was invited to fill his pipe and pray with the students—an inconceivable occurrence when nuns and priests held sway.[16]

By 2008 three lawsuits had been filed by former students against the Church entities that had been responsible for St. Paul's: the Catholic diocese of Sioux Falls, the Benedictine Fathers of Blue Cloud Abbey, the Sisters of the Blessed Sacrament, and the Oblate Sisters of the Blessed Sacrament.

One of the suits had 17 plaintiffs and named seven nuns and three priests as abusers:

Sisters of the Blessed Sacrament: Sr. M. Baptista, Sr. Eleta Marie, Sr. M. Theophane, and Sr. M. Davidica (Therese Helen Kistner, 1920–2006).

Oblate Sisters of the Blessed Sacrament: Sr. Agnes, Sr. John Marie, and Sr. Mary Francis (Delia Rose Poitra, 1916–2005).

Benedictine Monks of Blue Cloud Abbey: Fr. Francis Suttmiller (1927–1996), Fr. George Lyon (1924–2008), and Fr. Leo.[17]

Sister Mary Francis presents a curious case since she was an Oblate Sister and Native herself. Born in 1916 into the Turtle Mountain Chippewa community in Belmont, North Dakota, she was sent to complete her education at St. Paul's. Entering the Oblate Sisters in 1937, she spent most of her career at the mission working in the kitchen, laundry, and boys' dormitory. Getting behind the wheel of a car was one of her passions, and she once declared: "I want to drive all the way to heaven." She

Predatory Nuns

"went to her Lord" on April 22, 2005, but whether she drove there or not is a matter of speculation.[18]

When former students first began to speak out about mistreatment and abuse at St. Paul's, Sister Mary Francis was quick to dismiss the allegations as nothing but "gossip." While admitting that children were spanked, she explained: "They weren't treated wrong. They asked for everything that happened to them."[19] This hardly seems likely. When D.Z. Iron Wing was 10 years old, Sister Mary Francis was his dormitory supervisor. In one of the lawsuits filed in 2008, he accused her of sexual abuse. She would take him to her room in the middle of the night, he claimed, when everyone else was asleep. Once there, she would fondle his genitals—usually for about 15 minutes on each occasion. There were at least 10 such encounters over a three-year period.[20]

Father Francis Suttmiller was identified by plaintiffs as a persistent sexual predator. A native of Batesville, Indiana, he entered the Benedictine novitiate in 1952 and was ordained a priest at Blue Cloud Abbey in 1954. He was assigned to teach at the St. Paul Mission immediately afterwards. Hunting, fishing, and beekeeping were his favorite pastimes, and he was known to be a born storyteller. His crimes against children were not made public until more than a decade after his death in November 1996.[21]

Barbara Charbonneau-Dahlen was only five when she was sent to St. Paul's from her home on the Turtle Mountain Chippewa reservation in North Dakota. She described how Suttmiller used to take her to the church basement and threaten to put her in a coffin unless she agreed to his sexual demands. Other girls that she knew became pregnant at the school, she alleged, and were forced to have abortions. All eight of her sisters attended St. Paul's as well, and all complained of abuse.[22]

Suttmiller also targeted boys. D.Z. Iron Wing said that the priest would take him to his room in the early hours of the morning for oral sex. This happened eight or nine times. When the boy was in his junior year of high school, he told his father and his stepmother of the depredations of Sister Mary Francis and Father Suttmiller. His stepmother was outraged, but not at the abusers. Slapping him across the head, she berated him for spreading lies about "people of God" who would never behave in such a manner. Iron Wing never spoke of the abuse for many decades afterwards.[23]

Since several lawsuits involving different boarding schools were proceeding through the courts simultaneously and were all dealt with

5. Weaknesses of the Flesh

in a similar manner, we shall examine the problems in one more institution before considering the final outcome.

Tekakwitha Indian Home

By the Treaty of Traverse des Sioux, 1851, the U.S. government acquired the Native lands of Minnesota and Iowa in return for reservations, payments, and other considerations. The Santee, or eastern Sioux, were placed on reservations along the Minnesota River. The tribes known as the Sissetons and Wahpetons settled in the Northern Agency, while the Mdewakantons and Wahpekutes went to the Southern Agency. Provoked by treaty violations, the Minnesota Uprising of 1862, or Little Crow's War, involved the southern tribes. Although the Sissetons and Wahpetons stayed aloof from the conflict, they, along with the other Santee, were scattered in its aftermath in attempting to evade vengeful whites. Many fled northwards to seek refuge in the British territory of Rupert's Land. Meeting a cool reception across the boundary, most soon returned to settle around Enemy Swim Lake, Dakota Territory, where they signed a new treaty in 1863. They were thereby granted the wedge-shaped Lake Traverse Reservation in the northeastern corner of what is now South Dakota.[24]

Theresa von Wuellenweber (1833–1907) was the eldest daughter of a German baron. Raised in the aristocratic privilege of a Rhineland castle and educated at an exclusive Benedictine convent in Belgium, she decided not to marry but was unsure of what else to do with her life. She first tried religious life with the Society of the Sacred Heart and later with the Visitation Sisters, but found it unsatisfactory. After years of trial and error she founded her own order during a visit to Italy in 1888, the Sisters of the Divine Savior. Von Wuellenweber was known in religion as Mother Mary of the Apostles; members of her order were called "Salvatorians"—not to be confused with people from El Salvador, "Salvadorans." In 1895 some Salvatorians came to the U.S., where, from their headquarters in Milwaukee, they began to establish schools and hospitals for the German diaspora.[25]

In 1933 the nuns were invited to participate in the Catholic mission at the Lake Traverse Reservation in collaboration with the Oblate Fathers, who had been there since 1931. Their first missionary institution was the Tekakwitha Hospital (1933–1967), which was followed by the Tekakwitha Indian Children's Home. The home was in fact a

Predatory Nuns

boarding school and orphanage, and it remained in operation from 1939 until 1973. The part of it reserved for very young children was known as the Papoose House. Both institutions were named after Kateri Tekakwitha (1656–1680), a Mohawk convert to Catholicism and practitioner of self-inflicted pain who was canonized in 2012. In her official history of the Salvatorians, Sister Margaret Shekleton claimed, "from the beginning, the Sisters strove to respect the traditions of the Indian children and to cultivate within them a respect and love for their own heritage." And she added that "the Sisters who worked at Tekakwitha labored to help these youngsters appreciate an education and tried to inspire them to work to help their own people."[26]

In 1946, three-month-old Mary-Catherine Renville was taken from her mother and placed in the Papoose House. At the age of six she was moved to the main building to begin her schooling. Upon finishing the junior high grades, which was the maximum offered at Tekakwitha, she was enrolled in a Nebraska boarding school to complete her education. She remembered her youth as a time of hunger, punishment, and abuse. The nuns were a problem, she recalled: "The nuns would take us to their private quarters and do things to our bodies that even at that young age I knew were not right." In general, she found them cold and uncaring: "They wanted our souls and to teach us to fear God. Sometimes they'd whip us, holding us with the left hand while using the right to beat us with a rubber hose."

When Renville was eight or nine, Oblate Father John Pohlen, head of the mission, placed her with a family for the summer as a potential adoptee. Here she was raped by the men and boys of the household. Later, when she was around 10, another attempted adoption also resulted in rape. There was physical violence at the Nebraska school, but no sexual abuse. As an adult, she drifted from place to place while working as a waitress to survive. In time she returned to live at Lake Traverse. Her motivation for joining the 2010 lawsuit was clear: "What I want to do is to talk about Tekakwitha. They took away our sense of belonging to anyone, our opportunities to develop relationships. They kept us off balance by sending us here and there without warning. But they could never take away the truth: that what they were doing was wrong. I want everyone to know what happened to us there."[27]

In the mid–1950s, when he was around five years old, Howard Wanna and his siblings were placed in Tekakwitha by his parents, who believed that the nuns and priests would educate and care for them. At first the place seemed welcoming, but after a few weeks everything

5. Weaknesses of the Flesh

changed. Wanna was still resident at the Papoose House when Father Pohlen came by, took him to a room behind the church altar, and raped him. The priest rotated him with four other boys, and he dreaded the day when his turn would come around again. Worst of all, there was no one to turn to, not even God, because "God's representative on earth" was hurting him. Before long, a nun was targeting him too, and there were numerous other horrors and indignities as well. Here are his words:

> Soon a nun began to abuse me as well, placing me under her gown and rubbing my little hands between her legs. This was something the nuns did to other children there, too. It was horrifying, not just because of what she was doing but because it was dark and I couldn't breathe. Other abuse included beating us with sticks, hoses, and even a metal shovel. The cruelty was strangely inventive. At bath time, we'd line up, a line of naked girls and a line of naked boys, which was embarrassing to begin with. We'd take turns jumping into a laundry tub and being scrubbed—scratch, scratch, scratch—with a stiff brush you'd use for floors. We'd then hop out of the tub with scrapes all over our bodies.... Tekakwitha was a very quiet place. You'd think with all those children, there'd be noise and laughing. But so many of us were being abused and simply didn't talk. We were too frightened. It was like a horror movie in which people walk by each other but can't communicate.[28]

The abuse lessened as Wanna became older and more assertive. When he was around nine years old—he was not sure since birthdays were not celebrated—his mother discovered what was happening to her children at the mission and turned up in a rage. During the argument that ensued he heard the authorities say to her, "Take the little bastards." And they left. His adulthood was a struggle, but he eventually went to college and owned his own business. He decided to participate in the lawsuit so that the goings-on at Tekakwitha would no longer remain hidden from the public by the Church. In reflecting on his experiences at the mission, he had this to say: "I often wonder how so many pedophiles ended up at Native American schools. Father Pohlen was not only a pervert; he also hired the worst of the worst, which meant none of the Tekakwitha staff would protect us from the others. How did he find them? Is there someone in the Church you can call to request problem priests and nuns? Was there a dual plan to hurt Native Americans while taking care of the pedophiles? Was this genocide? It's so confusing, but it's also just plain evil."[29]

The suit against the Catholic mission at Lake Traverse was filed on July 19, 2010, by 24 plaintiffs who were identified solely by their initials. The accused were the Diocese of Sioux Falls, the Tekakwitha

Predatory Nuns

Indian Mission, the U.S. Province of the Missionary Oblates of Mary Immaculate, and the Sisters of the Divine Savior. Five Oblate priests and three brothers were named as predators, as were seven nuns. The suit alleged that the accused had been aware of sexual abuse of minors at the mission and had concealed it from law enforcement authorities in accordance with directives from the Vatican known as *Crimines Solicitationes* or the pontifical secret. Moreover, they had warned the victims that, should they disclose details of the abuse, they and their families would be humiliated, denied food, or be in other ways harmed.

The earliest instance of abuse was alleged by a boy who had been at the school between 1944 and 1945; the most recent was by a girl enrolled between 1960 and 1970. Which means that the abusive behavior at Tekakwitha endured for at least 25 years. The evidence suggests that the nuns were the most persistent offenders.

It began at the top with accusations by three girls against Sister Lucy Marie, superior of the community during the 1950s and 1960s. It was claimed that this nun had peculiar predilections. She allegedly brought her victims to her office, where she forced them to undress and smear oil on a life-sized female doll as a prelude to performing sexual activities with it. And then she abused the children herself.

Sisters Bogadina, Gabrini, Katherine, John, Lagenda, and Teresa were accused of abusing both boys and girls, although their individual preferences varied. The bathtub was frequently the scene of their crimes. Sister Lagenda had a particularly odious reputation. She digitally penetrated her female victim numerous times while telling her she was nasty and "had the devil in her." On one occasion she forced the girl and another one to touch each other sexually while she watched.

Three girls and six boys alleged abuse by nuns whose names they could not recall. It is impossible to say whether these predators were the same nuns whose names were identified by others, or additions to the list. The patterns of abuse were similar, although one female victim, who was only 12 when she left the school, alleged that she had been forced to perform oral sex on her nun abuser. Many of those abused by nuns were also assaulted by the Oblate priests and brothers at the mission.[30]

Rebecca Rhoades, one of the lawyers with the California firm representing the plaintiffs, had this to say: "We certainly have seen female perpetrators, but the severity of the abuse by the nuns in this case is particularly unusual.... Really, it was just very perverse, very strange, and the clients we have whose abusers were nuns were very, very traumatized."[31]

In addition to St. Paul's and Tekakwitha, the lawsuits filed in 2010 and

5. Weaknesses of the Flesh

in the years previously also targeted the following institutions and those responsible for them: Holy Rosary Mission, Pine Ridge Reservation, the Society of Jesus; St. Francis Mission, Rosebud Reservation, the Society of Jesus and the Sisters of St. Francis; St. Joseph's Indian School, Chamberlain, South Dakota, Priests of the Sacred Heart and the Franciscan Sisters.

The students who attended St. Joseph's were mainly from the Cheyenne River Reservation. Eight former students alleged that they had been sexually abused at the school during the 1970s by Fathers William Pitcavage and Thomas Lind, both of whom were retired at the time of the suit. To defend the suit, the Priests of the Sacred Heart hired Chamberlain attorney Steven R. Smith to represent them. Smith devised a plan to prevent the plaintiffs from ever getting their day in court, which, if successful, would also derail the other mission lawsuits.

At the time, South Dakota Statute 20–10–25 required victims of sexual assault during their childhood to file suit against their assailants within three years of the assault or within three years of establishing a connection between the assault and the injury experienced subsequently. Smith drafted an amendment that read: "However, no person who has reached the age of forty years may recover damages from any person or entity other than the person who perpetrated the actual act of sexual abuse." He took it to the state legislature as a constituent bill, where it was sponsored by Republican Party legislators Thomas Deadrick, Kent Juhrke, and Cooper Garnos as Bill HB1104. It passed through the house and senate with great speed and little opposition, Smith himself being the only witness to appear during discussion. It was signed into law by Governor Mike Rounds in March 2010. Smith admitted that potential opposition to the measure had had little time to get organized. "Nobody knew what I was doing," he remarked.[32]

The revised law meant in effect that the vast majority of the plaintiffs in the various mission school cases were ineligible to sue because of age. But even if they met the age requirement, they could only sue their individual abusers and not the organizations to which they belonged. And even then, assuming that the abusers were still living—and many were not—suing them would have been pointless since members of religious orders, whether male or female, were usually without assets. On March 11, 2011, a state judge dismissed the various lawsuits filed by former mission school students. The revision to the statute embodied in Bill HB1104 was critical to the decision.[33]

State Representative Steve Hickey, who had opposed HB1104, was appalled at what had transpired: "It's scandalous and shameful that someone who is litigating abuse cases drafted and supported passage of a bill that shelters his client. This was not made clear to our citizen legislature, which works very fast, handling some 500 bills in 38 days. Nor was it made clear to legislators that HB1104 was going to affect court cases already in the system."[34] But Steven Smith remained unrepentant. The Church attorney maintained that the lawsuits against the missions were the work of out-of-state lawyers seeking large payoffs. Describing them as "con men," he portrayed them as victims of their own folly: "When you're playing a predatory practice, you better get ready for a predatory response. They created the monster and that got them to this bill that just got passed."[35]

The matter didn't end there. The nine Charbonneau sisters who had attended St. Paul's during the 1950s and 1960s maintained an agitation for redress by turning up every year at the state legislature in Pierre to see if their stories of abuse would resonate with lawmakers. Some listened. In February 2020 Democratic Party Representative Shawn Bordeaux sponsored a bill that would have suspended the statute of limitations for a two-year period to allow abuse cases to proceed. The bill did not succeed.[36] In taking this decision, South Dakota was out of step with an emerging trend: California, New Jersey, and New York had already suspended their statutes in response to pressure from victims, and other states were planning to follow suit.[37]

The Church did not wish to appear indifferent in the aftermath of its triumph. Diocese of Sioux Falls chancellor Matt Altoff said his organization was willing to offer psychological counseling and "spiritual direction" to assist with the healing. Father Michael Mulloy, administrator with the Diocese of Rapid City, offered reconciliation and healing for anyone who had been hurt: "I believe that the one who can give that reconciliation and healing is Jesus Christ." That victims would turn for help to those who had abused and denied them compensation is difficult to imagine.[38]

Montana

The Flathead Indian Reservation in Montana is home to the Salish, Pend d'Oreille, and Kootenai peoples. Catholic missionary activity

5. Weaknesses of the Flesh

among these peoples began with the arrival of Belgian-born Father Pierre-Jean De Smet and a number of other Jesuits in 1841. Convinced that nomadism hampered evangelism, De Smet encouraged settlement in villages where greater control could be exercised. In 1854, he established the St. Ignatius Mission as a major center of evangelical work. A year later, the Treaty of Hellgate, which led to the creation of the Flathead Reservation, facilitated organizing the Native peoples into Christianizing villages. Ursuline nuns arrived in St. Ignatius in 1890 and began to build schools. Their principal educational institution, the Ursuline Academy, lasted until 1972.[39]

The Ursulines, an order originating in Italy following the Counter-Reformation, was one of the earliest to arrive in North America. Twelve of them stepped ashore in New Orleans in 1727 from France. They quickly established themselves as educators of girls in what was at the time the French colony of Louisiana and spread out from there when it became part of the United States in 1803. It is worth observing that the Ursulines were one of at least eight religious sisterhoods that owned slaves in the antebellum South.[40]

The problematic nature of the St. Ignatius Mission first came to light as a result of a lawsuit brought against the Jesuits of the Oregon Province—an administrative region comprising the states of Alaska, Idaho, Montana, Oregon, and Washington. The 500 plaintiffs party to the lawsuit, who were preponderantly Native American, claimed that Jesuit missionaries had subjected them to sexual abuse during their youth and that the abuse had continued unchecked for many years. The claim, settled in March 2011, required the Jesuits to provide a compensation package to the victims amounting to $166.1 million. They also agreed to publish on their website the names of everyone working in their missions who had been credibly accused of abuse. It was the largest settlement ever against a religious order.[41]

Bryan Smith, an attorney with Tamaki Law in Yakima, Washington, whose firm was involved in the case, took depositions from many of the plaintiffs in the course of his work. He was shocked to learn that Ursuline nuns, who were missionary partners with the Jesuits, were also accused of sexual depredations. Michael Pfau, whose Seattle law firm, Pfau, Cochran, Vertetis, Amala, was also party to the case, noted complicity between the nuns and priests in the abuse.[42] Since the lawsuit was only against the Jesuits, there were no penalties imposed on the Ursulines. But their day of reckoning was not far off.

In October 2011, just six months after the Jesuit case had been

Predatory Nuns

settled, a lawsuit was filed in the Montana First Judicial Court seeking damages from both the Ursuline Sisters of the Western Province and the diocese of Helena. The suit claimed that "plaintiffs suffered physical, sexual, and emotional abuse by nuns and sisters employed at the Ursuline Academy in St. Ignatius, Montana, and/or by priests employed by the Roman Catholic Diocese of Helena." There were 45 plaintiffs initially, but that number rose to 95 as the case progressed.

On the day the lawsuit was filed, Blaine Tamaki and his legal team from Yakima, Washington, gathered with a number of the plaintiffs on the lawn of the Missoula County Courthouse to answer questions from the press. Several of the plaintiffs spoke openly about their mistreatment by nuns and priests when they had been young students at the mission between the 1940s and 1970s. George Lee Thomas, bishop of Helena since 2004, issued a prepared statement in which he accused the plaintiffs and their lawyers of attempting "to try the case in the court of public opinion by a selective misrepresentation of the facts."[43]

The lawsuit alleged that the Ursulines and the diocese knew or should have known that they were harboring sexual predators in their institutions and failed to report their criminal activity to the secular authorities. Moreover, they engaged in a pattern of placing the predators in remote areas and moving them about between different missions to hamper efforts at detection. Nor did they inform parents that their children were in the custody of pedophiles. In this way, they acted to protect their own assets from actions that might have been initiated by the victims and their parents. As a consequence, the Ursulines and the diocese allegedly caused "life-long, persistent damages" to the plaintiffs as well as "physical, emotional, psychological distress, and extreme anguish, loss of earnings and earning capacity and other general and special damages." The suit called on the Ursulines and the diocese to acknowledge publicly the sexual abuse suffered by the plaintiffs, to implement measures to prevent abuse in the future, and to provide a financial settlement as fair compensation for the damages sustained.[44]

The following Ursulines were identified as abusers in the suit: Mother Camellia, Sister Cecilia, Mother Henrietta, Sister John, Mother Loyola, and Sister Marion. The male missionaries accused included Brother René Gallant (known as Brother Charlie), and Fathers Joseph Balfe, William Burke, A.J. Feretti, and Bernard Harris. Most of the alleged sexual predators were dead, and for those still living, the statute of limitations prevented prosecution. The plaintiffs were seeking financial compensation only.[45]

5. Weaknesses of the Flesh

Why did the victims take so long to come forward with their complaints? A complete answer to this question would require a complicated digression. The words of one of them, however, may serve as our guide. Jackie Trotchie was abused when attending St. Mary's Catholic School in Helena. She was threatened with hellfire by her abusers were she ever to make a complaint against them. She was also aware that a Native American girl making such an accusation would either not be believed or be told that she had gotten what she deserved.[46]

Trotchie was typical of the victims: young, Native American, and living away from home in a boarding school. Francis Burke, for example, was only six years old when he was sent to the St. Ignatius Mission. He only stayed two years before running away. He and two of his fellow students, Garry Salois and Leland Hewankorn, had never wanted to attend the mission school, but their parents enrolled them in response to threats of prosecution from the state authorities. They arrived at St. Ignatius speaking little English. "Dirty," "pigs," and "dumb Indians" —the favorite terms used by the nuns to describe them—were among the first words they learned. Burke recalled one student with a slight speech impediment who was ridiculed endlessly as a "slobberpuss and a moron."[47] As he remembered the experience: "It was hell, 24–7. You never knew if you were going to be jerked out of bed and slapped around. I never seen them smile or show affection. There is not enough money in the world to make up for what happened to us, what they did to the Indians in their care. I grew up to be an angry man hiding my shame with alcohol and drugs."[48]

Verbal insults and physical violence were only a beginning: much worse was to come. Salois recalled that the sexual abuse began shortly after his arrival at the mission as a skinny five-year-old in 1956. He had several tormentors, but Mother Loyola stood out as the very worst—a view shared by Burke.[49]

Mother Loyola, already deceased at the time of the lawsuit, was born Rufina Karges in Germany around 1907. She was at the Montana mission in 1940, having immigrated to the United States during the 1930s.[50] A large woman, she was described by one of her Ursuline companions as "a rather severe disciplinarian." Some of her students suspected that she was a Nazi war criminal hiding out in the guise of a nun. Others thought that she was really a man until confronted with indisputable evidence to the contrary.[51]

Mother Loyola was in charge of the dormitory at the mission school—an advantageous position for a predator. Over a 23-year period, between 1942 and 1965, she allegedly sexually abused at least 14 boys, some of them on a continuous basis. She only targeted boys, all of whom were between the ages of six and 12. The abuse involved fondling their genitals as she put them to bed, but in some cases it went much further. She took two boys, and perhaps more, to her bedroom and forced them to perform oral sex on her. In another case, the fondling eventually led to masturbation and even intercourse when the victim was only 12.[52]

It was claimed that several of Loyola's victims had also been abused by other nuns, the following being named in the indictment: Sister Cecilia, Sister John, and Sister Marion. And most of them were also targeted by Brother Charlie and the priests at the mission. The female plaintiffs were almost exclusively abused by male clerics, but three of them complained of unspecified mistreatment by Sister Camellia, Sister Cecilia, Mother Henrietta, and Sister John.[53]

In spite of initial bluster and denial, Bishop George Thomas came to the conclusion that it was best to settle the claim against the diocese of Helena through a negotiated settlement. The diocese had liability insurance, and the insurers, after some reluctance, agreed to pay for most of the compensation. The sum offered was $16.5 million. Of this, the diocese paid over $2 million, which it raised through the sale of a youth camp and a retreat center. It also filed for bankruptcy protection as these details were worked out. As 2014 dragged on, it looked as if the Ursulines were prepared to fight their part of the suit in the courts. Without insurance, their situation was more precarious, but in the end a trial was avoided. In February 2015, the Ursulines agreed to pay $4.45 million in compensation to the plaintiffs to be financed by the sale of property assets. The terms of both settlements were agreed to by the plaintiffs on March 4, 2015, at the courthouse in Coeur d'Alene, Idaho.[54]

As part of the settlement, Bishop Thomas apologized to the victims for what they had suffered and assured them that the abusers were either dead or inactive. And he agreed to a measure requiring much more intensive background checks on candidates for the religious life. Finally, the diocese was obliged to post on its website the names of all its employees credibly accused of sexually abusing a minor. The list of abusers, which went back to the 1930s, included 21 diocesan priests, 14 Jesuits, and three Norbertine priests. There were 27 nuns on the list, 21 of whom were Ursulines.[55]

While the victims of abuse drew satisfaction from the compensation and Church acknowledgment of wrongdoing, they were all too conscious of the manner in which the abusers had shattered their lives.

5. Weaknesses of the Flesh

Francis Burke and Gary Salois, for example, had had long struggles with drugs and alcohol over the years as they attempted to blank out the memories of their time at the mission. "I'm a big guy now," said Salois, "but in my nightmares Mother Loyola still owns me." Both men rejected Christianity, refused to have their children baptized, and turned to traditional Native religion for healing. They resent the fact that the mission building in which they were tormented is listed on the National Register of Historic Places and cannot be touched. They would love to either pull it down or blow it up.[56]

Conclusion

Why was the sexual abuse so pervasive in this context, and why did it endure so long before being exposed? Ken Bear Chief, a paralegal with the Gros Ventre nation, claimed that Native missions became dumping grounds for problem religious who circulated among the many reservations of the Northwest, moving on when suspicions arose about their behavior. Barbara Dorris, outreach director of the Survivors Network of those Abused by Priests (SNAP), had this to say: "What we see is that Church officials tend to put predators into situations where they are less likely to be caught and prosecuted, where children have fewer resources, less access to law enforcement, fewer people watching. So, we do see a pattern.... Ultimately, it is a great situation for a predator."[57]

It would be difficult to deny that Catholic missions to the Native American communities of the Northwest bore a disquieting resemblance to a well-organized pedophile ring. And the Church's efforts to perpetuate the system through denials, cover-ups, and legal and political chicanery suggest a callous disregard for the welfare of the children entrusted to its care. "It's all about protecting their assets and their asses, so to speak," as Ken Bear Chief put it succinctly.[58]

6

Unfaithful Servants
Catholic Schools

> Some experts believe sexual abuse by nuns may be underreported—as is sexual abuse by women in secular society—and unrecognized even by those children who are its victims. In fact, Kenneth Lanning, the FBI's expert on child sexual abuse, who attended Catholic schools as a child, wonders if some nuns' notorious penchant for physical discipline may betray a degree of sexual sadism.[1]
> —Elinor Burkett and Frank Bruni, *A Gospel of Shame: Children, Sexual Abuse, and the Catholic Church*

As the Catholic Church developed its network of institutions in America in conjunction with immigration and population growth, the teaching sister became its most visible figure. By 1965, when the convent system reached its pinnacle, there were almost 180,000 nuns in total, with 114,000 working in Catholic schools.[2] That they were the workhorses of the Church's school system—the largest private system in the world—is not in dispute. Nuns were principals, teachers, fundraisers, and willing volunteers for any task requiring attention. Some took on the additional duty of teaching religion classes on Saturdays or after regular school hours to Catholic children enrolled in the public system.[3]

When parents sent their children to Catholic schools, they expected them to be taught by nuns, and this was usually so, especially at the elementary level. The nun as the ideal teacher for girls—and for younger boys too—became an axiom of Catholic education. Since it was believed that she was called by God to an exalted way of life, the moral formation of youth was presumed to be safe in her hands. And her expertise in religious instruction—an essential part of the curriculum—was never in doubt. At times it was even claimed that her work in the classroom was inspired by divine guidance. Writing in 1952,

6. Unfaithful Servants

Mother Marie Helene, superior general of the Sisters of Providence (St. Mary-of-the-Woods, Indiana), noted: "The ease with which a frail little sister can interest and gain the hearts of a group of children shows that God gives the tools to those who are willing to do his work."[4]

Did teaching sisters always do God's work? Or were there some among them who took advantage of their unquestioned authority and image of holiness to sexually abuse children placed in their classrooms? And if so, how did religious orders respond when presented with evidence of criminal activity among their ranks? We shall seek answers in 18 representative case studies that include nuns from several congregations and one ex-nun.

Judith Fisher, Sisters of St. Joseph, Missouri

The origins of the Sisters of St. Joseph can be traced to seventeenth-century France. They were suppressed, along with all other religious orders, during the Revolution only to be revived in its aftermath by Mother Saint John Fontbonne. In 1836 six of the Sisters arrived in frontier Missouri and established a convent and school at Carondelet, a village adjacent to St. Louis and which ultimately became part of the city. In little more than a decade they were expanding their operations to Philadelphia; St. Paul, Minnesota; and Toronto. They became known as the Sisters of St. Joseph of Carondelet in order to distinguish themselves from orders of a similar name, such as the Sisters of St. Joseph of Cluny.

One hundred years later, they were still expanding. In 1947 the Sisters established Immacolata School in Richmond Heights, a western suburb of St. Louis. In 1971 Anne Gleeson was 13 years old and a Grade 8 student at the school. She was of a devoutly Catholic family, and her father was an active member of the parish. Her homeroom and history teacher was the charismatic 37-year-old Sister Judith Fisher. Early in the school year Sister Judith began to indicate a special interest in Gleeson—leaving presents for her, adding personal notes to her written assignments, pressing close to her in the darkness of the classroom when a movie was being shown. By December the teenager was having sleepovers at the convent, and it was here that the nun initiated sexual touching. According to Sister Judith, the abuse was a special form of "God's love" that nobody else would understand. Consequently, it had to remain a secret. She promised that the two of them would be together forever. In the meantime, she ingratiated herself with Gleeson's family and became particularly close to her mother, which helped to allay suspicion that anything out of the ordinary was going on.

The secrecy came to an end in 1974 when Gleeson's parents discovered to their horror the diary in which she had recorded all the sordid details. Her father, Dixon, was particularly shocked since he had deliberately sent his five children to Immacolata believing that nuns named after St. Joseph, the protector of families, were above reproach. Like typical Catholics of the time, the parents approached the parish priest, Father Cornelius Flavin, who promised to take care of the matter. But he counseled them against reporting the abuse to the police in order to avoid scandal. Shortly afterwards, Sister Judith was transferred to Denver, Colorado, where she became principal of St. Francis de Sales School. Moving the problem elsewhere was an all-too-familiar strategy of the Church when confronted with criminal activity among its personnel. Even so, the abusive relationship continued for several more years, this time in greater secrecy and with less frequent encounters because of distance. In 1979 Sister Judith Fisher left religious life.

More than two decades after these events, a therapist explained to Gleeson that her relationship with the nun had been one of sexual exploitation. In 2003 Gleeson decided to act by filing a lawsuit against her abuser as well as the archdiocese of St. Louis and the Sisters of St. Joseph. Her suit was less about money than about closure: she wanted Fisher to confess to the abuse and offer an explanation for it. But Fisher died on January 11, 2004, before she could be held accountable for her actions. The Sisters of St. Joseph did settle the suit with Gleeson and provided her with letters of apology for the harm done to her.

Anne Gleeson left the Catholic Church as a result of the abuse. She believes that the victims of pedophile nuns are much more numerous than people think but most of them are reluctant to come forward because of the saintly public image of women in religious life.[5]

Charlotte Skeabeck, Sisters of St. Joseph, Pennsylvania

The diocese of Erie is one of six that was investigated by the grand jury that reported on sex abuse by religious personnel in Pennsylvania in August 2018. In response to the inquiry, Erie published on its website the names of its employees credibly accused of crimes against young

6. Unfaithful Servants

people. By October the list identified 49 priests, 20 lay people, and one nun. Charlotte Skeaback was the nun in question.

Skeabeck joined the Sisters of St. Joseph in 1942 when she was 18. Following her novitiate, Sister Mary Carmel, as she was now known, began her teaching career in the Pennsylvania Catholic schools staffed by her community. In 1958 she was assigned to the staff at Villa Maria Academy, an all-girls high school in Erie. And it was here that she "sexually abused a student on numerous occasions." Complaints about her behavior were made at the time and unspecified "corrective actions" were taken that the Sisters later acknowledged to have been "insufficient by today's standards." Skeabeck continued her teaching career in the diocese until retirement in 2001. She died in 2015 at the age of 91, three years before her crimes became public.[6]

Alberta Veri, Sisters of St. Joseph, Pennsylvania

Pam Erdely kept her secret for more than two decades. In 1971–72 she was a senior at Bishop Canevin High School in Pittsburgh, Pennsylvania, when the librarian, Sister Bernardine, began to show a personal interest in her. At first, she was flattered since the nun appeared to be a good person. One evening, Sister Bernardine invited her to a poetry reading and afterwards asked that she spend the night at the convent of her community, the Sisters of St. Joseph. Later, the nun allegedly entered the bedroom, undressed, got into the bed, and molested Erdely. As the weeks and months passed by, she talked much of love and asked that their relationship remain a secret and that it become a life-long commitment. It is not clear if Sister Bernardine had other victims. In 1980 she left religious life and went once more by her real name, Alberta Veri. More than two decades later she was working in the collections department of a Cleveland bank.

Things did not go well for Pam Erdely after high school graduation. Psychological trauma, confusion about her sexual orientation, and problems in romantic relationships were compounded by an uneven employment record and the cost of extensive therapy. In 1994 she was advised by a therapist that the abuse by Veri was the probable cause of her difficulties. In 1997 she filed a lawsuit against Veri, the Sisters of St. Joseph, and the diocese of Pittsburgh. The Sisters were prepared to offer a settlement to their part of the suit if she were willing to sign a confidentiality clause—which she refused. But the lawsuit ran afoul of

Pennsylvania's strict statute of limitations, which required a minor who was a victim of sexual assault to file a claim before she/he reached the age of 20.[7]

Georgene Stuppy, Sisters of St. Francis, Minnesota

A native of Milwaukee, Wisconsin, Georgene Helen Stuppy entered the novitiate of the Sisters of St. Francis in Edina, Minnesota, in 1958, when she was 20 years old. She professed her vows in 1961 and was known in religion as Sister Dimitri. With a degree in education from the College of St. Teresa in Winona, she worked for two decades as a junior high teacher in various Catholic schools in Illinois, Ohio, and Minnesota. In 1976 she was teaching in Queen of Angels School in Austin, Minnesota, when she became on friendly terms with a female student in her religion class. For two years, she insinuated herself into the life of the student and her family, establishing herself as a spiritual mentor. In 1978, the student, now 13, began to receive counseling from Sister Dimitri, and she claimed that it was at this stage that the nun initiated physical contact of a sexual nature. The abuse continued until 1981.

In January 1992, the former student sued Sister Dimitri and the Sisters of St. Francis alleging that the nun had "regularly and repeatedly engaged in unpermitted, harmful and offensive sexual contact" with her for three years beginning in 1978. The abuse was said to have taken place both at Queen of Angels School and in the nun's convent in Rochester. In response to the allegation, Sister Dimitri admitted to physical contact with her student, but claimed that it had been of a nurturing and comforting nature and not for the purposes of sexual gratification. She explained that the two of them had been spiritual companions on a "shared journey" to discover God's divine love. Her extensive correspondence with the girl was filled with strange religious allusions that would have qualified as heresy if nothing else. One thing was clear: this was a woman obsessed. For example, when the girl left her class one day the nun penned a note that read: "When I moved your desk to the side, I found myself bowing and kissing it." The suit was settled for an undisclosed sum in 1993.

Georgene Stuppy died on May 23, 2009, at Assisi Heights, Rochester, Minnesota. Her obituary included the following description: "A gifted educator, she helped her students expand their awareness of justice and peace needs on a global scale."[8]

6. *Unfaithful Servants*

Janice Nadeau, School Sisters of Notre Dame, New York

In 1976, following a teaching stint at McQuaid Jesuit High School in Brighton, a southern suburb of Rochester, New York, Sister Janice Nadeau was appointed principal of St. Margaret Mary School in Irondequoit, a northern part of the city. In her forties at the time and determined to make an impression, the School Sister of Notre Dame quickly earned a reputation as a harsh disciplinarian and a stickler for rules. On her first day on the job she demanded that a student parade in front of a class with a piece of gum she had been chewing stuck on her nose. When the student refused, Nadeau slapped her in the face.

Early in 1977 the principal began to cast her disapproving eye in the direction of 12-year-old Christina Grana, observing that the kilt she wore as part of the school uniform was too short. Grana's mother, upon learning of the complaint, measured the kilt, found that it conformed to regulations, and wrote to the principal expressing this view. When Nadeau read the letter, she flew into a rage and dragged the seventh-grader by the ear to her office. With the door slammed shut, the nun slapped Grana in the face with a force that knocked her against the wall. A second blow sent her flat on the floor. At this stage Sister Janice straddled the girl yelling: "You're a slut, you're inviting rape and you're going to get raped." Then, reaching under the girl's kilt, she digitally penetrated her victim.

Grana told nobody of the incident at the time. When she was 18, she left home and eventually found work in the movie industry in Los Angeles. But during all those years she was afflicted with nightmares and depression. Nadeau continued to haunt her; she was the monster in the closet, under the bed. Abusive relationships with men were part of her life as well as constant therapy. It was not until June 2018, after she had returned to the Rochester area, that she recounted her experiences with the nun to family and friends. When she lodged a complaint about her assault with the diocese of Rochester, the administrator of its abuse victims reconciliation program found her story "completely credible." Grana was offered a five-figure settlement in compensation for her suffering. By this time, Sister Janice Nadeau was in her mid–eighties, had long since retired, and was living in a care facility with advanced dementia.[9]

Predatory Nuns

Marcene Schlosser, School Sisters of Notre Dame, Minnesota

Marcene Eva Schlosser was born in May 1938 on the family farm near Madison, Minnesota. When she was in Grade 7, she expressed an interest in religious life and was accepted into the Good Counsel Academy in Mankato for her secondary schooling. The academy was an aspirancy—a special boarding school run by the School Sisters of Notre Dame designed to protect from the contagion of the world the incipient religious vocations of teenagers who were considered "convent material." In Schlosser's case the protection worked out, and upon graduation she entered the School Sisters, an order of German origin that was brought to America in 1847 by its founder, Mother Teresa of Jesus (Caroline Gerhardinger). In religion she was known as Sister Mary Cletus, but after the reforms of the Second Vatican Council she was able to reclaim her own name and became Sister Marcene Schlosser.

In 1959 Schlosser began her teaching career in the Catholic parish schools of Minnesota. Between 1978 and 1986 she taught Grade 1 at St. Michael School in a northwest suburb of Minneapolis. Her principal at the time described her in these words: "She loves children. They are happy and eager to come to school. Sister Marcene is sincerely interested in each student." But one of them was not very happy. "John Doe" was in her class from 1978 to 1979. In 1996, following nightmares and flashbacks, he claimed that he had been sexually abused two or three times a week by Schlosser and filed a lawsuit against the School Sisters of Notre Dame. Schlosser "adamantly and vehemently" denied the allegations. And Sister Katherine DuVal, head of the order, said that an internal investigation found no evidence of the abuse. Nonetheless, the order offered a confidential settlement in October 2000. In DuVal's words, they agreed to "pay a small settlement that takes care of everything and finishes this off." She admitted, however, that the order had received two other complaints about sexual abuse by its members that had allegedly taken place in the 1940s, one of which had been in Minnesota. She also added that, in light of those complaints and that respecting Schlosser, the order had abandoned its practice of internal investigations; complaints would now be referred to diocesan officials, but not, apparently, to the police. The complaint did not put an end to Schlosser's teaching career. Her final assignment was at St. Bartholomew School, Wayzata, 1998–2010. She died in Mankato in December 2020 aged 82.[10]

6. Unfaithful Servants

Ramona Schweich, School Sisters of Notre Dame, Minnesota

The religious career of Mildred Margaret Schweich followed a pattern not unlike that of Marcene Schlosser. Born on the family farm near New Trier, Minnesota, in August 1922, she always considered herself a country girl. At St. Mary's parish school in New Trier she was strongly influenced by the School Sisters of Notre Dame to consider a life in the convent. With this in mind, she took her secondary education at the Sisters' aspirancy, the Good Counsel Academy in Mankato, becoming a postulant with the order upon graduation in 1940. The summer of 1943 brought profession of her first vows and the beginning of her lengthy career as a teacher of religion, math, and science in her order's high schools in Minnesota and neighboring states. From 1983 onwards she became involved in pastoral work in a number of settings.

In 2004 an episode from the past turned up which would tarnish Schweich's reputation. Between 1950 and 1954 she had been on the staff at Notre Dame Academy in Colton, Washington State, a boarding school that closed in 1960. There she had initiated a sexual relationship with a 16-year-old boarder, Betty Davis. When Davis lodged the complaint with the School Sisters, Schweich, now 81, admitted to the abuse and apologized to her victim. The Sisters agreed to a financial settlement of around $120,000 for Davis. Schweich died in March 2012 in Mankato.[11]

Gael Biondo, Adrian Dominicans, Michigan

The Dominicans of Adrian are a branch of the Order of Preachers, first established by St. Dominic in France in 1206. Four Sisters arrived in New York from Bavaria in 1853, and the order spread out from there with a focus on areas of German Catholic settlement. By the 1870s they had a foothold in Michigan, and the Sisters in that state became a separate congregation in 1923 with their provincial house at Adrian. In 1940 they established and staffed Dominican High School in an eastern suburb of Detroit. It closed in 2005.

Marya Dantzer-Rosenthal was raised in a difficult and devoutly Catholic home environment in Detroit. She was 14 years old when she began her studies at Dominican High School in 1964. Language was her passion, and in adulthood she would work as a journalist with the *Boston Globe* and a writing instructor with Harvard Extension School. Her

English teacher and spiritual advisor at Dominican was 38-year-old Sister Mary Gael (Gael Biondo), whom she trusted and considered a "second mother." Small wonder then that she was confused and frightened when the nun allegedly made sexual overtures to her. The abuse, which involved kissing, fondling, and oral sex, took place regularly at the school and on one occasion in the school chapel after a session of prayer. It continued throughout the teenager's years at Dominican, even after Sister Mary Gael was reassigned to St. Lawrence Catholic School, some distance to the north. It only came to an end in 1970 when the nun left religious life. In explaining why the abuse endured for so many years, Dantzer-Rosenthal asked: "Have you ever heard of a Catholic kid who got away with saying no to a nun?" And she added: "I was a devout and trusting teenager and she was my English teacher, my mentor and a nun with all the authority that accrued to her."

Two decades after the abuse had begun, Dantzer-Rosenthal was married with two children and living in Boston. It was there that she connected the abusive relationship with the emotional problems she was experiencing in adulthood. On June 21, 1995, she filed a lawsuit against Biondo, the archdiocese of Detroit, and the Dominican Sisters of Adrian. Her purpose in doing so was "to help the Church to a new level of honesty and accountability." The lawsuit led to a series of discussions with the nuns that she found chilling. Facing formidable legal costs and the probability of failure due to Michigan's statutes of limitations, she settled out of court in 1996.[12]

Benen Kent, Third Order of St. Francis, Illinois

Sister Benen Kent took her vows with the Third Order of St. Francis of the Congregation of Our Lady of Lourdes in 1938. The 20-year-old nun then began her lengthy career as a music teacher in St. Joseph parish, Winona, Minnesota. She taught at several Catholic schools in Minnesota and also in Norfolk, Nebraska. Her frequent relocations had an air of suspicion about them and may have been related to her history of mental instability. In 1963 she was assigned to St. Juliana's parish school in Chicago, where her previous difficulties were unknown. She quickly established a reputation as a fine musician and talented teacher and became on close terms with some of the families whose children she taught.

In 1964 six-year-old Karen Britten signed up for weekly piano

6. Unfaithful Servants

lessons with Kent. The first half of the lesson focused on practice, the second on music theory. It was during the theory instruction that the nun began to reach beneath her dress. In the years that followed, Britten experienced emotional and psychological problems including eating disorders, depression, low energy, suicidal tendencies, and feelings of guilt and shame. In 1967 Kent was transferred to the Franciscan motherhouse in Rochester, Minnesota, in order to receive treatment for her long-standing mental health issues at the nearby Mayo Clinic. In 1972, following treatment, she was assigned to another parish school where she continued to teach until retirement in 1993.

It was 1989 by the time Karen Britten realized that her problems had originated with Kent's music lessons back in the 1960s; she had repressed the memory of the sexual abuse all those years. She asked her older sister, Christine Bertrand, if she too had been abused by Kent, and the answer was no. The same question was asked of Patricia Swartz, a childhood friend, who had also taken lessons from the nun, and again the response was no. Britten wanted to confront her abuser at the time but was too embarrassed to do so all on her own. By 2002, however, Bertrand and Swartz remembered that they too had been abused by Kent, and they informed Britten. The three women arranged a meeting with Sister Delore Rockers, head of the congregation, seeking more information about Kent's history and whereabouts. They also wanted an opportunity to confront their abuser. Rockers was evasive and unhelpful and would only provide information that proved to be false. She offered them $10,000 each if they agreed to keep their silence on the matter, which they refused. In the summer of 2003 Britten received a letter from the congregation stating that a meeting with Kent was now out of the question; the predator nun had died on June 24, aged 85.

In 2005, the three survivors sued the Sisters of St. Francis for damages relating to their experiences. The suit noted that the Sisters must have been aware of Sister Benen Kent's proclivities when they had moved her from Chicago to Rochester, Minnesota, in 1967 "in response to complaints of her conduct with children attending St. Juliana's." In September 2008, the nuns settled the suit with a compensation package worth $400,000 accompanied by a statement that "there's no admission of liability on the part of the Sisters of St. Francis in the agreement." To this they added an all too familiar sanctimonious platitude: "It is the hope of the Sisters that the forgiving, healing love of God, that is offered in every celebration of the Eucharist, will bring reconciliation and peace to the hearts of victims of abuse and draw us all into the heart of Love, that we can become instruments of God's love and peace in a broken, wounded world."[13]

Mary Helen Thieneman, Dominican Sisters of Peace, Kentucky

Andrea Dessommes entered fourth grade in September 1974. Her school, St. Margaret Mary in Louisville, Kentucky, was conducted by the Dominican Sisters of Peace. Although there were no particular problems in her life requiring intervention, the school counselor, Sister Mary Helen Thieneman, began to remove her from class on occasion for private conversations in a convent room. The conversations soon became intimate in nature with Thieneman telling the girl that she loved her and that they would have secrets together. Later, the nun allegedly initiated sexual touching, which carried on for several months.

Dessommes did not inform her parents of the transgressions until she was 19 and the family had relocated to California. Patrick Callahan, a psychologist in Yorba Linda, conducted an evaluation and concluded that the abuse had indeed taken place. Dessommes's father reported the matter to the Dominican superior in January 1984. The superior failed to take action, claiming that they had had no other complaints against Thieneman. In 1992 the father met with Archbishop Thomas C. Kelly of Louisville to discuss what had happened to his daughter as well as his concern that Thieneman might be abusing others. He was assured by Kelly that the nun was no longer working with children and was serving as a hospital chaplain under special supervision.

In 2003 Dessommes, who was now married and living in Australia, engaged Louisville attorney Michael McMahon to file a lawsuit against the archdiocese of Louisville and the Dominican Sisters of Peace. The lawsuit, filed at the end of July, claimed that Thieneman's conduct constituted a felony and should have been reported to the police. In response, the archdiocese denied that it had been obliged to make such a report since Dessommes was an adult at the time her father had spoken to Archbishop Kelly. Sister Joye Gros, president of the Dominican community, said that Thieneman strongly denied the allegations and that she was unaware of other complaints against the nun. In November, with little prospect of success, the lawsuit was withdrawn.

Thieneman died on January 21, 2013, at the age of 80. Her obituary recorded her career switch to chaplain at a number of hospitals in

6. Unfaithful Servants

Ohio and Kentucky in the 1980s, but it was not explained why the former teacher and school principal had been removed from working with children.[14]

Cheryl Porte, Marianites of Holy Cross, Louisiana

Cheryl Ann Porte was born on September 2, 1950, to a working class family in New Orleans. Upon finishing school in 1968, she entered the Marianites of Holy Cross, taking her perpetual vows in 1975. In the meantime, she earned a bachelor's degree in elementary education and began to teach in the Catholic schools of Louisiana.

Myra Hidalgo was the youngest of six girls born to a Cajun family in the small city of Opelousas in southwestern Louisiana. She was 12 years old in August 1977 when she first met Porte, her new Grade 7 homeroom teacher at Opelousas Catholic Middle School. She was impressed with the charming and energetic 26-year-old Sister Ann, as she was known—the first nun she had seen dressed in civilian attire. A relationship between teacher and student was initiated that autumn when Porte slipped a card into Hidalgo's desk just before final bell. The message read: "You are special ... as a student and a friend." They began to sit with one another during lunch and had long conversations after school. The nun shared stories of her own adolescence in New Orleans, reminiscing about Mardi Gras, Beatles concerts, and the boys she had dated. And she shared examples of her poetry with her young listener. Conversations about popular music, psychology, social justice, and theology in time turned to sexuality and the puberty that the youngster was beginning to experience.

The next year, when Hidalgo was in Grade 8, Porte was her religion teacher. The friendship now became more intense, with nightly phone calls and gifts of candles and rosaries. As rumors about the two of them began to circulate, discretion prompted them to arrange meetings in the nun's bedroom away from prying eyes. Neither Hidalgo's parents nor the Marianites were concerned; they just assumed that Porte was grooming her student for entry into religious life. The parents had no objections, for example, when their daughter spent the night in the congregation motherhouse in New Orleans. Nor did they have a problem with the nun sleeping in their house when they were away for a weekend. It was during these overnight stays that the relationship allegedly became sexual. Porte would ask Hidalgo to rub her back then take the

Predatory Nuns

youngster's hand and steer it to more intimate places. Finding it all very strange, Hidalgo tried to resist, but then the nun would cry, and she assented to the sexual touching in order to comfort her. Porte explained that their relationship was "a very personal gift from God" that ought to be celebrated. Its sacredness meant that secrecy was required because others simply would not understand it. The secrecy ended in the spring of 1980 when a neighbor spotted them kissing in a parked car and reported it to the Marianites. Sister Juanita, provincial director of the congregation, removed Porte from her teaching position and informed Hidalgo's mother of the incident. The predator and her victim were forbidden to have any future contact.

An overachiever by her own admission, Hidalgo finished school and went on to university. And all the while she battled feelings of shame, bouts of depression, and suicidal tendencies. Psychiatric counseling helped her understand that her relationship with Porte had been one of sexual exploitation. In 1988, now a young adult, she decided to confront her abuser as part of her therapy. She discovered that the nun was attending university in St. Louis and phoned her to tell of her anger at the abuse. Porte was unrepentant and lashed out: "You have no idea what I've been through and how I have been made accountable." Hidalgo had been hoping for an apology or some indication of remorse, and in the absence of either, she hung up. She did feel a sense of satisfaction at having confronted her abuser.

As the years passed and Hidalgo witnessed priests held accountable for their sexual crimes, she determined that predator nuns should also face a reckoning. She approached a lawyer with litigation in mind, but, in view of the statute of limitations obstacle, decided against proceeding. She held lengthy discussions with the Marianites seeking assurances that Porte would not abuse others. The nuns were secretive, defensive, and not very helpful. Hidalgo went on to become a clinical therapist, and she treats people suffering from traumatic events such as childhood sexual abuse in her New Orleans practice.

Cheryl Porte's subsequent career with the Marianites does not appear to have been unduly impaired by her crimes. She was able to pursue her interests in theology at the graduate level, earning a master's in adult faith formation from St. Mary's University, San Antonio, Texas, and a doctorate in historical theology from St. Louis University. She held a number of positions in adult religious education over the years in O'Fallon, Illinois; St. Louis, Missouri; and at Our Lady of Holy Cross College in New Orleans. On April 17, 2020, she died at the age of 69 at

6. Unfaithful Servants

the Mercy Care Facility in her hometown after a battle with ALS, the debilitating affliction of the nervous system also known as Lou Gehrig's disease. Throughout her life she had had a special devotion to Our Lady Undoer of Knots, a novena of prayers that, we are assured, never fails.[15]

Loretta Barto, Sisters of Mercy, New York

Loretta Barto, known as "Chupie," was born in 1934 in Bay Shore, a hamlet on Long Island, New York. On February 2, when she was not yet 18, she entered the novitiate of the Sisters of Mercy in nearby Syosset, professing her final vows in 1957. In 1954 Sister Mary Juanita, as she was known in religion, began her lengthy teaching career in the Catholic schools of the state. Mater Christi was a diocesan high school in Queens in which the Sisters of Mercy taught the girls while the Irish Christian Brothers taught the boys. Sister Juanita was assigned to the teaching staff in 1966, and it was here that she met and befriended 15-year-old Cait Finnegan. According to the teenager, the relationship quickly evolved into sexual abuse. Initially confused about what was happening, Finnegan explained that, in her Irish Catholic family, "there was no such thing as sex." The abuse took place on school buses *en route* to and from sporting events, at religious retreats, at a Long Island convent, and even at the teenager's home.

When Finnegan graduated in 1969, she struggled to cope with the experience. The few people she told about it refused to believe her. In the early 1990s she decided to visit the Mercy Convent on Long Island in order to confront Sister Juanita, who had been living there since her retirement from teaching in 1988. But upon arrival, she realized that she could not face her abuser and just walked away. The trauma and anxiety she continued to suffer required extensive therapy, and the Sisters of Mercy agreed to pay for some of it. Finnegan never told her father about the abuse, fearing what he would do to the nun. She did, however, discuss it with her mother shortly before her death in 2002. Her mother encouraged her to get even with the nuns, but she discovered that there was little she could do because of New York's strict statute of limitations law. Sister Juanita died on May 2, 2014, her history of abuse virtually unknown. In 2019, when New York suspended its statute of limitations, Finnegan thought once more about a lawsuit. Preliminary discussions with the Sisters of Mercy led to a financial settlement in October 2020.[16]

Predatory Nuns

Dolores Crosby, Sisters of the Holy Names of Jesus and Mary, Washington State

Dolores Crosby, known as Dixie to her friends, was born in Spokane, Washington, in 1935 and grew up in the city. She was a niece of crooner Bing Crosby. As a young woman, Dixie joined the Sisters of the Holy Names of Jesus and Mary and began teaching in the Catholic schools of her hometown. Subsequent assignments took her to schools in Seattle, Edmonds, and Tacoma. She retired in 1999, having spent the previous seven years as principal of Immaculate Conception School in Everett. A big fan of the Seattle Mariners, she could recite their batting averages and pitching records at will. When she died of cancer in July 2007, gushing tributes from some of her former students praised her high academic standards and the positive influence she had had on their lives.

At first glance it looked like another great white nun biography, a genre all too familiar in Catholic literature. But there was a dark side to Sister Dixie that only emerged nine years after her death. The schools where she had spent her teaching career were part of the educational infrastructure of the archdiocese of Seattle, an entity that had had its fair share of America's pedophile priest problem. Indeed, since the late 1980s, the archdiocese had paid out around $74 million to settle 392 claims of sexual abuse of minors by its personnel. As part of these on-going settlements, on January 15, 2016, it published on its website the names of 77 religious it identified as abusers. Of this number, 76 were priests or brothers. There was one nun on the list: Sister Dolores Crosby, SNJM. Details of her misdeeds were not forthcoming, but Greg Magnoni, speaking on behalf of the archdiocese, had this to say:

> The one thing I can tell you is that the files were carefully reviewed by independent experts, and in every case for a name on the list the allegation or allegations were admitted, established or determined to be credible by them. A deceased person's reputation is very important, and the name would not be on the list unless an allegation was admitted, established or determined to be credible.

The revelation sent a frisson of fear through the parents of the many children Sister Crosby had taught during her lengthy career in the classroom. How many victims had there been? Where? How often? There were no answers, only a bleak void of uncertainty.[17]

6. Unfaithful Servants

Eileen Shaw, Sisters of Charity of St. Elizabeth, New Jersey

Patricia Cahill was born in 1952 to a prosperous but dysfunctional Irish-American family in Ridgewood, New Jersey. Her father, a violent man, had his own car dealership, and her mother, who had a fondness for the jar, sold real estate when the vodka bottle was empty. Cahill and her five siblings attended Our Lady of Mount Carmel parish school. She was only in Grade 1 when her uncle, Father Daniel Mallard of St. Maurice parish in Brooklawn, began to sexually assault her, threatening her with mortal sin were she ever to disclose their relationship to others. The abuse continued until she was 13 and was able to muster the courage to put a stop to it. Her troubles with Church personnel were, however, far from over.

At age 15 Cahill spoke of the priest's depredations to Sister Eileen Shaw, a family friend and principal of Our Lady of the Visitation parish school in nearby Paramus. Shaw, a member of the Sisters of Charity of St. Elizabeth based in Convent Station, New Jersey, was supportive and encouraging and began to assume the motherly role that was missing in Cahill's life. But soon enough the 36-year-old nun was supplying the teenager with alcohol and sedatives ostensibly to relax her; it was, according to Cahill, a prelude to sexual advances. Shaw told the youngster that she loved her and presented her with a special medal to be worn when the two of them were intimate. Coming from a family where there was little love, Cahill accepted the relationship, although with grave misgivings. The lovers were able to meet for their sexual trysts in various convents along the East Coast where Shaw had ready access. One of their hideaways was at the Xavier Center at Convent Station, a Sisters of Charity retreat. Another was the Glen Rock convent, where the nuns admitted Cahill through the back door and watched her going upstairs to Shaw's quarters without a word. On one occasion, as they were spending a weekend together in a Connecticut convent, a blizzard snowed them in and they were unable to turn up for school on Monday morning. The silence and active cooperation of the community in these arrangements may suggest either that Shaw's proclivities were known and tolerated, or that it was not unheard of for nuns to bring teenagers to their rooms. That convents rather than motels were the chosen venues for weekends of illicit sex with a minor is, at the very least, curious.

With Shaw's encouragement, Cahill went to college, qualified as a teacher, and in 1974 secured her first position at St. Cecelia's in Kearny,

New Jersey, where her mentor just happened to be principal. Shaw warned her not to date men and discouraged friendships with other teachers. After a year, Cahill realized that she needed some separation and went to teach in Hasbrouck Heights. By this time, she was drinking heavily, even on her way to work, and Shaw maintained the relationship by visiting on the weekend. The relationship was on and off over the years, and it was not until 1992 that Cahill finally put an end to it. Two years later she engaged an attorney who approached the Sisters of Charity seeking payment for therapy and demanded that Shaw be removed from her position as school principal. Shaw was indeed removed, but turned up later as director of the Caritas Community, a retirement home for the order in Jersey City. The Sisters of Charity agreed to provide Cahill with therapy and a compensation package worth in the region of $70,000. It came, of course, with a confidentiality clause. Cahill continued to battle alcohol and drugs and had difficulty relating sexually to either men or women. She is no longer a practicing Catholic.[18]

Sister Andre, Dominicans of Caldwell, New Jersey

Betty and Joe Robrecht settled in Hillside, New Jersey, in the mid–1950s. Devoutly Catholic, they quickly became active in their local parish that centered on St. Catherine of Siena Church. Their seven children, as they reached the required age, were enrolled in St. Catherine parochial school. Mary, the middle child, was 12 years old in 1965 when one of her teachers, Sister Andre, began to pay special attention to her. She was soon spending lots of time in the nun's company and was at the convent almost every evening of the week. The two even went away for a weekend together during the summer with parental approval. Sister Andre, 35 at the time, had a history of being moved about and was transferred that fall to Connecticut. Even so, she maintained contact with Mary by correspondence. The Robrechts thought nothing of the steady stream of letters and were even hopeful that it signaled that their daughter might have a religious vocation.

Then, in 1967, the truth came out. One day Betty Robrecht found one of the letters and decided to read it. In it, Sister Andre wrote of her romantic encounters with Mary. Presented with this evidence by her mother, Mary admitted to the sexual nature of the relationship. The local superior of the Dominicans of Caldwell, the nun's order, upon meeting with the Robrechts, went to Connecticut, where she retrieved

6. Unfaithful Servants

further evidence of the illicit goings-on. But she claimed, implausibly, that Sister Andre was nowhere to be found. When the Robrechts contacted Sister Joan Doyle, prioress of the Dominicans of Caldwell, she too denied any knowledge of the errant nun's whereabouts. It was not the only instance of a religious order making one of its members "disappear" when allegations of criminal activity surfaced. Mary's parents considered a lawsuit and even discussed the possibility with an attorney, but decided it would be better to put it all behind them.[19]

Lisa Zuccarelli, Dominican Sisters of Peace, Ohio

Lisa Zuccarelli was having a successful career in education. A Dominican Sister of Peace, she started out in 1975 as a science teacher in the Catholic high schools of Ohio. There were stints at De Sales in Columbus, Catholic Central in Steubenville, and Fisher Catholic in Lancaster. In 1985 she left school teaching to pursue an MS at New York University and, after spending the 1987–88 year teaching at Albertus Magnus College in New Haven, Connecticut, she returned to NYU for her PhD, which she earned in 1993. After a year as a postdoctoral student at Georgetown University's School of Medicine, she joined the faculty in 1994, transferring in 1996 to the School of Nursing, where she also served as chaplain-in-residence. Three years later she was appointed director of academic enrichment and student life in the Office of Student and Academic Affairs, a position she held until she left Georgetown. In 2003 she moved to Salve Regina University in Newport, Rhode Island, to take up a professorship in the Department of Biology and Biomedical Sciences. She was active in research, publishing a number of co-authored articles, including "Clavulanic Acid: A Competitive Inhibitor of Beta-Lactamases with Novel Anxiolytic-Like Activity and Minimal Side Effects," which appeared in *Pharmacology, Biochemistry and Behavior* (May 2009). And she was popular with her students, who described her as brilliant, personable, knowledgeable, and "quite possibly the sweetest woman on the face of the earth."

Sweet Sister Lisa was doing rather well for herself until a dark episode from her past turned up to derail everything. On July 28, 2018, the Dominican Sisters of Peace in Columbus received a letter from a woman who had been Zuccarelli's student at Fisher High in Lancaster during the 1980s. The woman alleged that one evening in 1982 she had left home following difficulties with her parents and sought Zuccarelli's guidance at St. Mary's Convent. The nun invited the teenager in, suggested she spend the night, and later made unwanted sexual advances to her. The Dominicans informed the Lancaster police about the letter and in July transmitted the allegations to Salve Regina University. The university placed Zuccarelli on a leave of absence, and her religious order forbade her from all unsupervised contact with any minor or former student. Meanwhile, an independent investigation into the affair was carried out by the law firm of Buckingham, Doolittle and Burroughs, which, when completed in October, determined that the allegations were credible. The Lancaster police described the incident as "borderline gross sexual imposition." The victim, however, decided not to press charges; besides, Ohio's 25-year statute of limitations respecting sexual assault of a minor had long since expired.[20]

Linda Baisi, Ex-Nun, New York

St. Frances de Chantal parish school in the Throgs Neck neighborhood of the Bronx is part of the educational system of the archdiocese of New York. Tuition is around $6,000 per annum and its motto is "Live Jesus." Opened in 1930 with a modest enrollment of 150 students in Grades 1 to 4, instruction was in the hands of the Sisters of Divine Compassion. At the time the working-class community was populated largely by Irish and Italian families. By 1979 most of the sisters had been replaced by lay teachers, and it was in that year that Linda Baisi, herself a former nun, joined the staff. Acquiring a reputation as a popular and respected teacher, she was described as "a very spiritual person."

In 1987 Baisi was the Grade 7 homeroom teacher when she began to take a special interest in 12-year-old Brian O'Rourke. She was 40 at the time. The teacher began to invite her student to her nearby apartment, and it was here that she initiated sexual activity. The encounters, which involved oral sex and intercourse, took place several times a month, and the entire affair lasted until 1992. In the meantime, fearful of being exposed, Baisi showered O'Rourke with gifts of cash and clothes and even did his homework on occasion to ensure his silence. The special attention was noticed by some students, who would taunt the victim about it. Other teachers may also have noticed something unusual going on, but nothing was said.

Upon high school graduation O'Rourke attended Iona College in New Rochelle, an institution founded by the Irish Christian Brothers.

6. Unfaithful Servants

Unable to focus on his studies because of drug and alcohol addiction that he attributed to the sexual abuse, he quit before the first semester was out. He could neither hold down a job nor develop healthy relationships with others. While attending a rehabilitation program in Florida, he was encouraged by counselors to report the abuse and take action against his former teacher. Returning to New York early in 1996, he confronted Baisi about her behavior. The former nun, who was now principal of Frances de Chantal, was horrified at the prospect of their affair becoming public. She claimed that she was a victim of love—that she had had too much love in her and that now it was going to destroy her. She begged O'Rourke to say nothing to the Church and not to reveal her name to his psychiatrist. Just say it was "an older chick," she said. And she threatened to commit suicide by driving her car into a river should she ever be exposed.

O'Rourke ignored the entreaties, and in February 1996 he sued the archdiocese of New York for $150 million, claiming serious emotional damage as a consequence of the liaison. The suit alleged that the archdiocese had neither supervised Baisi adequately nor trained its teachers to recognize abuse. At first, some parents whose children attended Frances de Chantal were dubious of the charges against their principal. But O'Rourke had secretly recorded his conversation with Baisi, and when part of the tape was played on ABC News *Primetime Live*, there could be no further room for doubt. The former nun was initially given a leave of absence from the school and later dismissed. The case was heard before the state supreme court in Manhattan in mid–September 2000. Before much progress was made, however, the archdiocese offered O'Rourke a settlement, which he readily accepted. No criminal charges were laid against Baisi nor was she obliged, being without resources, to contribute financially to the settlement. Her lawyer simply stated that she was no longer teaching and had left New York, but there was no word of her whereabouts.[21]

Conclusion

In assessing the cases examined above, we can make a few tentative generalizations. Sexual predator nuns were on the teaching staff of many Catholic schools. Their victims were preponderantly female, and were often experiencing puberty. The obsessive attachment to girls of this age group may indicate the predators' own social/psychological immaturity—perhaps a product of an adolescence that had passed them

Predatory Nuns

by in a fog of confusion. They often took advantage of the young girls' innocence on sexual matters while luring them into abusive behavior masquerading as something special, sacred, and spiritual.

The impact of the abuse on victims was always negative and often traumatic. We have seen several cases where the victims sought many years of expensive therapy as they coped with addictions, depression, eating disorders, suicidal tendencies, and feelings of guilt and shame.

How did religious orders respond to allegations of abuse? Their first instinct was to close ranks and protect the predators. The stories of Fisher, Porte, and Skeabeck show congregations simply moving abusers to other locations when complaints were received. Nor is it evident that effective measures were put in place to protect other potential victims. The case of Sister Andre reveals how an uncooperative religious order could spirit away its accused member in order to evade responsibility. The practice of conducting internal investigations when complaints were received was far from satisfactory and did not inspire the confidence of victims. There was only one case, that of Zuccarelli, in which the complaint was immediately reported to the police. And that was in the immediate aftermath of the Pennsylvania inquiry into sexual abuse reported in the summer of 2018 and its enormous repercussions for the Church.

When victims filed civil lawsuits, the sisters often came forward with compensation packages. This preferred strategy minimized publicity and legal fees while avoiding the uncertainty of court-ordered settlements. But there were also cases where legal mechanisms, such as hiding behind the statute of limitations, were employed to deny victims a measure of justice. The stories of Barto and Veri illustrate this approach.

Most of all, scandal had to be avoided. Catholic schools were private fee-paying institutions in competition with public schools, and anything that might have discouraged parents from supporting them required containment. Stories of teaching sisters as sexual predators would have been a disaster for the reputation of the system.

The case of Linda Baisi, the one ex-nun included here, reminds us that those who left religious life in the great exodus following the Second Vatican Council often returned to teach in Catholic schools and could still pose a problem. But *vive la différence*! Ex-nuns were not protected by the resources of a religious order and could simply be fired from their positions. Those who stayed in the convent system, however, had no such concern. The system looked after its own.

7

Days of Reckoning

> She is sick and twisted, a fraud and a degenerate who, just like the Church, is not being held responsible for what she has done.[1]
> —Linda Curran, victim of Eileen Rhoads, the former Sister Francis Therese, I.H.M.

In February 1977 Sister Maureen Murphy appeared before the Monroe District Court in Rochester, New York, charged with the manslaughter of the baby boy to whom she had given birth in the secrecy of her convent bedroom. Acquitted, she was spirited away from the courtroom and the glare of publicity by her religious order, the Sisters of St. Joseph, and subsequently disappeared.[2] Her unusual story caused a bit of a media sensation and inspired the 1985 movie *Agnes of God*. It was rare for nuns to face criminal prosecution whether for murder, manslaughter, or sexual assault. Apologists for the Church point to this as evidence of their holiness and the perfection of their lives. There are better explanations. Two cases involving prosecution for sex crimes have come to light in recent years, and they are instructive of the complex relationship between the Church and secular systems of justice.

Sister Francis Therese, I.H.M., "The face of evil"

The Sisters, Servants of the Immaculate Heart of Mary is a pontifical order of women religious founded by Father Louis Florent Gillet in Monroe, Michigan, in 1845. By the 1950s there were almost 4,000 sisters, mainly engaged in teaching. In addition to the original motherhouse in Monroe, there were two in Pennsylvania: one in Scranton, and the other, known as Villa Maria, in Chester County just west of Philadelphia. A promotional piece published in 1958 encouraged young women of "adequate health and average ability" and who possessed "a spirit of generosity and docility" to join their ranks. "The first purpose of the Sisters," it explained, "is to make saints of themselves. The second follows closely—the sanctification of others, chiefly through education of all types from kindergarten through college."[3] It didn't always work out that way.

A new recruit who entered the Villa Maria novitiate in 1957 appeared to be convent material, at least initially. Eileen Mary Rhoads was born in Philadelphia on June 18, 1939, and raised in the city. When she took her vows with the Sisters, Servants she was given the name Sister Francis Therese. She became one of the thousands of junior professed nuns who were pressed into service as teachers in Catholic school systems across the land that year. Her first decade of instructing the young took place in the schools of the archdiocese of Philadelphia.[4]

Early in September 1969, Sister Francis took up a new appointment teaching Grade 5 at St. Gregory the Great Catholic school in Virginia Beach—a medium-sized city on Virginia's Atlantic coast noted for its impressive stretch of waterfront sand. It was here that the troubled person in the nun's habit began to emerge. Before long she had developed a predatory relationship with one of her students, a 10-year-old boy. The abuse involved kissing and sexual touching. Her victim spoke to nobody about it at the time. His father was away in Vietnam, and his mother was busy raising a large family. He felt that there was no one to whom he could turn. Besides, Sister Francis said that she was in love with him and that they had "a special thing" going, just as adults did. It was not until many years later that he realized it had been a "predator-prey" relationship.[5]

Sister Francis left St. Gregory the Great during the summer of 1970 when the school year ended. She was returned to familiar surroundings and assigned a teaching position at Our Lady of Charity School in Brookhaven, a borough in Delaware County, west of Philadelphia. And here, once again, she sexually abused a male student. Before long she began to accept that she was unsuited to religious life. She was depressed and seeing a psychiatrist. Her superiors were now aware that she was having difficulty with the vow of chastity and that she was "inclined to be too familiar with the children." She was released from her vows in 1972. She was Eileen Rhoads once again.[6]

Defections from convents had been rare enough before the 1960s and had usually been tinged with a sense of failure and shame. Those who left were suspected of some great moral flaw. After 1965, however, the exodus from religious life became an unrelenting flood. Between

7. Days of Reckoning

1965 and 1981 most congregations lost around 30 percent of their members, and most of those who left were the younger and better educated ones. The departures were a disaster for the viability of the convent system. The effect on Catholic schools was also devastating since they had relied on the free labor of teaching sisters for countless decades. As the nuns vanished, Catholic schools were obliged to hire lay teachers. Although the salaries paid to lay teachers were considerably less than those paid in public schools, it still meant a huge increase in operating costs and tuition fees. In fact, one of the challenges facing the Church's schools was just finding qualified lay professionals willing to work for such meager remuneration. Sometimes they just could not be all that selective.[7]

In 1973, the archdiocese of Philadelphia hired Eileen Rhoads to teach Grade 6 at Holy Cross School in Springfield, a community of about 25,000 people just west of the city.[8] She was now 34 and as a layperson was free to develop relations with fellow adults. It made no difference; her obsessive attachment to her young students had not diminished.

In 1976 John McNeila transferred to Holy Cross and found himself in Rhoads's classroom. One day, early in the school year, he spied his teacher kissing another student, Christopher Nolan, behind a coat rack. Discretion seemed to be of little concern to her. Rhoads warned McNeila to say nothing of what he had seen and later invited him to join in. The kissing soon led to sexual touching and the abuse of the two boys became a regular occurrence when opportunities arose. In time, she invited them to her apartment in nearby Drexel Hill. Here she played Moody Blues and Simon and Garfunkel records while plying them with beer and cigarettes. She also produced *Playboy* and *Penthouse* magazines in order to arouse them with erotic images and stories. This was a prelude to having sexual intercourse with them. According to the victims, those encounters occurred dozens of times.[9]

Rhoads also targeted girls, and one in particular. She befriended Linda Curran in 1978 when the girl was only 11. Two years later, the sexual assaults began. Rhoads encouraged the youngster to try alcohol and marijuana and led on from there to masturbation and oral sex. The abuse continued until Curran was 18 and brought it to a halt. She suffered enormous shame and guilt during her teenage years as a result.[10]

One month before the end of the school year in 1994, Rhoads was laid off from her position at Holy Cross. Her teaching career was over. The archdiocese of Philadelphia never explained the reasons for her departure.[11]

Predatory Nuns

Almost a decade went by before these events were brought into public view. By 2002 Rhoads's victim at St. Gregory the Great was on medication for depression and in therapy. He was having problems developing relationships with others and his religious faith was compromised. He could no longer put aside what had happened to him. Early in 2003 he gave a full report to the Virginia Beach police. It took the police a number of months to track the predator down and to prepare a case against her. They found several witnesses prepared to testify; the evidence of her depredations was overwhelming. James C. Lewis, the victim's attorney, claimed that his client was not Rhoads's sole victim in Virginia. "She was an epidemic," he remarked.[12]

On February 2, 2004, a grand jury returned an indictment charging Rhoads with two felonies: "child enticement" and "indecent liberties with a child under 14." Early in the morning of February 10, the police arrested her at her home in Drexel Hill. Later that day she appeared before the Upper Darby District Court facing extradition to Virginia. She was ordered to surrender to the Virginia Beach police within three days. When she stood before the Virginia Beach Circuit Court on July 14, she entered an "Alford plea" to the two charges. The plea enabled her to avoid admitting wrongdoing while acknowledging that there was enough evidence against her to secure a conviction. It also saved on lawyers' fees. There would be no trial, just a sentencing.[13]

When Rhoads's arrest was reported in a Pennsylvania newspaper, it caught the attention of Linda Curran, John McNeila, and Christopher Nolan, whom she had abused many decades earlier at Holy Cross School. These three victims now came forward with their stories and took legal action against the former nun seeking compensation. Although the lawsuits ran up against the statute of limitations obstacle in that state, the publicity served as another black mark against Rhoads and those who had employed her. They reinforced her image as a persistent abuser.[14]

On September 21, 2004, the ex-nun appeared before the circuit court in Virginia Beach to receive her sentence. Her victim from many decades earlier at St. Gregory the Great School was present and testified for more than 30 minutes while never looking directly at her. Observing that she had abused at least two other children at the school, he said that he had fallen "into the clutches of a serial pedophile." And he concluded: "Judge, you have before you the face of evil and I ask for the most severe sentence that you can impose." Harvey L. Bryant, the prosecuting attorney, seconded the victim's demand for a lengthy prison term, noting

7. Days of Reckoning

that the abuse had not been an isolated act. Rhoads's defense attorney, William "Happy" O'Brien, holding up a fistful of letters he had received supporting his client, asked for a suspended sentence on account of her age and otherwise clean record.

The judge, Edward W. Hanson, said he could not see what purpose would be served by a lengthy prison term. He sentenced Rhoads to six months in jail and added a 10-year suspended prison sentence that would only be invoked should she reoffend upon release. Once this decision was handed down, Rhoads apologized to her victim: "I am sorry, so very sorry. I apologize with all my heart for any pain I may have caused you. Forgive me and I pray for you that this is over. I hope you can find some peace of mind." She was then led away in handcuffs.[15]

While the victim was pleased to see justice done, he felt that a longer prison sentence would have been more appropriate. Linda Curran, one of Rhoads's victims from Springfield, was present at the hearing and concurred. "It seems ridiculous," she said, "especially since the Pennsylvania statute of limitations prevented criminal charges being laid in her case and others in that state."[16]

In September 2005, some months after her release from jail, a reporter with the *Philadelphia Inquirer* interviewed Rhoads in her Drexel Hill home where she was living frugally with her cat, Honey. She admitted to spending a lot of time praying and weeping. "If I could bring every one of those kids here now," she said, "I would get on my knees and beg their forgiveness."[17]

Which begs the question: What did her employers know of her predilections, and what actions did they take to protect the children under her care during her lengthy teaching career? Sister Rose Marie De Carlo, superior at the Villa Maria House of Studies where Rhoads had done her novitiate, claimed that the Sisters, Servants of the Immaculate Heart of Mary knew nothing about the problem nun until the summer of 2003. The archdiocese of Philadelphia also took refuge in denial. It insisted that no complaint had ever been made against her during her tenure at Holy Cross School.[18] But Jay Abramovich, a lawyer representing the victims of pedophile priests in the archdiocese and in the neighboring diocese of Allentown, was incredulous at these denials. He said that there should have been an investigation into Rhoads's departure from Virginia Beach after only one year. And he added that the Pennsylvania abuse was so flagrant that the archdiocese could not possibly have been unaware of it.[19]

Predatory Nuns

The Depredations of Sister Norma, R.S.M. (Beverly Giannini)

Beverly Margaret Giannini was a child of the Depression, and there is much that was depressing about her life. Born in Chicago on August 26, 1928, she grew up in a city plagued with unemployment, poverty, crime, ethnic tensions, and no end of labor unrest and political intrigue.[20] And yet, by her own account, she led the sort of sheltered life that only a convent education could provide. Influenced by her teachers, the Sisters of Mercy, who had been a major force in staffing the city's parochial schools since their arrival in the 1840s, she joined the congregation when she was only 18. By 1949 she was emerging from the novitiate in Des Plaines, a northern suburb, had taken her vows, and was known as Sister Norma. And so began her lengthy teaching career in the Catholic school system. It was a path followed by many young women of the faith at the time, as religious congregations aggressively pursued new recruits to staff their classrooms in order to expand operations to accommodate the baby-boom generation.[21]

By 1964 Sister Norma had taught in five different schools staffed by her congregation in the Chicago area. She was now 36 and at that comparatively young age was sent to Milwaukee to take over as principal of St. Patrick's parochial school. The parish, in the inner-south part of the city, was a preponderantly Irish working-class neighborhood. In spite of poverty and an increasingly mixed ethnic makeup, it was a tightly knit community where everyone knew one another. Besides being principal, Grade 8 teacher, and superior of the local cohort of her order, Sister Norma was also expected to manage the parish since the local priest had a hankering for the grog. She was a dominating figure who commanded attention, and yet she seemed more modern and personable than her predecessor. She showed an unusual interest in her students' social lives and in the music they enjoyed.[22]

Gerald Kobs came from a troubled family. His father, an alcoholic, had left the home, and his older brother was in jail. His mother, Elese, worked two jobs to make ends meet. Although a devout Catholic, she felt shunned by the community because of her divorce. When Kobs was 13 he entered Grade 8 in St. Patrick's and had Sister Norma as his teacher. When the nun learned of the family's vulnerability, she befriended his mother and insinuated herself into their lives. One day, Sister Norma found a pretext to keep Kobs back after school. Once they were alone together in the classroom, she drew close and began kissing him. This

7. Days of Reckoning

was repeated on other occasions and in time she encouraged greater intimacy—inviting him to grope inside her habit, for instance. Before long, they were having sexual intercourse, and not just in the classroom. At times, she brought him to the convent basement, and there were even molestations in his home when she came to visit her friend, his mother. In all, there were between 60 and 80 sexual encounters between the two of them.[23]

In 1967 James Koszewski was a 12-year-old Grade 7 student in St. Patrick's. He had a newspaper route that required him to make a delivery at the Sisters of Mercy convent. One day, as he was making his delivery, Sister Norma appeared at the doorway and invited him into the parlor. As they sat on the sofa together, she nudged closer and began to kiss him. During the weeks and months that followed, she invited him in regularly, plied him with wine on occasion, and became more sexually aggressive. Eventually, they were having intercourse together. And sometimes she would remove him from class during the school day and take him to a bathroom next to her office for further sexual encounters. There were more than 100 such incidents while he was in Grades 7 and 8.[24]

In 1969, much to the relief of the youngsters she had abused, Sister Norma left Milwaukee to return to Chicago, where she taught in a number of Catholic schools. In 1989, she was appointed principal of the Most Holy Redeemer parochial school in Evergreen Park, a community on the southwestern fringes of the Windy City. A few years later, while still holding this position, her past began to catch up with her.

When James Koszewski finished school, he drifted from job to job and devoted much of his leisure time to alcohol and marijuana. In 1992, unable to put the Sister Norma nightmare behind him, he contacted the Sisters of Mercy and told of his experiences. He was invited to the archdiocese headquarters, where he met with the auxiliary bishop, Richard J. Sklba, and a representative of the Sisters. Koszewski was assured that Sister Norma would be barred from further contact with children. The Sisters offered him $50,000 in settlement if he agreed never to disclose the abuse he had suffered. It was the standard hush money response by the Church. In December 1992 Sister Norma was removed suddenly from her position as principal at the Most Holy Redeemer. She was sent for treatment to a facility in St. Louis and assigned afterwards to office work for the congregation. The parents whose children attended the school were offered no explanation for the disappearance of their principal. Nor were they told that a suspected sexual predator had been in daily contact with their young ones. And evidence of her criminal activity was not passed to the justice system.[25]

Upon completing high school Gerald Kobs learned how to cook and found employment in the restaurant business. His experiences with Sister Norma continued to haunt him, and he suffered from migraines that affected his ability to work. And yet he could share the story of the sexual abuse with nobody, not even his wife, Terri, whom he had married shortly after graduation. And he dared not breathe a word of it to his mother, who remained in contact with the nun who had molested him. When Elese died in 1986, Sister Norma returned to Milwaukee for the funeral—adding further to Kobs's distress at the time. Finally, in 1996, Kobs discussed the abuse with his doctor, who referred him to a therapist. The therapist in turn introduced him to Father Vic Capriolo, a former deacon at St. Patrick's church. It was Capriolo who arranged for him to meet with Project Benjamin, an entity whose purpose and function requires explanation.[26]

Rembert Weakland was the archbishop of Milwaukee, a post he had held since 1977. He was a former head of the Benedictine order, and his liberal theology often put him at odds with other members of the Catholic hierarchy. In 1989, in response to the emerging pedophile priest scandal, he established Project Benjamin—in effect, a committee of experts appointed by the archdiocese to provide guidance and counseling to victims of sexual abuse. At the time, Weakland was praised for his initiative, but doubts soon arose. Rita McDonald resigned from Project Benjamin when she saw how it was operating. "I left when it came out that victims would have to return to the church for treatment," she said. "That's like asking someone who had their legs broken by the Mafia to go to the mob for treatment."[27]

Dr. Elizabeth Piasecki, a psychologist, was director of Project Benjamin in 1996 when Kobs reported Sister Norma to them. She passed the matter on to the Sisters of Mercy, who provided $9,500 in hush money. Nothing was reported to the police. Even so, the complaints did prompt Project Benjamin to interview the errant nun in August of that year. Sister Norma admitted to having had intercourse and oral sex with Kobs and Koszewski and with three other boys at St. Patrick's who were not identified. She also confessed to having begun her depredations earlier in her teaching career in Chicago: "One thing happened at St. Ann's before Milwaukee, a young man, a student. First time it happened. He was 14 to 15. He was in 8th grade. Starting kissing and petting. I was talking to him and all of a sudden, he was kissing me. Then it went on.

7. Days of Reckoning

And then unfortunate." She had received counseling from a priest for two years afterwards, apparently without effect.[28]

Sister Norma explained her behavior to Project Benjamin in the context of her sheltered adolescence. She had taken her vows at 18, she said, when she knew nothing about sex and was emotionally immature. When she arrived at St. Patrick's, she found that the other nuns were much older than she was and were often sick—not exactly the company that a 30-something woman might hope for. In her loneliness, her mind turned to the boys she was teaching, and she became infatuated with some of them. She even thought she was in love. When asked if she had any understanding of how the boys felt about the sexual activity, she replied: "They were sowing their wild oats. How many teenagers would resist that opportunity?"[29]

The Church was having some success in containing its sexual predator scandal with liberal applications of hush money, palaver about prayer and forgiveness, and assurances to victims that the problems would be dealt with confidentially. Then, in 2002, everything began to fall apart. In January, the *Boston Globe* began its exposé respecting the pedophile priest problem in the local archdiocese and set in motion a scandal that led to Cardinal Bernard Law's resignation before the year was out.

On May 23, Paul Marcoux, a former theology student at Marquette University, appeared on the popular television program *Good Morning America* with a shocking tale to tell. He claimed that in 1979 Archbishop Weakland had sexually assaulted him and had provided $450,000 from diocesan funds to keep his silence about the incident. Weakland initially denied the allegation, but resigned shortly afterwards. After a week in seclusion he issued an apology for his sinfulness, which he said he had placed "in God's loving and forgiving heart." And he expressed concern for those whose faith might have been shaken by his behavior.[30]

This development gave victims new hope. The Church no longer seemed such an impregnable fortress, and its ability to cover up criminal activity with legal maneuvers and soothing words was wearing thin. As the passing of time brought further revelations, Gerald Kobs read a newspaper account of a priest who was prosecuted in Wisconsin for sex crimes he had committed many years earlier. Prosecution became possible because the priest had left the state, stopping the clock on the six-year statute of limitations. It occurred to Kobs that Sister Norma might also be prosecuted under the same provision since she had spent less than six years in Wisconsin. On January 26, 2006, he contacted the Milwaukee police to see if charges could actually be laid and learned that it was possible. Shortly afterwards, James Koszewski, who now went under the surname St. Patrick, also reported his experiences with the Sister of Mercy to the police.[31]

The two complaints against Sister Norma, the details of which were convincingly similar, were handled by Lori Gaglione, a detective with much experience in sexual assault cases. In the course of her investigations, she demanded and received extensive files relating to the complaints from the archdiocese, including the handwritten notes taken by Dr. Piasecki during the nun's interview with Project Benjamin a decade earlier. In September, following a "John Doe investigation," a Milwaukee judge determined that a crime had indeed been committed. On December 5, 2006, Sister Norma was charged with two counts of "indecent behavior with a child" under Wisconsin Statute 944.11.[32] Sister Betty Smith, head of the Sisters of Mercy in the Chicago region, admitted that two other members of her order had also been accused of sexual assault. She did not name them or disclose if the matter had been reported to law enforcement.[33]

On Monday, November 12, 2007, Sister Norma appeared before the Milwaukee County Courthouse to begin her trial on the two felony charges. The image of the 79-year-old nun in her dark clothes facing prosecution for sex crimes understandably attracted media attention. Although many nuns had been accused of sexual assault, most cases had been resolved through civil litigation and out-of-court financial settlements. This was the first instance of criminal prosecution. The proceedings, however, allowed for little courtroom drama and ended quickly. The Sisters of Mercy had decided to pay for Sister Norma's defense and had hired for that purpose Nikola Kostich, a lawyer of questionable reputation. Kostich entered a no-contest plea, which meant an automatic conviction. He explained that the plea was an acknowledgment that the prosecution had enough evidence to secure a guilty verdict.[34]

On Friday, February 1, 2008, the convicted nun was back in court to receive her sentence. "I ask forgiveness from the bottom of my heart," she said, as she stood before circuit court judge M. Joseph Donald. But she never looked directly at her victims, Kobs and Koszewski/St. Patrick, who were present. She faced a possible 20 years of incarceration on the two felony charges. Prosecutor Paul Tiffin asked for eight years and $28,000 in compensation. Defense attorney Kostich proposed probation only, on the grounds that his client had gone willingly for

7. Days of Reckoning

therapy and was elderly, in poor health, and effectively confined to an assisted-living complex. Sister Norma's frailty was on display that day; she had limped into the courthouse leaning on a cane. Judge Donald sentenced the nun to five years' imprisonment on each of the two felonies, but then announced that he would stay the sentences. He felt, nonetheless, that some incarceration was in order for what he described as the "evil destruction, pure heartache ... and other deviant behavior" for which she had been responsible with "young and impressionable boys." He gave her one year in the House of Correction and 10 years of supervised probation. He ruled out the compensation demanded by the prosecution since the nun had no assets.[35]

On April 23, 2008, Sister Norma entered the Milwaukee County House of Correction to serve her sentence. Health issues continued to dog her, making the spell under lock and key all the more difficult. She was rushed to the medical emergency facilities a number of times for heart conditions and other ailments. And she began to lose weight upon finding the food not to her taste. In December, her lawyer requested an early release in order to "save her life." Paul Tiffin, who had prosecuted the case, opposed the request, arguing that the nun was receiving the treatment she needed. Judge Donald agreed and ruled against an early release. He said that the court and the victims expected the full sentence to be served.[36]

One year after she had entered the House of Correction, Sister Norma regained her liberty. And two years later, on April 18, 2011, she died in Omaha, Nebraska.[37]

The case of Sister Norma was unique in only one respect: it was the first instance of a Catholic nun prosecuted successfully in the United States for the sexual abuse of minors. Otherwise, the story followed a familiar pattern documented on countless occasions when it came to predator priests and religious brothers. The Sisters of Mercy and the archdiocese of Milwaukee had known of the problem nun's depredations as early as 1992 and had failed to contact the civil authorities. Hush money and the usual palaver about prayer and forgiveness kept the matter out of the public domain. It was only in 2006, 14 years later, that the justice system was apprised of the crimes, and it was at the initiative of the victims, not the Church.

As Sister Norma languished in jail, the West Midwest Community of the Sisters of Mercy issued a statement in which they expressed their "profound regret for the pain experienced by the two men and their families." And they added: "We hope that our cooperation with the justice system provides some resolution for everyone affected."[38] The statement was anything but honest. If the Sisters had indeed cooperated with the civil authorities, it was only after their lengthy cover-up of criminal activity was finally exposed. And it is not inconceivable that they had been aware of the nun's proclivities as early as the 1960s, when they moved her from Chicago to Milwaukee and back again.

Conclusion

The two cases examined are similar and different in important ways. Both Rhoads and Giannini were nuns when the sexual crimes for which they were prosecuted took place. It is probable that their religious orders were aware of their depredations and accordingly moved them from school to school in order to avoid scandal—a familiar story. And were it not for complications respecting the statutes of limitations, it is unlikely that either of them would ever have been charged. Rhoads, for example, avoided prosecution for her crimes in Pennsylvania because the statute had expired. It was the different legal system in Virginia that led to her downfall. Had Giannini spent more than six years in Wisconsin, the statute would have expired and she would have evaded the law. Her short stay in the state made prosecution possible.

But the cases differ in the sense that Rhoads left religious life and most of her career was as a lay teacher in Catholic schools. As such she did not have the protective mechanisms of the convent system when complaints were lodged against her. Giannini, on the other hand, remained a nun and almost evaded justice when the Sisters of Mercy tried to buy the silence of her victims with hush money and pledges of secrecy. Only when the victims could no longer abide the terms of the dishonorable pacts and approached the police were her crimes exposed.

Conclusion

> Nuns kind of get a free ride. It's women. They're sweet. You think of women as being nurturing. And you trust them more. And when it's done gently and sweetly and they paint it to be for your benefit, you believe it.[1]
> —Anne Gleeson, abuse survivor

There were nuns who were wonderful teachers. Nuns who were great leaders. Holy, dedicated, self-sacrificing nuns. Nuns who were saints or on the road to sainthood. America had them all, we are told. If Catholic historians had their way, these are the only nuns you would ever hear about. The truth is more complicated, as it always is. The convent system harbored nuns with the complete range of human aptitudes and inclinations—the good, the bad, and the ugly. There were some, for instance, whose ability to instruct the young was mediocre or even hopeless. And there were others who had no business being even in the vicinity of children and adolescents—the sadistic brutes and sexual predators.

In looking back at the goings-on in convent institutions, we can conclude that there was no shortage of "bad" nuns and you didn't have to probe too deeply to find them. They turned up in convent novitiates; orphanages; boarding schools for Native Americans; and in Catholic schools, elementary and secondary.[2] Their victims, both male and female, ranged in age from young adults to six-year-olds. That being said, there was a discernable concentration of abuse directed at those in the 12–14 age range, suggesting that predator nuns may have had perverse attachments to those going through puberty. Moreover, it can be noted that abuse was more prevalent in orphanages and boarding schools for Native Americans than in other institutions since 24-hour custody and the absence of parents made the children particularly vulnerable. Strange theories about "bad blood," paganism, and racial inferiority probably made matters much worse in these settings.

Predatory Nuns

Is there a more odious and repellent crime than the sexual abuse of minors? It is hard to conceive of one. Small wonder that abusers are at the very bottom of the criminal hierarchy and are treated accordingly when incarcerated. The impact of their crimes is usually devastating and long-term. We have seen numerous cases of survivors spending years in therapy as they battled depression, trauma, addictions, and confusion about sexual identity. A rejection of Catholicism or even religion in any form was a frequent outcome.

Why so few prosecutions with so much convent criminality? In truth, the vast majority of victims preferred filing civil lawsuits against their nun assailants and their religious orders. Success was thereby better assured since the standard of proof was the "balance of probabilities," and financial settlements were a likely outcome. Criminal prosecution required the higher standard of "beyond reasonable doubt," and a favorable result, even if more elusive, brought only the satisfaction of seeing your assailant led away in handcuffs. The preference for civil suits is readily understood.

Why did predators emerge in a population of women pledged to lives of chastity and the renunciation of sensual pleasure? There are no easy answers, but clues may be found in the austere regimentation of convent novitiate programs where nuns-in-training were taught to live without emotions while their psychosexual growth was arrested at an adolescent level. Immature, confused about human sexuality, and denied opportunities to develop relationships with adults, some nuns turned for intimacy to those most accessible and least likely to resist: the children under their care. The case of the notorious Sister of Mercy, Norma Giannini, lends credence to this. By her own admission, Sister Norma entered religious life following a sheltered adolescence, was emotionally immature, and knew nothing about sex. In her loneliness and confusion, she became infatuated with the boys in her classroom.

How did religious orders and their leaders respond when complaints about sexual abuse by their members were brought to their attention? The Sisters of Charity, the Sisters of Mercy—with names such as these you might have expected them to be charitable, merciful, or at least just a little bit compassionate towards those whose well-being had been impaired by nun predators. Not a chance. When confronting such complaints, the mothers superior drew on an arsenal of defensive tactics almost identical to that of the bishops. In various combinations, they resorted to suspect internal investigations, moving the predators elsewhere, offering hush money, negotiating confidential out-of-court

7. Conclusion

settlements, and hiding behind statutes of limitations. And they were loud in their refusal to accept any responsibility for the crimes committed under their watch. In a general sense, they closed ranks to protect the predators and in doing so endangered countless other children. As for the complainants, they were treated as a nuisance to be brushed aside with minimum publicity and expense. It was all about propping up the system, its reputation, and its considerable assets.

At the national level too, the culture of secrecy and denial reigned supreme. The Leadership Conference of Women Religious refused to acknowledge for the longest time that the wayward and the wicked even existed within their ranks. Only after years of agitation by survivors and mounting evidence contradicting their denials did they finally face reality in August 2019. But even then, there was no decisive action to address the problem—no equivalent to the Dallas Charter, flawed though it was, and no publishing of lists of credibly accused nuns on congregational websites.

How widespread was the problem of the predatory nun? Were there just "a few bad apples" as apologists for the Church claim? Precise numbers remain elusive and shall continue that way. The stories that have emerged have only done so because of the extraordinary courage and persistence of some of those who were abused. It is not unreasonable to assume, as others have done, that what we know is a mere glimpse at what was really going on. The tip of the iceberg is a metaphor often employed to describe a situation in which the vast majority of victims/survivors never file complaints and there are no records in the public domain. While this is true for those abused by both men and women, there are some complicating peculiarities respecting female abuse.

Dr. Myriam S. Denov, professor and Canada research chair at McGill University's School of Social Work, argues that the public at large, and even the police and social workers, view sexual abuse by women as much less harmful to children than abuse by men. Although there is no evidence to support it, this belief results in victims of female predators not being taken seriously and being discouraged from lodging complaints.[3] A.W. Richard Sipe, an experienced psychotherapist who has handled dozens of cases involving abusive nuns, says society is more comfortable with women touching children, which can allow abuse to be initiated in subtle ways, almost without suspicion.[4]

It is not difficult to see why alleging sexual misconduct by a nun would be greeted with greater skepticism than a similar allegation against a laywoman. Nuns are, after all, holy women whose renunciation of the world and its pleasures clothes them in an aura of sanctity and places them above suspicion. To accuse them of sexual impropriety invites not only disbelief, but indignation and even outrage. It is tantamount to an attack on the Church itself—or maybe even God. Many with good reason to lodge complaints may have sensed the futility of it and failed to act.

How might the full story be better revealed? There are two measures that would make a major difference. The first has to do with the statute of limitations on sexual crimes against minors. When New York temporarily suspended its statute in 2019, followed shortly afterwards by a number of other states, a flood of litigation against the Church and its personnel was unleashed. It is not difficult to imagine the result were all states to do likewise. The second measure would be the establishment of public inquiries with power to subpoena secret files and interrogate witnesses under oath. The only instance of this in the United States was the Pennsylvania grand jury inquiry that reported in 2018. Again, consider the possibilities of such inquiries on a national scale with nuns included, not just diocesan priests as in Pennsylvania.

The "few bad apples" argument has little plausibility. There is already ample evidence at hand to rewrite this book several times over with a similar structure but different case studies.

Even if the quest for justice by those abused by nuns did not always succeed, the culture of denial, *omertà*, and cover-up that protected and sustained convent crimes ultimately failed. It is far too late to put that genie back in the bottle. As for the work of Catholic historians who approach the past as a search for holy heroes, substantial revisions are surely in order.

Chapter Notes

Preface

1. Claire McGettrick, Katherine O'Donnell, Maeve O'Rourke, James M. Smith, and Mari Steed, *Ireland and the Magdalene Laundries: A Campaign for Justice* (London: Bloomsbury, 2021); Paul Jude Redmond, *The Adoption Machine: The Dark History of Ireland's Mother and Baby Homes and the Inside Story of How 'Tuam 800' Became a Global Scandal* (Newbridge, Co. Kildare: Merrion Press, 2018); Brian Titley, "Heil Mary: Magdalen asylums and moral regulation in Ireland," *History of Education Review* 35, no. 2 (October 2006): 1–15.

2. For a personal account of the referendum, see my essay "Keep your rosaries off my ovaries" on my website, briantitley.com.

3. For example: Deirdre Raftery, Catriona Delaney, and Catherine Nowlan-Roebuck, *Nano Nagle: The Life and the Legacy* (Newbridge, Co. Kildare: Merrion Press, 2018). This book makes no reference to the Ryan Commission Report of 2009, which revealed the horrors of Irish orphanages and industrial schools, some of which were operated by the Sisters of the Presentation, the subject of the book. You will read about these nuns in America in Chapter 4.

4. For example, Claire McGettrick, Katherine O'Donnell, Maeve O'Rourke, James M. Smith, and Mari Steed, the authors of *Ireland and the Magdalene Laundries: A Campaign for Justice*, 2021.

5. James R. Miller, *Shingwauk's Vision: A History of Native Residential Schools* (Toronto: University of Toronto Press, 1996).

6. There is no mention of lay sisters in Margaret McGuinness, *Called to Serve: A History of Nuns in America* (New York: New York University Press, 2013). They are examined in Brian Titley, "Convent Class Struggle: Lay Sisters and Choir Sisters in America," *Historical Studies in Education/Revue d'histoire de l'éducation* 32, no. 1 (Spring, printemps 2020): 97–112.

7. The two Catholic historians who have written about the asylums, Maureen Fitzgerald and Suellen Hoy, do not question the official "mission" of the Good Shepherd Sisters as they themselves define it: healing the unfortunate while bandaging their wounds. See Maureen Fitzgerald, *Habits of Compassion: Irish Catholic Nuns and the Origins of New York's Welfare System, 1830–1920* (Urbana: University of Illinois Press, 2006) and Suellen Hoy, *Good Hearts: Catholic Sisters in Chicago's Past* (Urbana: University of Illinois Press, 2006).

8. Rachel L. Swarns, "The nuns who bought and sold human beings," *New York Times*, August 2, 2019. In her detailed study of the various campaigns to promote Americans for sainthood, Kathleen Sprows Cummings fails to mention Duchesne's slave ownership or whether it was even considered as an impediment before her canonization in 1988. Moreover, she spends several pages attempting to prove—without success—that Saint Katherine Drexel was not racist even though she restricted membership of her Sisters of the Blessed Sacrament for Indians and Colored People to white women. Kathleen Sprows

Notes—Chapter 1

Cummings, *A Saint of Our Own: How the Quest for a Holy Hero Helped Catholics Become American* (Chapel Hill: University of North Carolina Press, 2019), 188–191.

Chapter 1

1. Quoted in Kieran Tapsell, *Potiphar's Wife: The Vatican's Secret and Child Sexual Abuse* (Adelaide: ATF Press, 2014), 229–230.
2. Evan Moore, "Church abuse case haunts lawyer who defended priest," *USA Today*, October 5, 2013; Michael D'Antonio, *Mortal Sins: Sex, Crime, and the Era of Catholic Scandal* (New York: Thomas Dunne Books, 2013), 13–40.
3. Desmond Cahill and Peter Wilkinson, *Child Sexual Abuse in the Catholic Church: An Interpretive Review of the Literature and Public Inquiry Reports* (Melbourne: Centre for Global Research, School of Global, Urban and Social Studies, RMIT University, 2017), 40–41; Tapsell, *Potiphar's Wife*, 61.
4. Tomas C. Bruneau, "Church and State in Portugal: Crises of Cross and Sword," *Journal of Church and State* 18, no. 3 (Autumn 1976): 463–490; Othon Guerlac, "The Separation of Church and State in France," *Political Science Quarterly* 23, no. 2 (June 1908): 259–296.
5. Tapsell, *Potiphar's Wife*, 77–78.
6. Cahill and Wilkinson, *Child Sexual Abuse in the Catholic Church*, 33–35; Tapsell, *Potiphar's Wife*, 56.
7. Tapsell, *Potiphar's Wife*, 52, 53, 127–130.
8. Jason Berry, "The Tragedy of Gilbert Gauthe," *The Times of Acadiana*, May 23, 1985. Berry would later publish a book-length study of the case, *Lead Us Not into Temptation*, in 1992.
9. "The Church's Sexual Watergate," Geraldo transcript #303, air date November 14, 1988, http://www.bishop-accountability.org/news5/1988_11_14_Rivera_TheChurchs.pdf (accessed February 15, 2021).
10. D'Antonio, *Mortal Sins*, 194, 195.
11. Cahill and Wilkinson, *Child Sexual Abuse in the Catholic Church*, 269.
12. Carol Lynn Mithers, "Incest and the law," *New York Times Magazine*, October 21, 1990.
13. D'Antonio, *Mortal Sins*, 164.
14. *Ibid.*, 168.
15. Jason Berry, "The Shame of John Paul II: How the sex abuse scandal stained his papacy," *National Catholic Reporter*, April 27, 2011. Much has been written about Father Maciel. A good short account is found in Frédéric Martel, *In the Closet of the Vatican: Power, Homosexuality, Hypocrisy* (London: Bloomsbury, 2019), 231–250.
16. D'Antonio, *Mortal Sins*, 179–182.
17. Walter V. Robinson, "Scores of priests involved in sex abuse cases," *Boston Globe*, January 31, 2002; "The cardinal's departure," *Boston Globe*, December 14, 2002; Stephanie Kirchgaessner and Amanda Holpuch, "How cardinal disgraced in Boston child abuse scandal found a Vatican haven," *The Guardian*, November 6, 2015. *Spotlight*, the 2015 American film directed by Tom McCarthy, is a brilliant dramatized version of the work of the *Boston Globe*'s Spotlight team in investigating and exposing the pedophile priest problem in the archdiocese of Boston.
18. D'Antonio, *Mortal Sins*, 265–272.
19. Tapsell, *Potiphar's Wife*, 275, 276.
20. *Ibid.*, 169.
21. Bernard Condon and Jim Mustian, "Catholic Church could face legal reckoning as state laws pave way for thousands of potential abuse lawsuits," *Globe and Mail*, December 2, 2019; Laurie Goodstein, "Oregon archdiocese files for bankruptcy protection," *New York Times*, July 7, 2004.
22. Berry, "The Shame of John Paul II"; D'Antonio, *Mortal Sins*, 293.
23. Jamie Manson, "Pope Benedict explains things to me," *National Catholic Reporter*, April 12, 2019; Joshua J. McElwee, "In new letter, Benedict blames clergy abuse on sexual revolution, Vatican II theology," *National Catholic Reporter*, April 11, 2019.
24. Tapsell, *Potiphar's Wife*, 130.
25. Nicholas Vaux-Montagny, "French court convicts cardinal of not reporting child abuse," *PBS News*, March 7, 2019;

Notes—Chapter 1

Noemie Bisserbe and Francis X. Rocca, "French court overturns cardinal's conviction for failing to report child sex abuse," *Wall Street Journal*, January 30, 2020.

26. Tapsell, *Potiphar's Wife*, 140.

27. Steve Rennie, "Bishop in child-porn case on probation after serving eight months," *Globe and Mail*, January 4, 2012.

28. Elisabetta Povoledo, "Bishop, 73, in Belgium steps down over abuse," *New York Times*, April 23, 2010.

29. Joshua McElwee and Dennis Coday, "Final days of Benedict full of unclear calls for change," *National Catholic Reporter*, March 11, 2013.

30. Conall Ó Fátharta, "Ryan Report that shocked nation offers much but gaps in the detail still remain," *Irish Examiner*, May 19, 2019; Government of Ireland, *The Report of the Commission to Inquire into Child Abuse (The Ryan Report)*, 2009, https://www.gov.ie/en/publication/3c76d0-the-report-of-the-commission-to-inquire-into-child-abuse-the-ryan-re/ (accessed January 20, 2021).

31. Government of Canada, Truth and Reconciliation Commission of Canada, https://www.rcaanc-cirnac.gc.ca/eng/1450124405592/1529106060525 (accessed February 1, 2021).

32. Government of Australia, Royal Commission into Institutional Responses to Child Sexual Abuse, Final Report, 2017, https://www.childabuseroyalcommission.gov.au/final-report (accessed February 1, 2021).

33. John Hooper, "Vatican bank's former president accused of negligence," *The Guardian*, June 10, 2012.

34. Tamar Lapin, "'Vatileaks' butler who betrayed Pope Benedict dead at 54 after illness," *New York Post*, November 24, 2020.

35. Ian Traynor, Karen McVeigh, and Henry McDonald, "Pope Benedict 'complicit in child sex abuse scandals,' say victims groups," *The Guardian*, February 11, 2013.

36. Anthony Faiola, "8 of Pope Francis's most liberal statements," *Washington Post*, September 7, 2015; Ross Douthat, "Will Pope Francis break the Church?" *The Atlantic*, May 2015.

37. This information is found on the Bishopaccountability.org website under the heading "Data on the crisis" at https://www.bishop-accountability.org/AtAGlance/data.htm (accessed November 20, 2018).

38. Peter Daly, "McCarrick report shows former cardinal's character: ambitious, brazen, untouchable," *National Catholic Reporter*, December 8, 2020; Elizabeth Bruenig, "Everyone knew about Theodore McCarrick," *New York Times*, November 10, 2020; Laurie Goodstein and Sharon Otterman, "He preyed on men who wanted to become priests. Then he became a cardinal," *New York Times*, July 16, 2018; Jason Horowitz, "Sainted too soon? Vatican report cast John Paul II in harsh new light," *New York Times*, November 14, 2020.

39. John Bacon and Mike James, "'Men of God hid it all': Church protected more than 300 'predator priests' in Pa., grand jury says," *USA Today*, August 14, 2018; Michelle Boorstein and Gary Gately, "More than 300 accused priests listed in Pennsylvania report on Catholic Church sex abuse," *Washington Post*, August 14, 2018.

40. Jason Horowitz, Elizabeth Dias, and Laurie Goodstein, "Pope accepts Wuerl's resignation as Washington bishop, but calls him a model bishop," *New York Times*, October 12, 2018. It should be noted that Pope Francis abolished the pontifical secret in December 2019: https://www.vaticannews.va/en/pope/news/2019-12/pope-abolishes-pontifical-secret-sexual-abuse-clergy.html (accessed April 6, 2021).

41. Maryclaire Dale, "DOJ probe of Catholic Church abuse goes quiet two years later," *National Catholic Reporter*, December 14, 2020.

42. Lexi Churchill, Ellis Simani, and Topher Sands, "Catholic leaders promised transparency about child abuse. They haven't delivered," *ProPublica*, January 28, 2020, https://www.propublica.org/article/catholic-leaders-promised-transparency-about-child-abuse-they-havent-delivered (accessed March 9,

Notes—Chapter 2

2021); Campbell Robertson, "Lists of priests accused of sexual abuse are spilling out across the country," *New York Times*, December 14, 2018.

43. Diocese of Helena, List of accused personnel, https://diocesehelena.org/list-of-accused-personnel/ (accessed March 9, 2021).

44. Emma Green, "Why does the Catholic Church keep failing on sexual abuse?" *The Atlantic*, February 14, 2019.

45. Pete Madden, "Exclusive: Leaked transcript shows NY Church's attempt to block Child Victims Act," *ABC News*, January 14, 2021.

46. "Church influencing state: How the Catholic Church spent millions against survivors of clergy abuse," https://www.shewinslaw.com/wp-content/uploads/sites/1600712/2020/05/1234publications-church-influencing-state-how-the-catholic-church-spent-millions-against-survivors-of-clergy-abuse.pdf (accessed March 29, 2021).

47. Bernard Condon and Jim Mustian, "Catholic Church could face legal reckoning as state laws pave way for thousands of potential abuse lawsuits," *The Globe and Mail*, December 2, 2019; Katha Pollitt, "It's about time for New York's Child Victims Act," *The Nation*, August 22, 2019.

48. Bernard Condon and Jim Mustian, "Catholic abuse legal reckoning: New wave of lawsuits could cost church over $4B," *Associated Press*, December 2, 2019.

49. *Ibid.*; Michael Gold, "Facing 200 abuse claims, diocese becomes US's largest to seek bankruptcy," *New York Times*, October 1, 2020; "NY diocese files for bankruptcy amid clergy abuse lawsuits," *Claims Journal*, October 2, 2020. Penn State University Law maintains an excellent website documenting bankruptcy protection measures by Catholic entities: https://elibrary.law.psu.edu/bankruptcy/index.2.html (accessed February 22, 2021).

50. "Four nuns in one family: Reflections on a Mercy-filled life," Sisters of Mercy website, April 10, 2019, http://www.sistersofmercy.org/blog/2019/04/10/four-nuns-one-family-kay-graber/ (accessed April 1, 2021); John Cropley, "52 new suits against Albany Diocese allege sex abuse by priests, nuns," *The Daily Gazette* (Albany), June 15, 2020, https://dailygazette.com/2020/06/15/52-new-suits-against-albany-diocese-allege-sex-abuse-by-priests-nuns/ (accessed April 1, 2021).

51. Child USA, "Child Sex Abuse Statute of Limitations Reform," https://childusa.org/sol/ (accessed April 2, 2021).

52. Haidee Eugenio Gilbert, "Amended lawsuit: 2 nuns abused boy, one of them turning him into a sex slave in 1950s," *Pacific Daily News*, September 5, 2019, https://www.guampdn.com/story/news/2019/09/05/amended-lawsuit-1-2-abusive-nuns-turned-boy-into-her-sex-slave/2217952001/ (accessed April 2, 2021).

53. SNAP, "Abuse by Women Religious (Nuns and Sisters)," https://www.snapnetwork.org/nun_abuse (accessed April 3, 2021).

54. "Six new sex abuse lawsuits filed against Portland archdiocese," *Oregonlive*, August 2, 2007, https://www.oregonlive.com/breakingnews/2007/08/6_new_sex_abuse_lawsuits_filed.html (accessed April 3, 2021); Christopher Landau, "Sex abuse by nuns: the unknown story," *BBC News*, October 2, 2007, http://news.bbc.co.uk/2/hi/americas/7022694.stm (accessed April 3, 2021).

55. Dan Stockman, "Face facts, says LCWR president: Sisters have been part of Catholic Church sexual abuse scandal," *National Catholic Reporter*, August 16, 2019.

56. Dawn Araujo-Hawkins, "Leadership groups condemn abuse by nuns but leave solutions to local congregations," *National Catholic Reporter*, February 25, 2021.

Chapter 2

1. Saint Alfonso Di Liguori, *The True Spouse of Jesus Christ* (New York: Benziger Brothers, 1888), 32.

Notes—Chapter 2

2. Karen Armstrong, *Through the Narrow Gate: A Memoir of Spiritual Discovery* (New York: St. Martin's Griffin, 2000), 71, 286.

3. This idea has no foundation in the official books of the Bible and is usually traced to the *Infancy Gospel of James*, or the *Protoevangelium*, which was written around 150 CE.

4. Charles Freeman, *The Closing of the Western Mind: The Rise of Faith and the Fall of Reason* (New York: Vintage Books, 2005), 246–248.

5. Saints Agnes, Lucy, Margaret of Antioch, and Catherine of Alexandria fall into this fictional category, and they were eliminated from the liturgical calendar in 1969. See Katherine Ludwig Jansen, *The Making of the Magdalen: Preaching and Popular Devotion in the Later Middle Ages* (Princeton, NJ: Princeton University Press, 2001), 335, 336.

6. Pius XII, *Sacra Virginitas*, 6.

7. *Ibid.*, 9, 10.

8. Desmond F. McGoldrick, *The Martyrdom of Change: Simple Talks to Postulant Sisters on the Religious Mentality and Ideal* (Pittsburgh: Duquesne University Press, 1961), 31, 32.

9. Charles W. Harris, "Virginity," *National Catholic Educational Association Bulletin* 55, no. 1 (August 1958): 347, 348; Pius XII, *Sacra Virginitas*, 3.

10. Diarmaid MacCulloch, *Christianity: The First Three Thousand Years* (New York: Viking Penguin, 2010), 203–205; Geneviève Reynes, *Couvents de femmes: La vie des religieuses cloîtrées dans la France des XVIIe et XVIIIe siècles* (Paris: Fayard, 1987), 8, 9.

11. Freeman, *The Closing of the Western Mind*, 251–252; MacCulloch, *Christianity*, 317–318; Jo Ann Kay McNamara, *Sisters in Arms: Catholic Nuns Through Two Millennia* (Cambridge, MA: Harvard University Press, 1996), 33, 34.

12. Elizabeth Rapley, *The Lord as Their Portion: The Story of the Religious Orders and How They Shaped the World* (Toronto: Novalis, 2001), 39.

13. Elizabeth Kuhns, *The Habit: A History of the Clothing of Catholic Nuns* (New York: Image/Doubleday, 2003), 53–55, 65–67.

14. Elizabeth Rapley, *The Dévotes: Women and the Church in Seventeenth Century France* (Montreal and Kingston: McGill-Queen's University Press, 1990), 48–60.

15. Brian Titley, *Into Silence and Servitude: How American Girls Became Nuns, 1945–1965* (Montreal and Kingston: McGill-Queen's University Press, 2017), 54–82.

16. *Ibid.*, 183–102. It is well to remember that American public schools had a very uneven record when it came to providing sex education. The fact that education was first a state responsibility and much decision-making was devolved to local school boards meant that a nation-wide program was out of the question. Zimmerman outlines the problem in his international survey of sex education but does point out the consistent opposition of the Catholic Church to the subject in every country where it exercised influence. See Jonathan Zimmerman, *Too Hot to Handle: The Global History of Sex Education* (Princeton, NJ: Princeton University Press, 2015), 27, 36, 37, 60–63, 74.

17. Nazareno Camilleri, *The Problem of Teen-Age Purity: The Teachings of Pope Pius XII* (New Rochelle, NY: Salesiana Publishers, 1961), 42–43.

18. *Ibid.*, 71.

19. Jude Senieur, "Why Do My Parents Object?" in *Meeting the Vocation Crisis*, ed. George L. Kane (Westminster, MD: The Newman Press, 1956), 82.

20. Godfrey Poage, *For More Vocations* (Milwaukee: The Bruce Publishing Co., 1955), 148–50.

21. Titley, *Into Silence and Servitude*, 124–145.

22. O'Donnell-Gibson, *The Red Skirt*, 183

23. Turk, *The Buried Life*, 9.

24. Mullaly, *Spiritual Reflections for Sisters*, 90.

25. Di Liguori, *The True Spouse of Jesus Christ*, 219, 220.

26. Madeline DeFrees, *The Springs of Silence* (London: The Catholic Book Club, 1954), 59–60; Di Liguori, *The True Spouse of Jesus Christ*, 478; Mary Gilligan Wong, *Nun: A Memoir* (New York:

Notes—Chapter 2

Harper Colophon, 1984), 170; Deborah Larsen, *The Tulip and the Pope: A Nun's Story* (New York: Vintage, 2006), 57–8, 68; Patricia O'Donnell-Gibson, *The Red Skirt: Memoirs of an Ex Nun* (Watervleit, MI: StuartRose Publishing, 2011), 122–3; Catherine Whitney, *The Calling: A Year in the Life of an Order of Nuns* (New York: Crown Publishers, 1999), 49.

27. Patricia Grueninger-Beasley, *The Tears I Couldn't Cry: Behind Convent Doors* (Bloomington, IN: Authorhouse, 2009), 19; Sister Mary Jane Masterson, *One Nun's Story: Then and Now* (Salt Lake City: Millennial Mind Publishing, 2009), 97–8; Midge Turk, *The Buried Life: A Nun's Journey* (London: New English Library, 1972), 34–35.

28. Felix M. Kirsch, *The Spiritual Direction of Sisters: A Manual for Priests and Superiors* (New York: Benziger Brothers, 1931), 53.

29. Mullahy, "Sanctification Through the Vows," 94.

30. Fran Fisher, *In the Name of God, Why? Ex-Catholic Nuns Speak Out About Sexual Repression, Abuse, and Ultimate Liberation* (Granite Bay, CA: Griffin Publishing, 2012), 199.

31. Marie Therese Gass, *Unconventional Women: 73 Ex-Nuns Tell Their Stories* (Clackamas, OR: Sieben Hill, 2001), 176–77.

32. Fisher, *In the Name of God, Why?*, 190, 259.

33. Larsen, *The Tulip and the Pope*, 105. Deborah Larsen was 19 years old in 1960 when she entered the novitiate of the Sisters of Charity of the Blessed Virgin Mary in Dubuque, Iowa. She left in 1965.

34. Susan Bassler Pickford, *Removing the Habit of God: Sister Christina's Story* (Charleston, SC: Createspace, 2012), 77, 78.

35. Orice Klaas, *Once Upon a Convent: A Memoir of a Lesbian Nun* (Portland, OR: Orice Klaas/Uponanon Publishing, 2015), 181–183.

36. Theresa Price, *Letters from a Black and White World: The Making of a Nun* (Bloomington, IN: WestBow Press, 2013), 202–205.

37. Larsen, *The Tulip and the Pope*, 132–36.

38. Nancy Henderson, *Out of the Curtained World* (New York: Pyramid Books, 1972), 161, 162.

39. Joyce H. Vandever, *The Nun, the Pope, and the Wind: A Memoir* (Frederick, MD: America Star Books, 2014), 13, 188.

40. Klaas, *Once Upon a Convent*, 97–99.

41. Mary Zenchoff, *The In-Between Years: A Former Nun's Story of Life in a Convent* (Morgan Hill, CA: Bookstand Publishing, 2017), 66.

42. Marion Kenneally, *One Nun's Odyssey: A Memoir* (Denver: Outskirts Press, 2016), 91.

43. Marge Rogers Barrett, *Called: The Making and Unmaking of a Nun* (Simsbury, CT: Antrim House, 2016), 199, 224.

44. Price, *Letters from a Black and White World*, 202–205.

45. Margaret Lynch, *Triptych: A Memoir* (Bloomington, IN: Authorhouse, 2005), 60–61.

46. Rose Gordy, *The Green That Never Died: A Convent Memoir of the 50s and 60s* (Roseword Books, 2015), 10, 175.

47. John H. McGoey, *The Sins of the Just* (Milwaukee: The Bruce Publishing, 1963), 118.

48. Philip E. Dion, *Sister's Vow of Chastity* (New York: Joseph F. Wagner, 1965), 7–9, 20. Dion's frank discussion of sexuality, designed to be read by novices, probably had minimal impact. It was published in 1965 just as novitiates emptied and the convent system began its unexpected decline.

49. Karol Wojtyla, *Love and Responsibility*, trans. H.T. Willetts (San Francisco: Ignatius Press, 1981), 271.

50. Paulo Provera, *Live Your Vocation*, trans. Thomas F. Murray (St. Louis: B. Herder, 1959), 111.

51. James Alberione, *The Superior Follows the Master* (Boston: The Daughters of St. Paul, 1965), 73.

52. Frederick T. Hoeger, *The Convent Mirror: A Series of Conferences for Religious* (New York: Frederick Pustet Co., 1951), 86, 87.

53. Wong, *Nun*, 221, 225–26.

54. Joan Glisky, "The Official IHM Stance on Friendship, 1845–1960," in

Notes—Chapter 3

Building Sisterhood (Syracuse, NY: Syracuse University Press, 1997), 153–171.

55. Klaas, *Once Upon a Convent*, 35–36.

56. Alberione, *The Superior Follows the Master*, 73. Father James Alberione (1884–1971) was no obscure cleric. The Italian was known as the priest of the media for his energetic use of magazines and periodicals to promote the interests of the Church. He was also the founder of no fewer than four female religious congregations: the Daughters of St. Paul, the Pious Disciples of the Divine Master, the Sisters of Jesus the Good Shepherd (Pastorelle Sisters), and the Queen of Apostles Institute for Vocations (Apostoline Sisters): www.vatican.va/news_services/liturgy/saints/ns_lit_doc_20030427_alberione_en.html (accessed June 19, 2020).

57. Kirsch, *The Spiritual Direction of Sisters*, 406–407.

58. Paul Philippe, *The Novitiate: Religious Life in the Modern World, Vol. 2* (South Bend, IN: University of Notre Dame Press, 1961), 34–39.

59. Paul VI, *Persona Humana: Declaration on Certain Questions Concerning Sexual Ethics, Section IX*, 1975.

60. Alberione, *The Superior Follows the Master*, 111–12.

61. Hoeger, *The Convent Mirror*, 132.

62. René Biot and Pierre Galimard, *Medical Guide to Vocations*, trans. Robert P. Odenwald (Westminster, MD: The Newman Press, 1956), 210. The book was translated from the original French and given an imprimatur by Archbishop Francis Keough of Baltimore.

63. Hubert Van Zeller, *The Yoke of Divine Love: A Study of Conventual Perfection* (Springfield, IL: Templegate, 1957), 53.

64. John E. Moffatt, *Step This Way, Sister: Reflections for Nuns, Young and—Less Young* (New York: Farrar, Strauss and Cudahy, 1960), 80.

65. Dion, *Sister's Vow of Chastity*, 35, 40, 91–92.

66. Turk, *The Buried Life*, 59.

67. Bassler, *Removing the Habit of God*, 58.

68. Joanne Howe, *A Change of Habit: The Autobiography of a Former Catholic Nun* (Nashville, TN: Christian Communications, 1986), 53; Masterson, *One Nun's Story*, 128.

69. Anne Clark Bartlett and Thomas Howard Bestul, eds., *Cultures of Piety: Medieval English Devotional Literature in Translation* (Ithaca, NY: Cornell University Press), 8.

70. Cahill and Wilkinson, *Child Sexual Abuse in the Catholic Church*, 230.

Chapter 3

1. John T. Chibnall, Ann Wolf, and Paul N. Duckro, "A National Survey of the Sexual Trauma Experiences of Catholic Nuns," *Review of Religious Research* 40, no. 2 (December 1998): 160.

2. Christian D. Knudsen, "Naughty nuns and promiscuous monks in late Medieval England" (PhD diss., University of Toronto, 2012), 114, 115.

3. Masterson, *One Nun's Story*, 70.

4. Marta Danylewycz, *Taking the Veil: An Alternative to Marriage, Motherhood, and Spinsterhood in Quebec, 1840–1920* (Toronto: McClelland and Stewart, 1987), 49.

5. Carole Garibaldi Rogers, *Habits of Change: An Oral History of American Nuns* (New York: Oxford University Press, 2011), 264.

6. Jeanne Córdova, *Kicking the Habit: A Lesbian Nun Story* (Los Angeles: Multiple Dimensions, 1990), 107, 208, 226–236, 241–246.

7. Turk, *The Buried Life*, 38–41.

8. Wong, *Nun*, 225–6.

9. Córdova, *Kicking the Habit*, 242.

10. Nancy Manahan and Rosemary Keefe Curb, eds., *Lesbian Nuns: Breaking Silence* (Tallahassee, FL: Naiad Press, 1985), Foreword by Joanne E. Passet, xii-xxvi.

11. Halstead and Halstead, "A Sexual Intimacy Survey of Former Nuns and Priests."

12. Chibnall, Wolf, and Duckro, "A National Survey of the Sexual Trauma Experiences of Catholic Nuns," 146–147, 158–160.

13. Judith C. Brown, *Immodest Acts:*

Notes—Chapter 3

The Life of a Lesbian Nun in Renaissance Italy (New York: Oxford University Press, 1985). This is a summary of the 137-page book. The quotation is found on p. 118.

14. Hubert Wolf, *The Nuns of Sant'Ambrogio: The True Story of a Convent in Scandal*, trans. Ruth Martin (New York: Alfred A. Knopf, 2015). This is a summary of the 371-page book.

15. Sister M. Liguori, "Imported Polish American Sisterhoods," *Polish American Studies* 14, no. 3/4 (July-Dec. 1957): 95–98; Thomas P. McCarthy, *Guide to the Catholic Sisterhoods in the United States* (Washington, DC: Catholic University of America Press, 1958), 133.

16. "Obituary, Sister Gloria Czarniewicz, September 27, 1927-August 20, 2016," https://www.dignitymemorial.com/obituaries/monroe-ct/sister-gloria-czarniewicz-7056376 (accessed October 10, 2020).

17. Stuart Vincent, "Nun alleges sex abuse in convent," *Newsday* (New York), July 14, 1994; Stuart Vincent, "Judge kills nun's sex suit," *Newsday* (New York), January 11, 1995. These news reports are to be found on the website BishopAccountability.org: https://www.bishop-accountability.org/news3/1994_07_14_Vincent_NunAlleges_Gloria_Czarniewicz_1.htm (accessed April 30, 2021) and https://www.bishop-accountability.org/news3/1995_01_11_Vincent_JudgeKills_Gloria_Czarniewicz_2.htm (accessed April 30, 2021).

18. "In Memoriam, Sr. Gloria Czarniewicz (1927–2016)," https://nazarethcsfn.org/in-memoriam?rec_id=145 (accessed October 10, 2020).

19. McCarthy, *Guide to the Catholic Sisterhoods*, 315.

20. "Passing of Sr. Mary Finn," Sisters, Home Visitors of Mary, https://sistershvm.org/2021/01/04/passing-of-sr-mary-finn/ (accessed April 13, 2021).

21. Michael Betzold, "Elderly nun resigns, admitting 'inappropriate conduct' in past years," *Deadline Detroit*, January 17, 2019, https://www.deadlinedetroit.com/articles/21455/elderly_nun_resigns_admitting_inappropriate_conduct_with_novitiate_in_past_years?fb_comment_id=1829737630485880_1831504510309192 (accessed April 13, 2021).

22. Mary Farrow, "Sister resigns from Detroit seminary after sex abuse allegations," *Catholic News Agency*, January 18, 2019, https://www.catholicnewsagency.com/news/40345/sister-resigns-from-detroit-seminary-after-sex-abuse-allegations (accessed April 13, 2021).

23. Michael Betzold, "Elderly nun resigns, admitting 'inappropriate conduct' in past years," *Deadline Detroit*, January 17, 2019, https://www.deadlinedetroit.com/articles/21455/elderly_nun_resigns_admitting_inappropriate_conduct_with_novitiate_in_past_years?fb_comment_id=1829737630485880_1831504510309192 (accessed April 13, 2021).

24. "May they rest in peace: Sr. Mary Finn, HVM," *Detroit Catholic*, January 6, 2021.

25. Dawn Araujo-Hawkins, "Survivors of sex abuse by nuns suffer decades of delayed healing," *National Catholic Reporter*, February 22, 2021.

26. Sister Louise Parent, "The Mission of the Sisters of the Holy Cross in the New England States," Paper prepared for the Conference on the History of the Congregation of Holy Cross in the U.S.A., Moreau Seminary, Notre Dame, IN, March 18–20, 1982.

27. Immaculata was one of three Manchester Catholic schools that merged in 1970 to form the coeducational Trinity High School. The two others were St. Anthony's, a girls' school run by the Sisters of Mercy, and Bishop Bradley, a boys' school belonging to the Brothers of the Christian Schools.

28. Kathryn Marchocki, "To ex-nun, 'therapy was abuse,'" *Union Leader* (Manchester, NH), June 2, 2003.

29. "Affidavit—Jane Mary McDonald, May 10, 2002," https://www.bishop-accountability.org/affidavits/2002_05_10_McDonald_On_Jeanne_Wilfort_1.htm (accessed April 2, 2021).

30. Titley, *Into Silence and Servitude*, 175–203.

31. Rosa Bruno-Jofré, *The Sisters of Our Lady of the Missions: From*

Notes—Chapter 4

Ultramontane Origins to a New Cosmology (Toronto: University of Toronto Press, 2019), 168; Rosa Bruno-Jofré, Heidi MacDonald, and Elizabeth Smith, *Vatican II and Beyond: The Changing Mission and Identity of Canadian Women Religious* (Montreal and Kingston: McGill-Queen's University Press, 2017), 66.

32. Krista Foss, "The novice nun, the holy retreat and the barefoot apostle of love," *Globe and Mail*, June 25, 2002.

33. "Affidavit—Jane Mary McDonald, May 10, 2002."

34. Kathryn Marchocki, "To ex-nun, 'therapy was abuse,'" *Union Leader*, June 2, 2003.

35. "Affidavit—Jane Mary McDonald, May 10, 2002."

36. "Affidavit—Jane Mary McDonald, May 10, 2002"; Tony Dalmyn, posting on Sylvia's Site, May 17, 2004. Sylvia's Site is a WordPress-based blog and database. Launched in 2010 by Sylvia MacEachern from her home in Fitzroy Harbour, Ontario, it documents sexual abuse by Catholic Church personnel in Canada: www.theinquiry.ca/wordpress/ (accessed April 15, 2021).

37. Tony Dalmyn, posting on Sylvia's Site, May 17, 2004.

38. Kevin Spurgaitis, "Desolation Angel," *Catholic New Times*, May 18, 2003.

39. Kathryn Marchocki, "Sister Jane McDonald, 51; had filed sex assault lawsuit," *Union Leader*, August 2, 2003; "Sister Mary Jane McDonald, obituary," *Winnipeg Free Press*, August 1, 2003.

40. "The 38th Conference features 'Holy Cross Ministry in Canada and Beyond.'"

41. http://holycrosshistory.com/-index-past-papers/ (accessed April 20, 2021).

Chapter 4

1. Susanne Robertson, *Throw Away Child* (Baltimore: Publish America, 2003), 252, 253.

2. Canada's Human Rights History, "Duplessis Orphans," https://historyofrights.ca/encyclopaedia/main-events/duplessis-orphans/ (accessed February 21, 2021); Clyde H. Farnsworth, "Orphans of the 1950s, telling of abuse, sue Quebec," *New York Times*, May 21, 1993; Sister Mary James, *Providence: A Sketch of the Sisters of Charity of Providence in the Northwest, 1856–1931* (Seattle: Sisters of Charity of Providence, 1931), 4–18; Marguerite Jean, "Tavernier, Emilie," in *Dictionary of Canadian Biography, Vol. VIII* (Toronto: University of Toronto Press, 1985).

3. *Commission to Inquire into Child Abuse*, Justice Sean Ryan, chair, Dublin, 2009: See Vol. 1, 1.135, 1.136; Vol. 3, 9.103. Witnesses reported sexual abuse by 16 nuns, although they are not identified by name or order; McCarthy, *Guide to the Catholic Sisterhoods in the United States*, 238; "Orders offer abuse compensation," *BBC News*, November 26, 2009; Patsy McGarry, "Sister Act," *Irish Times*, October 3, 2003.

4. John Mack Faragher, *Daniel Boone: The Life and Legend of an American Pioneer* (New York: Henry Holt, 1992), 98–106.

5. Dolores Delahanty, "Catherine Spalding: A legacy worth preserving," *Courier-Journal* (Louisville, KY), September 23, 2014.

6. John Freund, "Sisters of Charity of Nazareth confront own history of slavery," Vincentian Family Communications Commission, July 14, 2012, https://famvin.org/en/2012/07/14/sisters-of-charity-nazareth-confront-own-history-of-slavery/ (accessed April 5, 2019).

7. Peter Smith, "Order reaches out to accusers: abuse by nuns, priest alleged," *Courier-Journal*, July 23, 2004.

8. Peter Smith, "Accused priest recalled as both 'saint' and abuser," *Courier-Journal*, September 12, 2004.

9. "Sexual abuse suit accuses orphanage's priest, nuns," *Lexington Herald-Leader*, July 16, 2004; Peter Smith, "Sibling sisters share accusations against priest and nuns," *Courier-Journal*, July 20, 2004.

10. Peter Smith, "Order reaches out to accusers: abuse by nuns, priest alleged," *Courier-Journal*, July 23, 2004; Gregory

Notes—Chapter 4

A. Hall, "Class action sought in orphanage lawsuit," *Courier-Journal*, July 23, 2005.

11. Kim Michele Richardson, *The Unbreakable Child: A story about forgiving the unforgivable* (self-published, 2012), 3, 4, 20, 21, 34, 57–60.

12. Peter Smith, "Order reaches out to accusers: abuse by nuns, priest alleged," *Courier-Journal*, July 23, 2004; "Claims alleging sex abuse rise to 19," *Associated Press*, July 28, 2004; "5 join abuse suit; priest, nun coach named," *Courier-Journal*, August 11, 2004; "6 join lawsuit claiming abuse by Catholic nuns," *Associated Press*, August 25, 2004; Richardson, *The Unbreakable Child*, 80–82.

13. "24 people say nuns abused them at orphanage," *Associated Press*, August 7, 2004, updated August 9, 2004; Peter Smith, "Memoir details alleged abuse at orphanage," *Courier-Journal*, March 18, 2009.

14. Richardson, *The Unbreakable Child*, 1, 10, 12, 24, 46, 47, 65.

15. Peter Smith, "Order reaches out to accusers: abuse by nuns, priest alleged," *Courier-Journal*, July 23, 2004.

16. Peter Smith, "4 more women claim sex abuse," *Courier-Journal*, July 26, 2004; Kentucky Revised Statutes, 500.050.

17. Peter Smith, "47 file Catholic sex-abuse suits," *Courier-Journal*, October 23, 2005.

18. Peter Smith, "Order of nuns agrees to pay $1.5 million in abuse suit," *Courier-Journal*, August 25, 2006.

19. Joseph Gerth, "Catholic pioneer Mother Spalding honored with statue in Louisville," *Courier-Journal*, July 26, 2015.

20. Leslie Choquette, "French Canadian Immigration to Vermont and New England (1840–1930)," *Vermont History* 86 (Winter/Spring 2018): 2; Yves Roby, "Les Canadiens francais des Etats-Unis (1860–1900): dévoyés ou missionnaires," *Revue d'histoire de l'Amérique française* 41, no. 1 (1987): 3, 4, 11, 18–20.

21. "Diocese to raise funds to improve orphanage here," *Burlington Free Press*, April 28, 1954; Sam Hemingway, "Echoes of abuse grip orphans," *Burlington Free Press*, October 27, 1996; David Massell, Greer Cowan, and Richard Watts, "Vermont's French connection," *Burlington Free Press*, March 5, 2017.

22. Sally Johnson, "Adults worry the Church won't confess its sins," *Insight on the News*, August 22, 1994, www.bishop-accountability.org/news5/1994_08_22_Johnson_AdultsWorry.htm (accessed February 19, 2020); Christine Kenneally, "The Ghosts of St. Joseph's Catholic Orphanage," *Buzzfeed News*, August 27, 2018, 11–14; "State, diocese settle abuse case," *Burlington Free Press*, July 13, 1996.

23. "Abuse allegations rise over closed orphanage," *Burlington Free Press*, November 16, 1993.

24. *Ibid.*; Kenneally, "The Ghosts of St. Joseph's Catholic Orphanage," 11–14.

25. Sally Johnson, "Adults worry the Church won't confess its sins," *Insight on the News*, August 22, 1994, www.bishop-accountability.org/news5/1994_08_22_Johnson_AdultsWorry.htm (accessed February 19, 2020); Kenneally, "The Ghosts of St. Joseph's Catholic Orphanage," 15–16.

26. Joseph R. Barquin, Plaintiff, v. The Roman Catholic Diocese of Burlington, Vermont, Inc., Vermont Catholic Charities, Inc., St. Joseph's Orphanage Asylum, Inc., and/or Its Successors or Assigns in Interest, and Sister Jane Doe, Defendants.

27. Sally Johnson, "Adults worry the Church won't confess its sins," *Insight on the News*, August 22, 1994, www.bishop-accountability.org/news5/1994_08_22_Johnson_AdultsWorry.htm (accessed February 19, 2020); "The response of the diocese: Please accept this deep apology…," *Burlington Free Press*, October 28, 1996.

28. *Ibid.*; "State, diocese settle abuse case," *Burlington Free Press*, July 13, 1996.

29. Sam Hemingway, "Echoes of abuse grip orphans," *Burlington Free Press*, October 27, 1996, 1, 4.

30. Kenneally, "The Ghosts of St. Joseph's Catholic Orphanage," 20–22.

31. "Diocese settles abuse case,"

Notes—Chapter 4

Burlington Free Press, July 13, 1996; "First accuser seeks healing," *Burlington Free Press*, October 28, 1996.

32. "Suits filed by St. Joseph's Residents," *Burlington Free Press*, October 28, 1996.

33. Kenneally, "The Ghosts of St. Joseph's Catholic Orphanage," 7, 8, 55, 56.

34. "Deposition of Robert Cadorette as recorded on 16 May 1997, 9.25 am, at the offices of Paul, Frank and Collins, Inc., Church Street, Burlington, Vermont," United States District Court for the District of Vermont, https://www.bishop-accountability.org/depo/Cadorette_1997_05_16_full_Gelineau_part_R.pdf (accessed February 20, 2021); Kenneally, "The Ghosts of St. Joseph's Catholic Orphanage," 80, 81.

35. "Orphanage abuse lawsuit dismissed," *Burlington Free Press*, August 29, 1998; "Orphans struggle to escape past," *Burlington Free Press*, October 28, 1996.

36. Kenneally, "The Ghosts of St. Joseph's Catholic Orphanage," 43, 53.

37. Ibid., 41, 71.

38. "Abuse lawsuits against orphanage dismissed," *Burlington Free Press*, September 23, 1998; "Orphanage abuse lawsuit dismissed," *Burlington Free Press*, August 29, 1998.

39. Sam Hemingway, "Church to settle orphanage abuse claims," *Burlington Free Press*, April 9, 1999; Kenneally, "The Ghosts of St. Joseph's Catholic Orphanage," 72.

40. Kenneally, "The Ghosts of St. Joseph's Catholic Orphanage," 79; Sam Hemingway, "Vermont diocese slow to cooperate, state says," *Burlington Free Press*, April 27, 2002.

41. Sisters of the Presentation, Watervliet, NY, website: https://presentationsisterswatervlietny.com/history/ (accessed February 25, 2021).

42. Chris Glorioso, "Abuse claim haunts Albany's LaSalle School," *Times Union* (Albany, NY), April 5, 2019; Judy Gregory to Louise Sharpe, April 8, 2002, in Robertson, *The Throw Away Child*, 254, 255.

43. Robertson, *The Throw Away Child*, 13, 14, 25.

44. Aliza Nadi, Emily R. Siegel, Anne Thompson, and Rich Schapiro, "Nun abused me at Catholic orphanage, woman says," *NBC News*, August 13, 2019.

45. "Mary Regina Losee, obituary," *Times Union*, March 6, 2012.

46. Robertson, *The Throw Away Child*, 12, 13.

47. Testimony of Peter R. Gerace, March 10, 2002, in Robertson, *The Throw Away Child*, 230–234; Judy Gregory to Louise Sharpe, April 8, 2002, in Robertson, *The Throw Away Child*, 254, 255.

48. Posting by Leona (Winney) Adams on the Justice for Gilbert website: http://www.justiceforgilbert.com/OtherStories.html (accessed February 27, 2021).

49. Robertson, *The Throw Away Child*, 30–32.

50. Bob V. to Susanne Robertson, March 21, 2002, in Robertson, *The Throw Away Child*, 221; Testimony of Peter R. Gerace, March 10, 2002, in *ibid.*, 230–234; Robertson, *The Throw Away Child*, 60.

51. Nano Nagle website: http://nanonagle.org/education/ (accessed March 2, 2021).

52. A witness to Ireland's Ryan Commission, for example, had this to say: "Sr. X. beat me regularly for being left-handed, saying, no convent girl is going to be left-handed, left-handed people are for the devil," 14.57 Chapter 14, Children's Homes, *Commission to Inquire into Child Abuse*, Dublin 2009. It was believed that the devil baptized his followers with his left hand, although it is doubtful if anyone has seen it happening. See also, Lily Rothman, "How lefties first gained acceptance," *Time*, August 13, 2015.

53. Robertson, *The Throw Away Child*, 21–23, 47.

54. Posting by Leona (Winney) Adams on the Justice for Gilbert website: http://www.justiceforgilbert.com/OtherStories.html (accessed February 27, 2021).

55. Steve Hughes, "CVA lawsuits bring spotlight back to St. Colman's Home," *Times Union*, August 15, 2019; Aliza Nadi, Emily R. Siegel, Anne Thompson, and Rich Schapiro, "Nun sexually abused

me at Catholic orphanage, woman says," *NBC News*, August 13, 2019; Robertson, *The Throw Away Child*, 52, 53, 73–77.

56. Testimony of Peter R. Gerace, March 10, 2002, in Robertson, *The Throw Away Child*, 230–234; Testimony of June Maloney, April 2002, in *ibid.*, 248–253.

57. Testimony of Peter R. Gerace, March 10, 2002, in Robertson, *The Throw Away Child*, 230.

58. Robertson, *The Throw Away Child*, 82, 106–108, 119.

59. Michele Morgan Bolton, "Searching for answers: An 8-year-old- boy's death in 1953 is still a mystery to his brothers, who hunt to find those responsible," *Times Union*, October 17, 2005.

60. "Answers to a 42-year-old mystery may have eroded away," *Times Union*, December 21, 1995.

61. Robertson, *The Throw Away Child*, 122, 123.

62. "Despite lack of evidence, St. Colman's saga lives," *Times Union*, February 29, 1996; "Mary Regina Losee, obituary," *Times Union*, March 6, 2012.

63. Aliza Nadi, Emily R. Siegel, Anne Thompson, and Rich Schapiro, "Nun sexually abused me at Catholic orphanage, woman says," *NBC News*, August 13, 2019.

Chapter 5

1. Stephanie Woodard, "South Dakota boarding school survivors detail sexual abuse," *Indian Country Today*, July 28, 2011.

2. James Wilson, *The Earth Shall Weep: A History of Native America* (New York: Grove Press, 1998), 247–285.

3. Roxanne Dunbar-Ortiz, *An Indigenous Peoples' History of the United States* (Boston: Beacon Press, 2014), 151; Vinnie Rotondaro, "Boarding Schools: A Black Hole of Native American History," *National Catholic Reporter*, September 1, 2015.

4. Cory Allen Heidelberger, "Guest Column: Rename Custer State Park," *Dakota Free Press*, October 16, 2018, https://dakotafreepress.com/2018/10/16/-guest-column-rename-custer-state-park/ (accessed March 3, 2021); Wilson, *The Earth Shall Weep*, 281, 282, 284, 285; Dunbar-Ortiz, *An Indigenous People's History of the United States*, 145, 146, 154–57.

5. "Alleged abuse prompts lawsuit," *Yankton Daily Press and Dakotan*, June 7, 2003.

6. Chet Brokaw, "Court asked to reinstate abuse suit at Indian school," *Associated Press*, *Rapid City Journal*, October 3, 2006.

7. "Champion of Excellence: Struck by the Ree," South Dakota Hall of Fame, https://sdexcellence.org/Struck_By_The_Ree_1978 (accessed March 10, 2021).

8. Gerald W. Wolff, "Father Sylvester Eisenman and Marty Mission," *South Dakota History* 5, no. 4 (Fall 1975): 363, 364, 376, 377.

9. Anne M. Butler, *Across God's Frontiers: Catholic Sisters in the American West, 1850–1920* (Chapel Hill: University of North Carolina Press, 2012), 192–195, 216–225; McGuinness, *Called to Serve*, 129–131; "Obituary of Sr. Mary Francis Poitra," *Yankton Press and Dakotan*, April 26, 2005; "Oblate Sisters of the Blessed Sacrament," https://martycatholic.wordpress.com/meet-the-oblate-sisters/ (accessed March 10, 2021).

10. For a fuller discussion of this distinction, see Titley, "Convent Class Struggle."

11. Stephanie Woodard, "South Dakota boarding school survivors detail sexual abuse," *Indian Country Today*, July 28, 2011.

12. Sharon Waxman, "Abuse charges hit reservation," *Washington Post*, June 2, 2003.

13. David Melmer, "School victims want reparation: Decades of abuse results in court action," *Indian Country Today*, April 28, 2003.

14. Stephanie Woodard, "South Dakota boarding school survivors detail sexual abuse," *Indian Country Today*, July 28, 2011.

15. Sharon Waxman, "Abuse charges hit reservation," *Washington Post*, June 2, 2003; David Melmer, "School victims want reparation: Decades of abuse

Notes—Chapter 5

results in court action," *Indian Country Today*, April 28, 2003.

16. Stephanie Woodard, "South Dakota boarding school survivors detail sexual abuse," *Indian Country Today*, July 28, 2011.

17. Supreme Court of the State of South Dakota, Theresa Bernie et al, vs Catholic Diocese of Sioux Falls et al, 2012.

18. "Obituary of Sr. Mary Francis Poitra," *Yankton Press and Dakotan*, April 26, 2005.

19. Sharon Waxman, "Abuse charges hit reservation," *Washington Post*, June 2, 2003.

20. Supreme Court of the State of South Dakota, D.Z. Iron Wing vs Catholic Diocese of Sioux Falls, et al, 2011.

21. "Francis Suttmiller Obituary," Under the Blue Cloud, https://www.underthebluecloud.com/francis-suttmiller-obituary/ (accessed September 17, 2020).

22. Cecily Hilleary, "For Native American clergy abuse survivors, justice is elusive," *VOA News*, September 27, 2018.

23. Supreme Court of the State of South Dakota, D.Z. Iron Wing vs Catholic Diocese of Sioux Falls, et al, 2011.

24. Gontran Laviolette, "Tatanke-Najin (known as Standing Buffalo)," in *Dictionary of Canadian Biography, IX* (Toronto: University of Toronto Press, 2003); Alan L. Neville and Alyssa Kaye Anderson, "The Diminishment of the Great Sioux Reservation: Treaties, Tricks, and Time," *Great Plains Quarterly* 33, no. 4 (Fall 2013), 238–241; Natasha Rausch, "Sisseton Wahpeton Nation created through movement, sometimes willing but sometimes forced," *Grand Forks Herald*, November 30, 2019; Wilson, *The Earth Shall Weep*, 270–272.

25. McCarthy, *Guide to the Catholic Sisterhoods in the United States*, 250; Sister Margaret Shekleton, *Bending in Season: History of the North American Province of the Sisters of the Divine Savior, 1895–1985* (Milwaukee: Sisters of the Divine Savior, 1985), 11–22.

26. Sharon Otterman, "Complex emotions over first American Indian saint," *New York Times*, July 24, 2012; John Rasmussen, "Saint Kateri (Kateri Tekakwitha)," in *Canadian Encyclopedia*; Shekleton, *Bending in Season*, 233–34.

27. Stephanie Woodard, "South Dakota boarding school survivors detail sexual abuse," *Indian Country Today*, July 28, 2011.

28. Ibid.

29. Ibid.

30. State of South Dakota, County of Minnehaha, Second Judicial Circuit Court, W.M.D. et al., plaintiffs vs. The Catholic Diocese of Sioux Falls, et al., July 19, 2010.

31. Dirk Lammers, "Abuse by priests, nuns alleged at S.D. orphanage," *Sioux City Journal*, August 6, 2010; Jeff Martin, "Sexual abuse alleged at orphanage," *Argus Leader* (Sioux Falls), August 6, 2010.

32. Peter Harriman, "Lawmakers want to limit sex abuse lawsuits," *Argus Leader*, March 8, 2010; Statute 26–10–25 South Dakota, Bill HB-1104, Legislative assembly of South Dakota: "An Act to limit the source of recovery in certain civil actions for childhood sexual abuse injuries, 2010."

33. Stephanie Woodard, "Catholic Church evades sex charges in South Dakota," *Women's eNews*, April 8, 2011.

34. Stephanie Woodard, "South Dakota legislature gets new sex-abuse bill," *Indian Country Today Network*, October 30, 2011.

35. Peyton Healy, "A change in South Dakota's child sexual abuse statute of limitations," *American Indian Law Journal* 7, no. 2 (2019): 86, 87; Peter Harriman, "Lawmakers want to limit sex abuse lawsuits," *Argus Leader*, March 8, 2010.

36. Mary Farrow, "S. Dakota dioceses focus on healing after statute of limitations bill fails," *Catholic News Agency*, February 25, 2020.

37. "California expands statute of limitations for childhood sex abuse," *Catholic News Agency*, October 15, 2019.

38. Mary Farrow, "S. Dakota dioceses focus on healing after statute of limitations bill fails," *Catholic News Agency*, February 25, 2020.

39. A sympathetic portrayal of De Smet is found in a book by a fellow Jesuit:

John J. Killoren, *Come Black Robe: De Smet and the Indian Tragedy* (Norman: University of Oklahoma Press, 1994).

40. Emily Clark, *Masterless Mistresses: The New Orleans Ursulines and the Development of a New World Society, 1727–1834* (Chapel Hill: University of North Carolina Press, 2007), 41–58, 161–194; Rachel L. Swarns, "The nuns who bought and sold human beings," *New York Times*, August 2, 2019.

41. Gwen Florio, "Anguish has never healed for Natives physically, sexually abused at St. Ignatius mission," *The Missoulian*, June 5, 2011; Gwen Florio, "Silence shrouds St. Ignatius Jesuit abuse case as settlement date nears," *The Missoulian*, June 6, 2011.

42. Gwen Florio, "Anguish has never healed for Natives physically, sexually abused at St. Ignatius mission," *The Missoulian*, June 5, 2011.

43. B.L. Azure, "Sexual, physical and emotional abuse suit filed," *Char-Koosta News* (Pablo, MT), October 6, 2011.

44. Montana First Judicial District Court, Lewis and Clark County, John Does and Jane Does v. Ursuline Sisters, October 2011.

45. *Ibid.*

46. Gwen Florio, "Lawsuit filed alleging sexual abuse by nuns at St. Ignatius Mission," *The Missoulian*, September 27, 2011.

47. Gwen Florio, "Anguish has never healed for Natives physically, sexually abused at St. Ignatius mission," *The Missoulian*, June 5, 2011; Gwen Florio, "Lawsuit filed alleging sexual abuse by nuns at St. Ignatius Mission," *The Missoulian*, September 27, 2011.

48. B.L. Azure, "Sexual, physical and emotional abuse suit filed," *Char-Koosta News*, October 6, 2011.

49. Jimmy Tobias, "Forgive You, Father," *Missoula Independent*, March 27, 2014.

50. U.S. Federal Population Census, 1940.

51. Gwen Florio, "Anguish has never healed for Natives physically, sexually abused at St. Ignatius mission," *The Missoulian*, June 5, 2011.

52. Montana First Judicial District Court, Lewis and Clark County, John Does and Jane Does v. Ursuline Sisters, October 2011.

53. *Ibid.*

54. Dan Morris-Young, "Helena diocese reaches sex abuse settlement via 'consensus model,'" *National Catholic Reporter*, March 20, 2015; Dan Stockman, "Settlement reached in Ursuline abuse suit," *National Catholic Reporter*, February 6, 2015.

55. Stephanie Woodard, "Nun abuse case goes to bankruptcy court; survivor speaks out," *Indian Country Today*, February 6, 2015; Alexander Deedy, "Diocese names priests, sisters, staff accused of sex abuse," *Independent Record* (Helena, Montana), April 29, 2015; Diocese of Helena, List of accused personnel, https://diocesehelena.org/list-of-accused-personnel/ (accessed March 9, 2021).

56. Gwen Florio, "Anguish has never healed for Natives physically, sexually abused at St. Ignatius mission," *The Missoulian*, June 5, 2011; Jimmy Tobias, "Forgive You, Father," *Missoula Independent*, March 27, 2014.

57. Jimmy Tobias, "Forgive You, Father," *Missoula Independent*, March 27, 2014.

58. *Ibid.*

Chapter 6

1. Elinor Burkett and Frank Bruni, *A Gospel of Shame: Children, Sexual Abuse, and the Catholic Church* (New York: Penguin/Viking, 1993), 88.

2. Titley, *Into Silence and Servitude*, 177, 198.

3. Carol K. Coborn and Martha Smith, *Spirited Lives: How Nuns Shaped Catholic Culture and American Life, 1836–1920* (Chapel Hill: University of North Carolina Press, 1999), 129, 130, 144.

4. Mother Marie Helene, "The Spiritual Possibilities of Teaching as a Vocation," in *Religious Community Life in the United States*, 117–25.

5. Araujo-Hawkins, "Survivors of sex abuse by nuns suffer decades of delayed healing"; Coborn and Smith, *Spirited Lives*, 84, 85; "Former nun accused in

Notes—Chapter 6

sex lawsuit," *CBS News online*, June 9, 2003; Carol Kuruvilla and Jessica Blank, "Women Sexually Abused by Catholic Nuns Speak Up: She Told Me It Was 'God's Love,'" *Huffington Post*, April 11, 2019; McCarthy, *Guide to the Catholic Religious Sisterhoods*, 156, 157; "Obituary, Judith R. Fisher," *Indianapolis Star*, January 30, 2004; "Woman speaks up about alleged abuse by Colo. nun," *Associated Press*, August 6, 2008.

6. Ed Palattella, "Erie nuns knew about abusive sister decades ago" and "Erie nuns set up hotline in light of abuse revelation," GoErie.com, October 30, 2018, https://www.goerie.com/news/20181030/erie-nuns-knew-about-abusive-sister-decades-ago (accessed October 20, 2020).

7. Ann Rodgers-Melnick, "Former student's suit says nun seduced her in secret 70s romance," *Pittsburgh Post-Gazette*, October 18, 1997; Paul Van Osdol, "Team 4 examines alleged abuse by nun," WTAE (Pittsburgh), April 26, 2002, http://www.thepittsburghchannel.com/tem4/1420912/detail.html (accessed July 20, 2019).

8. Rick Linsk and Stephen Scott, "Oakdale woman warns of sexual abuse by nuns," *St. Paul Pioneer Press*, July 15, 2002; Burkett and Bruni, *A Gospel of Shame*, 88, 89; "Sister Georgene Stuppy—Rochester," *PostBulletin* (Rochester, MN), May 27, 2009.

9. David Andreatta, "Webster woman alleges sexual abuse by nun, settles with Rochester diocese," *Rochester Democrat and Chronicle*, March 1, 2019.

10. Rick Linsk and Stephen Scott, "Oakdale woman warns of sexual abuse by nuns," *St. Paul Pioneer Press*, July 15, 2002; "In loving memory: Sister Marcene (Mary Cletus) Schlosser," https://www.ssndcentralpacific.org/file/obituary/marcene-schlosser.pdf (accessed September 9, 2021).

11. "Catholic nun sexual abuse case is settled," *Detroit Free Press*, June 27, 2004; "Girls school student calls atmosphere free," *Argus-Leader* (Sioux Falls, SD), March 21, 1978; Deanna B. Narveson, "Good Counsel Academy gone for 38 years, still remembered by its alumnae," *Mankato Free Press*, April 29, 2018, https://sites.google.com/site/guardianangelstbonifaceschool/history (accessed July 5, 2019); "In loving memory: Sister M. Ramona Schweich, SSND," https://www.ssndcentralpacific.org/document.doc?id=101 (accessed September 9, 2021).

12. Araujo-Hawkins, "Survivors of sex abuse by nuns suffer decades of delayed healing"; McCarthy, *Guide to the Catholic Sisterhoods in the United States*, 281; Wylie Gerdes, "Woman names ex-nun in sexual abuse lawsuit," *Detroit Free Press*, June 22, 1995; Alison Bass, "Woman sues, says she was molested by nun," *Boston Globe*, June 22, 1995; Louis Rom, "Vows of Silence?" *Gambit, the best of New Orleans*, August 12, 2002.

13. Pamela Miller, "Complaints of sex abuse by nuns begin to emerge," *Star Tribune* (Minneapolis-St. Paul, MN), June 24, 2006; Jim Kouri, "Nuns on the run? New child sex abuse lawsuits filed against Catholic nun," *The Conservative Voice*, June 15, 2006, https://www.bishop-accountability.org/news2006/05_06/2006_06_14_Kouri_NunsOn.htm (accessed April 28, 2021); Karen Maezen Miller, "Shattered faith in two parts," *Killing the Buddha*, May 4, 2009, https://killingthebuddha.com/mag/dispatch/shattered-faith-in-two-parts/ (accessed April 28, 2021); "Sister Benen Kent –Rochester (obituary)," *Post-Bulletin* (Rochester, MN), June 25, 2003; State of Minnesota in Court of Appeals A07–1054, Karen Britten, appellant, vs. the Franciscan Sisters, 29 April 2008; "Suffering in Silence: 3 women tell the story of sex abuse by nun," KARE, September 27, 2008, bishop-ccountability.org/news2008/09_10/2008_09_27_Kare_SufferingIn.htm (accessed December 28, 2018); Manya A. Brachear, "Woman sues order of nuns for alleged '60s sex abuse," *Chicago Tribune*, June 1, 2005.

14. Gregory Hall, "Suit alleges nun abused girl in 1970s," *Courier-Journal* (Louisville, KY), August 1, 2003; "Obituary, Sister Mary Helen Thieneman, OP," *Courier-Journal*, January 24, 2013; SNAP, "KY- Louisville area nuns who are or have

been accused of sexual abuse," March 15, 2015, https://www.snapnetwork.org/ky_snap_fact_sheet_3_15 (accessed December 20, 2020).

15. Myra L. Hidalgo, *Sexual Abuse and the Culture of Catholicism: How Priests and Nuns Become Perpetrators* (New York: The Haworth Press, 2007), 4–20; Louis Rom, "Victim, experts tell of abuse by nuns," *National Catholic Reporter*, November 1, 2002; "Sister Cheryl Ann Porte MSC, Obituary," https://www.schoenfh.com/tributes/-SisterCheryl-Porte (accessed February 18, 2021).

16. Araujo-Hawkins, "Survivors of sex abuse by nuns suffer decades of delayed healing"; Isabel Vincent, "Inside the horrifying, unspoken world of sexually abusive nuns," *New York Post*, February 16, 2018; "Obituary: Mercy Sister Juanita Barto," *The Tablet* (Diocese of Brooklyn), June 25, 2014.

17. Susan Gilmore, "Sister Dolores Crosby, longtime educator, dies at 72," *Seattle Times*, July 27, 2007; Julie Muhlstein, "Knowing, and not knowing, a Catholic pedophile," *Everett Herald* (Everett, WA), January 19, 2016.

18. Cris Foehlinger, "Betrayal of Faith," *Sunday News* (Lancaster, PA), January 16, 2005; Abbott Koloff, "Questions raised over handling of nun abuse," *Daily Record* (Parsippany-Troy Hills, NJ), October 24, 2004; "Woman claims nun plied her with booze, drugs and taught her to have sex with women," *Kingston Whig Standard* (Kingston, ON), January 3, 2019.

19. Rom, "Vows of Silence?"

20. Riley Rogerson, "Before GU, Nursing Dean Zuccarelli assaulted student seeking counsel," *The Hoya* (Georgetown University), March 15, 2019; Jeff Barron, "Former Fisher Catholic nun accused of molesting a student," *Lancaster Eagle-Gazette* (Lancaster, OH), November 29, 2018; Danae King, "Former Fisher Catholic nun accused of sexually abusing a student," *Columbus Dispatch* (Columbus, OH), December 11, 2018; Rate my professors, https://www.ratemyprofessors.com/ShowRatings.jsp?tid=451988 (accessed September 20, 2019).

21. Laura Mansnerus, "Archdiocese settles sex lawsuit involving former nun and boy," *New York Times*, September 19, 2000; Barbara Ross, "Archdiocese settles teacher sex-abuse case," *Daily News* (New York, NY), September 19, 2000; Laura Mansnerus, "School and archdiocese ignored ex-teacher's molesting of pupil, lawyer says at trial," *New York Times*, September 16, 2000; Laura Mansnerus, "Sex-abuse lawsuit names ex-teacher and archdiocese," *New York Times*, September 15, 2000; "Sex suit accuses ex-nun," *Daily News*, February 25, 1996; "Student says ex-nun forced sex on him," *Daily News*, March 2, 1996.

Chapter 7

1. Nancy Phillips and Mark Fazlollah, "Former nun grapples with history of abuse" *Philadelphia Inquirer*, September 14, 2005.

2. "The People of NY vs. Sister Maureen," *Los Angeles Times*, February 27, 1977; "Nun cleared of charge she killed newborn son," *New York Times*, March 5, 1977.

3. McCarthy, *Guide to the Catholic Religious Sisterhoods*, 149. These nuns could easily be confused with other congregations with very similar names. For example: the Sister-Servants of the Immaculate Heart of Mary (S.C.I.M., origins in Quebec); the Sisters of the Immaculate Heart of Mary (S.I.H.M., origins in Spain); and the Sisters Servants of Mary Immaculate (S.S.M.I., origins in Ukraine). The Sisters, Servants in question here employ the post-nominal letters I.H.M. Some of their students liked to joke that the letters stood for "I hate men."

4. Nancy Phillips and Mark Fazlollah, "Former nun grapples with history of abuse" *Philadelphia Inquirer*, September 14, 2005.

5. "Former nun gets six months for molestation," *Pocono Record* (Stroudsburg, PA), September 23, 2004; Rose Quinn, "Grand jury indictment awaits former nun," *The Daily Times* (Delaware County, PA), February 12, 2004.

6. Nancy Phillips and Mark Fazlollah,

Notes—Chapter 7

"Former nun grapples with history of abuse," *Philadelphia Inquirer*, September 14, 2005.

7. Titley, *Into Silence and Servitude*, 185, 198, 199.

8. Rose Quinn, "Grand jury indictment awaits former nun," *The Daily Times*, February 12, 2004.

9. Nancy Phillips and Mark Fazlollah, "Former nun grapples with history of abuse," *Philadelphia Inquirer*, September 14, 2005; "New suits allege clergy abuses," *Morning Call* (Allentown, PA), March 25, 2004; Jon Frank and Kate Wiltrout, "Two Pennsylvania men file suits against former Beach nun," *Virginian-Pilot* (Virginia Beach, VA), March 25, 2004.

10. Nancy Phillips and Mark Fazlollah, "Former nun grapples with history of abuse," *Philadelphia Inquirer*, September 14, 2005.

11. Rose Quinn, "Grand jury indictment awaits former nun," *The Daily Times*, February 12, 2004.

12. Jon Frank and Kate Wiltrout, "Two Pennsylvania men file suits against former Beach nun," *Virginian-Pilot*, March 25, 2004; "Former nun gets six months for molestation," *Ponono Record*, September 23, 2004.

13. "Ex-nun arrested on assault charges," The Associated Press, February 11, 2004; Jon Frank, "Former nun convicted of 2 felony sex crimes," *Virginian-Pilot*, July 15, 2004; "Former nun gets six months for molestation," *Ponono Record*, September 23, 2004.

14. Jon Frank and Kate Wiltrout, "Two Pennsylvania men file suits against former Beach nun," *Virginian-Pilot*, March 25, 2004; Nancy Phillips and Mark Fazlollah, "Former nun grapples with history of abuse," *Philadelphia Inquirer*, September 14, 2005.

15. Jon Frank, "Former nun sentenced for molestation 35 years ago," *Virginian Pilot*, September 22, 2004; "Former nun gets six months for molestation," *Pocono Record*, September 23, 2004.

16. "Former nun gets six months for molestation," *Pocono Record*, September 23, 2004; Nancy Phillips and Mark Fazlollah, "Former nun grapples with history of abuse," *Philadelphia Inquirer*, September 14, 2005.

17. Nancy Phillips and Mark Fazlollah, "Former nun grapples with history of abuse," *Philadelphia Inquirer*, September 14, 2005.

18. Rose Quinn, "Grand jury indictment awaits former nun," *The Daily Times*, February 12, 2004.

19. Jon Frank, "Former nun sentenced for molestation 35 years ago," *Virginian Pilot*, September 22, 2004.

20. Information on Sister Norma's birth and death are found on www.tributes.com/obituary/show/Beverly-Giannini-91339260 (accessed September 3, 2019); Saul Bellows's *The Adventures of Augie March*, about a young man growing up in the poverty of the Depression, captures well the challenges of life in 1930s Chicago.

21. Mary Beth Fraser Connolly, *Women of Faith: The Chicago Sisters of Mercy and the Evolution of a Religious Community* (New York: Fordham University Press, 2014), 75–78, 105–128.

22. Jessica McBride, "Devil in Disguise," *Milwaukee Magazine*, June 23, 2008.

23. Georgia Pabst, "Catholic nun sentenced in abuse of boys 40 years ago," *Milwaukee Journal Sentinel*, February 1, 2008; McBride, "Devil in Disguise."

24. Margaret Ramirez, "Nun, 79, declines to fight sex case," *Chicago Tribune*, November 12, 2007; McBride, "Devil in Disguise."

25. Manya A. Brachear, "Indictment against nun in abuse case from 1960s," *Chicago Tribune*, December 6, 2006; McBride, "Devil in Disguise."

26. McBride, "Devil in Disguise."

27. Jason Berry, "Victims caught up in Milwaukee's 'shell game,'" *National Catholic Reporter*, January 31, 2012; Marie Rohde, "The Prophet," *Milwaukee Magazine*, September 19, 2011.

28. "Nun accused of sexual assault to spend 1 year in jail," WISN-ABC12, February 1, 2008, https://www.bishopaccountability.org/news2008/01_02/2008_02_01_WISNABC12_NunAccused.htm (accessed March 5, 2020); Margaret Ramirez, "Nun Norma Giannini admitted abusing Chicago

Notes—Conclusion

boy, 3 others, court record shows," *Chicago Tribune*, February 1, 2008; McBride, "Devil in Disguise."

29. Manya A. Brachear, "Indictment against nun in abuse case from 1960s," *Chicago Tribune*, December 6, 2006; Margaret Ramirez, "Nun Norma Giannini admitted abusing Chicago boy, others, court record shows," *Chicago Tribune*, February 1, 2008; McBride, "Devil in Disguise."

30. Peter Miller, "Archbishop Weakland's Legacy: The liberal liturgist's shameful departure," *Seattle Catholic*, June 7, 2002. *The Seattle Catholic*, in which this article appeared, was an internet publication that ran from 2001 until 2006. It promoted an extremely conservative Catholicism and was scathing in its criticism of the reforms of the Second Vatican Council, which it viewed as a modernist conspiracy. The writer of this piece, Peter Miller, was virtually gloating at the downfall of Archbishop Weakland, who was seen as a despised liberal.

31. McBride, "Devil in Disguise."

32. McBride, "Devil in Disguise"; Milwaukee County Case Number 2006CF006443, State of Wisconsin vs. Norma Giannini. A "John Doe investigation" is a legal proceeding that allows a judge to determine if the evidence suggests that a crime has been committed. It is similar to a grand jury except that a judge rather than a jury of peers assesses the evidence. Witnesses can be subpoenaed but cannot discuss the case in public.

33. Manya A. Brachear, "Indictment against nun in abuse case from 1960s," *Chicago Tribune*, December 6, 2006.

34. McBride, "Devil in Disguise"; "Milwaukee/Attorney of abuser, victim reprimanded," *Twin Cities Pioneer Press*, December 21, 2010, https:www.twincities.com/2010.../milwaukee-attorney-of-abuser-victim-reprimanded (accessed March 21, 2020); Margaret Ramirez, "Nun, 79, declines to fight sex case," *Chicago Tribune*, November 12, 2007; Catrin Einhorn, "Nun pleads no contest in sex abuse," *New York Times*, November 13, 2007.

35. Georgia Pabst, "Catholic nun sentenced in abuse of boys 40 years ago," *Milwaukee Journal Sentinel*, February 1, 2008; "Nun gets one year for abusing two teens," *Associated Press*, February 1, 2008.

36. Marie Rohde, "Early release denied for nun in sex abuse case," *Milwaukee Journal Sentinel*, December 12, 2008, archive.jsonline.com/news/milwaukee/36061779.html/; "Nun convicted of sexual abuse back in court," WISN-ABC12, December 13, 2008, http://www.wisn.com/news/18263434/detail.html (accessed March 30, 2020).

37. Jerry Kobbs, "Pedophile nun released from Milwaukee Jail," SNAP press statement, April 23, 2009; "Beverly Margaret Giannini," http://www.tributes.com/obituary/show/Beverly-Giannini-91339260 (accessed March 30, 2020).

38. Sisters of Mercy of the Americas, "Statement: Sister Norma Giannini's Sentence," December 12, 2008, https://www.sistersofmercy.org/about-us/.../statement-sister-norma-gianninis-sentence/ (accessed March 30, 2020).

Conclusion

1. "Woman speaks up about alleged abuse by Colo. nun," *Associated Press*, August 6, 2008.

2. There were also specialized institutions staffed by some predator nuns, such as the notorious St. John's School for the Deaf in St. Francis, Wisconsin. One student at the school, Carolyn, claimed she had been sexually abused by four Sisters of St. Joseph as well as by the director, Father Lawrence Murphy. Arlene Krieger, *Behind the Walls of St. John's: A Story of Catholic Abuse* (Minneapolis-St. Paul: Freethought House, 2017), 153, 154.

3. Myriam Denov, "To a safer place? Victims of sexual abuse by females and their disclosures to professionals," *Child Abuse and Neglect* 27, no. 1 (2003) and Myriam Denov, "The long-term effect of child sexual abuse by female perpetrators: A qualitative study of male and female victims," *Journal of Interpersonal Violence* 19, no. 10 (2004).

4. Rom, "Vows of Silence?"

Bibliography

Articles and Books

Alberione, James. *The Superior Follows the Master.* Boston: The Daughters of St. Paul, 1965.

Araujo-Hawkins, Dawn. "Leadership groups condemn abuse by nuns but leave solutions to local Congregations." *National Catholic Reporter,* February 25, 2021.

Araujo-Hawkins, Dawn. "Survivors of sex abuse by nuns suffer decades of delayed healing." *National Catholic Reporter,* February 22, 2021.

Armstrong, Karen. *Through the Narrow Gate: A Memoir of Spiritual Discovery.* New York: St. Martin's Griffin, 2000.

Barrett, Marge Rogers. *Called: The Making and Unmaking of a Nun.* Simsbury, CT: Antrim House, 2016.

Bartlett, Anne Clark, and Thomas Howard Bestul, eds., *Cultures of Piety: Medieval English Devotional Literature in Translation.* Ithaca, NY: Cornell University Press, 1999.

Bellows, Saul. *The Adventures of Augie March.* New York: Viking, 1953.

Berry, Jason. *Lead Us Not into Temptation: Catholic Priests and the Sexual Abuse of Children.* Urbana: University of Illinois Press, 2000.

Berry, Jason. "The Shame of John Paul II: How the sex abuse scandal stained his papacy." *National Catholic Reporter,* April 27, 2011.

Biot, René, and Pierre Galimard. *Medical Guide to Vocations.* Translated by Robert P. Odenwald. Westminster, MD: The Newman Press, 1956.

Brown, Judith C. *Immodest Acts: The Life of a Lesbian Nun in Renaissance Italy.* New York: Oxford University Press, 1985.

Bruneau, Tomas C. "Church and State in Portugal: Crises of Cross and Sword." *Journal of Church and State* 18, no. 3 (Autumn 1976): 463–490.

Bruno-Jofré, Rosa. *The Sisters of Our Lady of the Missions: From Ultramontane Origins to a New Cosmology.* Toronto: University of Toronto Press, 2019.

Bruno-Jofré, Rosa, Heidi MacDonald, and Elizabeth Smyth. *Vatican II and Beyond: The Changing Mission and Identity of Canadian Women Religious.* Montreal and Kingston: McGill-Queen's University Press, 2017.

Burkett, Elinor, and Frank Bruni. *A Gospel of Shame: Children, Sexual Abuse, and the Catholic Church.* New York: Penguin/Viking, 1993.

Butler, Anne M. *Across God's Frontiers: Catholic Sisters in the American West, 1850–1920.* Chapel Hill: University of North Carolina Press, 2012.

Cahill, Desmond, and Peter Wilkinson. *Child Sexual Abuse in the Catholic Church: An Interpretive Review of the Literature and Public Inquiry Reports.* Melbourne: Centre for Global Research, School of Global, Urban and Social Studies, RMIT University, 2017.

Camilleri, Nazareno. *The Problem of Teenage Purity: The Teachings of Pope Pius XII.* New Rochelle, NY: Salesiana Publishers, 1961.

Chibnall, John T., Ann Wolf, and Paul N. Duckro. "A National Survey of the Sexual Trauma Experiences of Catholic Nuns." *Review of Religious Research* 40, no. 2 (December 1998): 142–67.

Bibliography

Choquette, Leslie. "French Canadian Immigration to Vermont and New England (1840–1930)." *Vermont History* 86 (Winter/Spring 2018): 1–8.

Clark, Emily. *Masterless Mistresses: The New Orleans Ursulines and the Development of a New World Society, 1727–1834*. Chapel Hill: University of North Carolina Press, 2007.

Coburn, Carol K., and Martha Smith. *Spirited Lives: How Nuns Shaped Catholic Culture and American Life, 1836–1920*. Chapel Hill: University of North Carolina Press, 1999.

Collins, A. Leonard, ed. *Proceedings of the 1955 Sisters' Institute of Spirituality*. South Bend: University of Notre Dame Press, 1956.

Connolly, Mary Beth Fraser. *Women of Faith: The Chicago Sisters of Mercy and the Evolution of a Religious Community*. New York: Fordham University Press, 2014.

Córdova, Jeanne. *Kicking the Habit: A Lesbian Nun Story*. Los Angeles: Multiple Dimensions, 1990.

Cummings, Kathleen Sprows. *A Saint of Our Own: How the Quest for a Holy Hero Helped Catholics Become American*. Chapel Hill: University of North Carolina Press, 2019.

Dale, Maryclaire, "DOJ probe of Catholic Church abuse goes quiet two years later." *National Catholic Reporter*, December 14, 2020.

Daly, Peter, "McCarrick report shows former cardinal's character: ambitious, brazen, untouchable." *National Catholic Reporter*, December 8, 2020.

D'Antonio, Michael. *Mortal Sins: Sex, Crime, and the Era of Catholic Scandal*. New York: Thomas Dunne Books, 2013.

Danylewycz, Marta. *Taking the Veil: An Alternative to Marriage, Motherhood, and Spinsterhood in Quebec, 1840–1920*. Toronto: McClelland and Stewart, 1987.

DeFrees, Madeline (Sister Mary Gilbert). *The Springs of Silence*. London: The Catholic Book Club, 1954.

Denov, Myriam. "The long-term effect of child sexual abuse by female perpetrators: A qualitative study of male and female victims." *Journal of Interpersonal Violence* 19, no. 10 (2004): 1137–1156.

Denov, Myriam. "To a safer place? Victims of sexual abuse by females and their disclosures to professionals." *Child Abuse and Neglect* 27, no. 1 (2003): 47–61.

Di Liguori, Saint Alfonso. *The True Spouse of Jesus Christ*. New York: Benziger Brothers, 1888.

Dion, Philip E. *Sister's Vow of Chastity*. New York: Joseph F. Wagner, 1965.

Douthat, Ross. "Will Pope Francis Break the Church?" *The Atlantic*, May 2015.

Dunbar-Ortiz, Roxanne. *An Indigenous People's History of the United States*. Boston: Beacon Press, 2014.

Faragher, John Mack. *Daniel Boone: The Life and Legend of an American Pioneer*. New York: Henry Holt, 1992.

Fisher, Fran. *In the Name of God, Why? Ex-Catholic Nuns Speak Out About Sexual Repression, Abuse, and Ultimate Liberation*. Granite Bay, CA: Griffin Publishing, 2012.

Fitzgerald, Maureen. *Habits of Compassion: Irish Catholic Nuns and the Origins of New York's Welfare System, 1830–1920*. Urbana: University of Illinois Press, 2006.

Freeman, Charles. *The Closing of the Western Mind: The Rise of Faith and the Fall of Reason*. New York: Vintage Books, 2005.

Gass, Marie Therese. *Unconventional Women: 73 Ex-Nuns Tell Their Stories*. Clackamas, OR: Sieben Hill, 2001.

Glisky, Joan. "The Official IHM Stance on Friendship, 1845–1960." In *Building Sisterhood*, Sisters, Servants of the Immaculate Heart of Mary, 153–71. Syracuse, NY: Syracuse University Press, 1997.

Gordy, Rose. *The Green That Never Died: A Convent Memoir of the 50s and 60s*. Roseword Books (self-publishing): 2015.

Green, Emma. "Why does the Catholic Church keep failing at sexual abuse?" *The Atlantic*, February 14, 2019.

Grueninger-Beasley, Patricia. *The Tears I Couldn't Cry: Behind Convent Doors*. Bloomington, IN: Authorhouse, 2009.

Bibliography

Guerlac, Othon. "The Separation of Church and State in France." *Political Science Quarterly* 23, no. 2 (June 1908): 259–296.

Halstead, Margaret M., and Lauro S. Halstead. "A Sexual Intimacy Survey of Former Nuns and Priests." *Journal of Sex and Marital Therapy* 4, no. 2 (1978): 83–90.

Harris, Charles W. "Virginity." *National Catholic Educational Association Bulletin* 55, no. 1 (August 1958): 346–50.

Healy, Peyton. "A change in South Dakota's child sexual abuse statute of limitations: An equal protection violations?" *American Indian Law Journal* 7, no. 2 (2019): 72–97.

Henderson, Nancy. *Out of the Curtained World*. New York: Pyramid Books, 1972.

Hidalgo, Myra L. *Sexual Abuse and the Culture of Catholicism: How Priests and Nuns Become Perpetrators*. New York, London, Oxford: The Haworth Press, 2007.

Hoeger, Frederick T. *The Convent Mirror: A Series of Conferences for Religious*. New York and Cincinnati: Frederick Pustet Co., 1951.

Howe, Joanne. *A Change of Habit: The Autobiography of a Former Catholic Nun*. Nashville, TN: Christian Communications, 1986.

Hoy, Suellen. *Good Hearts: Catholic Sisters in Chicago's Past*. Urbana: University of Illinois Press, 2006.

James, Sister Mary. *Providence: A Sketch of the Sisters of Charity of Providence in the Northwest, 1856–1931*. Seattle: Sisters of Charity of Providence, 1931.

Jansen, Katherine Ludwig. *The Making of the Magdalen: Preaching and Popular Devotion in the Later Middle Ages*. Princeton, NJ: Princeton University Press, 2001.

Jean, Marguerite. "Tavernier, Emilie." *Dictionary of Canadian Biography, Vol. VIII*. Toronto: University of Toronto Press, 1985.

Kane, George L., ed. *Meeting the Vocation Crisis*. Westminster, MD: Newman Press, 1953.

Kenneally, Christine. "The Ghosts of St. Joseph's Orphanage." *Buzzfeed News*, August 27, 2018.

Kenneally, Marion. *One Nun's Odyssey: A Memoir*. Denver: Outskirts Press, 2016.

Killoren, John J. *Come Black Robe: De Smet and the Indian Tragedy*. Norman: University of Oklahoma Press, 1994.

Kirsch, Felix M. *The Spiritual Direction of Sisters: A Manual for Priests and Superiors*. New York: Benziger Brothers, 1931.

Klaas, Orice. *Once Upon a Convent: A Memoir of a Lesbian Nun*. Portland, OR: Orice Klaas/Uponanon Publishing, 2015.

Krieger, Arlene. *Behind the Walls of St. John's: A Story of Catholic Abuse*. Minneapolis-St. Paul: Freethought House, 2017.

Kuhns, Elizabeth. *The Habit: A History of the Clothing of Catholic Nuns*. New York: Image/Doubleday, 2003.

Larsen, Deborah. *The Tulip and the Pope: A Nun's Story*. New York: Vintage, 2006.

Laviolette, Gontran, "TATANKA-NAJIN." *Dictionary of Canadian Biography, IX*. Toronto: University of Toronto Press, 2003.

Liguori, Sister M. "Imported Polish American Sisterhoods." *Polish American Studies* 14, no. 3/4 (July-Dec. 1957): 92–102.

Lynch, Margaret. *Triptych: A Memoir*. Bloomington, IN: Authorhouse, 2005.

MacCulloch, Diarmaid. *Christianity: The First Three Thousand Years*. New York: Viking Penguin, 2010.

Manahan, Nancy, and Rosemary Keefe Curb, eds. *Lesbian Nuns: Breaking Silence*. Tallahassee, FL: Naiad Press, 1985.

Manson, Jamie. "Pope Benedict explains things to me." *National Catholic Reporter*, April 12, 2019.

Martel, Frédéric. *In the Closet of the Vatican: Power, Homosexuality, Hypocrisy*. London: Bloomsbury, 2019.

Masterson, Sister Mary Jane. *One Nun's Story: Then and Now*. Salt Lake City: Millennial Mind Publishing, 2009.

McBride, Jessica. "Devil in Disguise." *Milwaukee Magazine*, June 23, 2008.

McCarthy, Thomas P. *Guide to the Catholic Sisterhoods in the United States*.

Bibliography

Washington, DC: Catholic University of America Press, 1958.

McElwee, Joshua, and Dennis Coday. "Final days of Benedict full of unclear calls for change." *National Catholic Reporter*, March 11, 2013.

McElwee, Joshua J. "In new letter, Benedict blames clergy abuse on sexual revolution, Vatican II theology." *National Catholic Reporter*, April 11, 2019.

McGettrick, Claire, Katherine O'Donnell, Maeve O'Rourke, James M. Smith, and Mari Steed. *Ireland and the Magdalene Laundries: A Campaign for Justice*. London: Bloomsbury, 2021.

McGoey, John H. *The Sins of the Just*. Milwaukee: The Bruce Publishing, 1963.

McGoldrick, Desmond F. *The Martyrdom of Change: Simple Talks to Postulant Sisters on the Religious Mentality and Ideal*. Pittsburgh: Duquesne University Press, 1961.

McGuinness, Margaret. *Called to Serve: A History of Nuns in America*. New York: New York University Press, 2013.

McNamara, Jo Ann Kay. *Sisters in Arms: Catholic Nuns Through Two Millennia*. Cambridge, MA: Harvard University Press, 1996.

Miller, James R. *Shingwauk's Vision: A History of Native Residential Schools*. Toronto: University of Toronto Press, 1996.

Miller, Peter. "Archbishop Weakland's Legacy: The liberal liturgist's shameful departure." *Seattle Catholic*, June 7, 2002.

Moffat, John E. *Step This Way, Sister: Reflections for Nuns, Young and—Less Young*. New York: Farrar, Strauss and Cudahy, 1960.

Morris-Young, Dan. "Helena diocese reaches sex abuse settlement via 'consensus model.'" *National Catholic Reporter*, March 20, 2015.

Mullahy, Bernard I. "Sanctification Through the Vows." In *Proceedings of the 1955 Sisters' Institute of Spirituality*, edited by Collins, 91–158.

Mullay, Charles J. *Spiritual Reflections for Sisters*. New York: Apostleship of Prayer, 1937.

Neville, Alan L., and Alyssa Kaye Anderson. "The Diminishment of the Great Sioux Reservation: Treaties, Tricks, and Time." *Great Plains Quarterly* 33, no. 4 (Fall 2013): 237–251.

O'Donnell-Gibson, Patricia. *The Red Skirt: Memoirs of an Ex Nun*. Watervleit, MI: StuartRose Publishing, 2011.

Parent, Sister Louise. "The Mission of the Sisters of the Holy Cross in the New England States." Paper prepared for the Conference on the History of the Congregation of Holy Cross in the U.S.A., Moreau Seminary, Notre Dame, IN, March 18–20, 1982.

Philippe, Paul. *The Novitiate: Religious Life in the Modern World, Vol. 2*. South Bend, IN: University of Notre Dame Press, 1961.

Pickford, Susan Bassler. *Removing the Habit of God: Sister Christina's Story*. Charleston, SC: Createspace, 2012.

Poage, Godfrey. *For More Vocations*. Milwaukee: The Bruce Publishing Co., 1955.

Pollitt, Katha. "It's about time for New York's Child Victims Act." *The Nation*, August 22, 2019.

Price, Theresa. *Letters from a Black and White World: The Making of a Nun*. Bloomington, IN: WestBow Press, 2013.

Provera, Paulo. *Live Your Vocation*. Translated by Thomas F. Murray. St Louis: B. Herder, 1959.

Raftery, Deirdre, Catriona Delaney, and Catherine Nowlan-Roebuck. *Nano Nagle: The Life and the Legacy*. Newbridge, Co. Kildare: Merrion Press, 2018.

Rapley, Elizabeth. *The Dévotes: Women and the Church in Seventeenth Century France*. Montreal and Kingston: McGill-Queen's University Press, 1990.

Rapley, Elizabeth. *The Lord as Their Portion: The Story of the Religious Orders and How They Shaped the World*. Toronto: Novalis, 2001.

Rasmussen, John. "Saint Kateri (Kateri Tekakwitha)." *Canadian Encyclopedia*, published online, November 19, 2012: https://www.thecanadianencyclopedia.ca/en/article/tekakwitha-kateri.

Redmond, Paul Jude. *The Adoption Machine: The Dark History of Ireland's*

Bibliography

Mother and Baby Homes and the Inside Story of How 'Tuam 800' became a Global Scandal. Newbridge, Co. Kildare: Merrion Press, 2018.

Religious Community Life in the United States: Proceedings of the Sisters' Section of the First National Congress of Religious Life in the United States. New York: Paulist Press, 1952.

The Report of the Commission to Inquire into Child Abuse (Ryan Commission). Dublin: Government of Ireland, 2009: https://www.gov.ie/en/publication/3c76d0-the-report-of-the-commission-to-inquire-into-child-abuse-the-ryan-re/ (accessed 15 April 2021).

Reynes, Geneviève. *Couvents de femmes: La vie des religieuses clôitrées dans la France des XVIIe et XVIIIe siècles*. Paris: Fayard, 1987.

Richardson, Kim Michele. *The Unbreakable Child: A Story About Forgiving the Unforgivable*. Self-published, 2012.

Robertson, Susanne. *Throw Away Child*. Baltimore: Publish America, 2003.

Roby, Yves. "Les Canadiens français des États-Unis (1860–1900): dévoyés ou missionnaires." *Revue d'histoire de l'Amérique française* 41, no. 1 (1987): 3–22.

Rogers, Carole Garibaldi. *Habits of Change: An Oral History of American Nuns*. New York: Oxford University Press, 2011.

Rohde, Marie. "The Prophet." *Milwaukee Magazine*, September 19, 2011.

Rom, Louis. "Victim, experts tell of abuse by nuns." *National Catholic Reporter*, November 1, 2002.

Rom, Louis. "Vows of Silence?" *Gambit, the best of New Orleans*, August 12, 2002.

Rotondaro, Vinnie. "Boarding Schools: A Black Hole of Native American History." *National Catholic Reporter*, September 1, 2015.

Senieur, Jude. "Why Do Parents Object?" In *Meeting the Vocation Crisis*, edited by George L. Kane. Westminster, MD: The Newman Press, 1956.

Shekleton, Sister Margaret. *Bending in Season: History of the North American Province of the Sisters of the Divine Savior, 1895–1985*. Milwaukee: Sisters of the Divine Savior, 1985.

Sisters, Servants of the Immaculate Heart of Mary. *Building Sisterhood: A Feminist History of the Sisters, Servants of the Immaculate Heart of Mary*. Syracuse, NY: Syracuse University Press, 1997.

Stockman, Dan. "Face facts, says LCWR president: Sisters have been part of Catholic Church sexual abuse scandal." *National Catholic Reporter*, August 16, 2019.

Stockman, Dan. "Settlement reached in Ursuline abuse suit." *National Catholic Reporter*, February 6, 2015.

Tapsell, Kieran. *Potiphar's Wife: The Vatican's Secret and Child Sexual Abuse*. Adelaide: ATF Press, 2014.

"The 38th Conference features 'Holy Cross Ministry in Canada and Beyond.'" *Holy Cross History* 37, no. 2 (Autumn 2019): 5–6.

Titley, Brian. "Convent Class Struggle: Lay Sisters and Choir Sisters in America." *Historical Studies in Education/Revue d'histoire de l'éducation* 32, no. 1 (Spring/printemps 2020): 97–112.

Titley, Brian. "Heil Mary: Magdalen Asylums and Moral Regulation in Ireland." *History of Education Review* 35, no. 2 (October 2006): 1–15.

Titley, Brian. *Into Silence and Servitude: How American Girls Became Nuns, 1945–1965*. Montreal and Kingston: McGill-Queen's University Press, 2017.

Travers, Nicole. "A Brief Examination of Pedophilia and Sexual Abuse Committed by Nuns Within the Catholic Church." *William and Mary Journal of Women and the Law* 12, no. 3 (2006): 761–778.

Turk, Midge. *The Buried Life: A Nun's Journey*. London: New English Library, 1972.

Vandever, Joyce H. *The Nun, the Pope, and the Wind: A Memoir*. Frederick, MD: America Star Books, 2014.

Van Zeller, Hubert. *The Yoke of Divine Love: A Study of Conventual Perfection*. Springfield, IL: Templegate, 1957.

Whitney, Catherine. *The Calling: A Year in the Life of an Order of Nuns*. New York: Crown Publishers, 1999.

Bibliography

Wilson, James. *The Earth Shall Weep: A History of Native America*. New York: Grove Press, 1998.

Wojtyla, Karol. *Love and Responsibility*. Translated by H.T. Willetts. San Francisco: Ignatius Press, 1981.

Wolf, Hubert. *The Nuns of Sant'Ambrogio: The True Story of a Convent in Scandal*. Translated by Ruth Martin. New York: Alfred A. Knopf, 2015.

Wolff, Gerald W. "Father Sylvester Eisenman and Marty Mission." *South Dakota History* 5, no. 4 (Fall 1975): 360–389.

Wong, Mary Gilligan. *Nun: A Memoir*. New York: Harper Colophon, 1984.

Zenchoff, Mary. *The In-Between Years: A Former Nun's Story of Life in a Convent*. Morgan Hill, CA: Bookstand Publishing, 2017.

Zimmerman, Jonathan. *Too Hot to Handle: A Global History of Sex Education*. Princeton, NJ: Princeton University Press, 2015.

Dissertation

Knudsen, Christian D. "Naughty Nuns and Promiscuous Monks: Monastic Sexual Misconduct in Late Medieval England." PhD diss., University of Toronto, 2012.

Legal Documents

Joseph R. Barquin, Plaintiff, v. The Roman Catholic Diocese of Burlington, Vermont, Inc., Vermont Catholic Charities, Inc., St. Joseph's Orphanage Asylum, Inc., and/or Its Successors or Assigns in Interest, and Sister Jane Doe, Defendants. Civ. A. No. 2:93-CV-169. United States District Court, D. Vermont. November 10, 1993.

Milwaukee County Case Number 2006CF006443 State of Wisconsin vs. Norma Giannini, May 12, 2006.

Montana First Judicial District Court, Lewis and Clark County. John Does 1–16 and John Does 17–100; and Jane Does 1–29 and Jane Does 30–100, Plaintiffs, v. Ursuline Sisters of the Western Province, a non-profit corporation, aka Ursuline Western Province; The Roman Catholic Diocese of Helena, a non-profit corporation, aka Helena Diocese of the Roman Catholic Church; ABC Corporation 1–10, Defendants John Doe A-M, and Defendants Jane Doe N-Z, Defendants. Complaint for Damages. October 2011.

State of Minnesota in Court of Appeals, A07–1054. Karen Britten, Appellant vs. the Franciscan Sisters d/b/a Sisters of the Third Order Regular of Saint Francis of the Congregation of Our Lady of Lourdes, et al., Respondents. Filed April 29, 2008. Affirmed Schellhas, Judge. Olmsted County District Court File No. 55-CV-06-4887.

State of South Dakota, County of Minnehaha, Second Judicial Circuit Court. M.W.D. et al., Plaintiffs, vs. Catholic Diocese of Sioux Falls; Tekakwitha Indian Mission of Sisseton, South Dakota; U.S. Province of the Oblates of Mary Immaculate; Sisters of the Divine Savior et al. Demand for Jury Trial, July 19, 2010.

In the Supreme Court of the State of South Dakota. Teresa Bernie, Plaintiff and Appellant, v. Blue Cloud Abbey; Sisters of the Blessed Sacrament; and the Oblate Sisters of the Blessed Sacrament, Defendants and Appellees, and Catholic Diocese of Sioux Falls, Doe Priest, Doe Perpetrators 1–4, Defendants. 2012 S.D. 64.

In the Supreme Court of South Dakota. D.Z. Iron Wing, Plaintiff and Appellant, v. Catholic Diocese of Sioux Falls; Blue Cloud Abbey; Fr. Francis Sutmueller; Oblate Sisters of the Blessed Sacrament; and Sr. M. Frances, Defendants and Appellees. 2011 S.D. 79.

Papal Documents

Paul VI. *Persona Humana: Declaration on Certain Questions Concerning Sexual Ethics*, 1975.

Pius XII. *Sacra Virginitas*, 1954.

Newspapers

Argus Leader (Sioux Falls, SD)
Boston Globe (Boston, MA)

Bibliography

Burlington Free Press (Burlington, VT)
Catholic New Times (Toronto, ON)
Char-Koosta News (Pablo, MT)
Chicago Tribune (Chicago, IL)
Columbus Dispatch (Columbus, OH)
Courier-Journal (Louisville, KY)
Daily Gazette (Albany, NY)
Daily News (New York, NY)
Daily Record (Parsippany-Troy Hills, NJ)
Daily Times (Delaware County, PA)
Dakota Free Press (Aberdeen, SD)
Deadline Detroit (Detroit, MI)
Detroit Catholic (Detroit, MI)
Detroit Free Press (Detroit, MI)
Everett Herald (Everett, WA)
Globe and Mail (Toronto, ON)
Guardian (Manchester, England)
Hartford Courant (Hartford, CT)
Independent Record (Helena, MT)
Indian Country Today (Washington, DC)
Indianapolis Star (Indianapolis, IN)
Irish Examiner (Cork, Ireland)
Jersey Journal (Jersey City, NJ)
Lancaster Eagle-Gazette (Lancaster, OH)
Lexington Herald-Leader (Lexington, KY)
Los Angeles Times (Los Angeles, CA)
Mankato Free Press (Mankato, MN)
Milwaukee Journal Sentinel (Milwaukee, WI)
Missoulian (Missoula, MT)
Morning Call (Allentown, PA)
New York Post (New York, NY)
New York Times (New York, NY)
Newsday (New York, NY)
Pacific Daily News (Hagatna, GU)
Philadelphia Inquirer (Philadelphia, PA)
Pioneer Press/Twin Cities Pioneer Press (St. Paul, MN)
Pittsburgh Post-Gazette (Pittsburgh, PA)
Pocono Record (Stroudsburg, PA)
Post-Bulletin (Rochester, MN)
Rapid City Journal (Rapid City, SD)
Rochester Democrat and Chronicle (Rochester, MN)
St. Paul Pioneer Press (St. Paul, MN)
Seattle Catholic (Seattle, WA)
Seattle Times (Seattle, WA)
Sioux City Journal (Sioux City, IA)
Star-Ledger (Newark, NJ)
Star Tribune (Minneapolis-St. Paul, MN)
Sunday News (Lancaster, PA)
Time (New York, NY)
Times of Acadiana (Lafayette, LA)
Times-Picayune (New Orleans, LA)
Times-Union (Albany, NY)
Union-Leader (Manchester, NH)
Union-Tribune (San Diego, CA)
USA Today (Tysons, VA)
Virginian-Pilot (Virginia Beach, VA)
Wall Street Journal (New York, NY)
Washington Post (Washington, DC)
Whig Standard (Kingston, ON)
Yankton Daily Press and Dakotan (Yankton, SD)

Index

ABC News, *Good Morning America* 123
ABC News, *Prime Time Live* 113
Abramovich, Jay 119
Adams, Leona 70, 71
Adrian, Michigan 101
African Americans 46, 59
Agnes of God 115
Agnes, Sister 81
Alaska 89
Albany, diocese of 18
Albany, New York 17, 18, 48, 68, 73
Alberione, Father James 34–36
Albert, Sister 67
Alberta, Canada 2, 54
Albertus Magnus College 111
Alford plea 118
Allentown, diocese of 119
Altoff, Matt 88
American Civil War 48, 76
Anderson, Jeff 7, 8
Andre, Sister 110, 111, 114
Andrea, Sister 19
Angell, Bishop Kenneth 65, 68, 75
Anglo-Americans 76
Annunciata, Sister 70
Anthony, Sister 61
Antonia Marie, Sister 40
Apache 76
Appalachian Mountains 58
Arapaho 76, 78
Archambeau, Mike 81
Armstrong, Karen 22
Assisi Heights 98
Augustine, Saint 11, 23, 24
Australia 56

Baisi, Linda 112, 114
Balfe, Father Joseph 90
Baltimore, Maryland 37
Barbarin, Cardinal Philippe 11
Bardstown, Kentucky 58
Barquin, Joseph R. (Clifton Lawrence Balazs) 63, 64, 66
Barquin family 63

Barre, Vermont 63
Barres, Bishop John O. 17, 18
Barto, Loretta (Sister Mary Juanita) 107
Barton, Patti 8
Basil of Caesaria, Saint 24
Bassler, Susan 29, 37
Battle of Point Pleasant 58
Bavaria, Germany 101
Bay Shore, Long Island, New York 107
Bear Chief, Ken 93
Beatles 105
Beauregard, Father Raymond 50
Belgium 12, 83
Belmont, North Dakota 81
Benedict, Mother 30
Benedict of Nursia, Saint 24, 37
Benedict XVI 11, 12, 13
Benedictine Fathers 81
Benedictine Sisters 29, 30, 34, 83
Berry, Jason 7, 8
Bertrand, Christine 103
Bessborough, Cork, Ireland 1
Bethea, Rainey 59
Biondo, Gael (Sister Mary Gael) 101, 102
Biot, René 36
Bishop Canevin High School, Pittsburgh, Pennsylvania 97
Black Hills, South Dakota 77
Blanche, Sister 66
Blessed Virgin Mary 23, 36, 42, 45
Blue Cloud Abbey, South Dakota 81
Bogadina, Sister 86
Bonneau, Bill 73
Bonneau, Dannie 72
Bonneau, Ernie 72, 73
Bonneau, Gilbert 72, 73
Bonneau family 72
Boone, Daniel 58
Bordeaux, Shawn 88
Borgoglio, Cardinal Jorge 13
Boston, archdiocese of 9
Boston, Massachusetts 102
Boston Globe 9, 101, 123
Bourget, Bishop Ignace 48, 56

157

Index

Boy Scouts of America 17
Britain 76
British Columbia, Canada 54
Britten, Karen 102, 103
Brooklyn, diocese of 45
Brooklyn, New York 69
Brothers of the Christian Schools 69
Broussard, Louisiana 5
Brown, Judith 43
Bruni, Frank 94
Bryant, Harvey L. 118
Bryn Mawr, Pennsylvania 30
Buchanan, Peter 70
Buckingham, Doolittle and Burroughs Law 112
Buffalo, diocese of 17
Bureau of Indian Affairs 77
Burke, Francis 91, 93
Burke, Father William 90
Burkett, Elinor 94
Burlington, diocese of 63, 64, 67, 68
Burlington, Vermont 62, 63
Burlington Free Press 65

Cadorette, Robert 66, 67
Caesarius of Arles 24
Cahill, Patricia 109, 110
California 17, 18, 86, 88, 104
Callahan, Michelle 40, 41
Callahan, Patrick 104
Camalin, Sister 19
Camden, Theresa 46, 47, 55
Camellia, Mother 90, 92
Canadian history 2
canon law 6
Capriolo, Father Vic 122
Caritas, Sister 32
Caritas Community, Jersey City, New Jersey 110
Carlini, Sister Benedetta 42
Carlisle Indian Industrial School, Carlisle, Pennsylvania 77
Carondelet, Missouri 95
Cashel, Ireland 57
Catches, Pete 81
Cathedral of the Assumption, Louisville, Kentucky 62
Catholic Central High School, Steubenville, Ohio 111
Catholic Conference Policy Group 17
Catholic historians 2, 3, 127, 130
Catholic Information Center, Detroit, Michigan 46
Cecilia, Sister (Sister of Charity of Nazareth) 70
Cecilia, Sister (Ursuline) 90, 92
Chamberlain, South Dakota 87
Champlain Valley 63

Chapter 11 bankruptcy 10, 14, 17, 18
Charbonneau sisters 88
Charbonneau-Dahlen, Barbara 82
Charlie, Sister 60, 61
Cheyenne 76, 77
Cheyenne River Reservation, South Dakota 87
Chibnall, John T. 39, 41, 55
Chicago, Illinois 7, 44, 46, 103, 120–122, 124, 126
Child USA 17
Child Victims Act 17, 73
choir sisters 80
Christian martyrs 23
Christopher, Sister 70
Claire, Sister 66, 67
Clare, Saint 27
Clark, Kelly 19
Clayton, Judge Denise 61
Cleveland, Ohio 37, 40, 97
Clohessy, David 13
Coeur d'Alene, Idaho 92
College of Cardinals 14
College of St. Teresa, Winona, Minnesota 98
Colman, Saint 68
Columbus, Ohio 111
Comanche 76
Conference on the History of Women Religious 3
Congregation for Bishops 15
Congregation for the Clergy 5, 11
Congregation for the Doctrine of the Faith 10, 11, 36
Congregation for the Religious 53
Congregation of the Holy Cross 48
Congressional Medal of Honor 77
Connecticut 109, 110
Connolly, Cornelia 22
Consolata, Mother 31
Convent Station, New Jersey 32, 109
Córdova, Jeanne 40
Cork, Ireland 1, 57, 68
Council of Elvira 5
Counter-Reformation 25, 89
County Tipperary, Ireland 57
County Tyrone, Ireland 46
Crazy Horse 78
Crimen Sollicitationis 6, 86
Crivelli, Sister Bartolomea 42
Crosby, Bing 108
Crosby, Dolores 108
Crystal City, Missouri 29, 31
Cumberland Gap 58
Cuomo, Andrew 73
Curia 13
Curran, Linda 115, 117–119
Cushwa Center for the Study of American Catholicism 3

158

Index

Custer, George Armstrong 77, 78
Custer State Park, South Dakota 77
custody of the eyes 27, 28
Cyprian, Saint 23
Czarniewicz, Victoria (Sister Gloria) 43–45

Dakoske, Sister Barbara 46, 47
Dale, Sally 66, 67
Dallas, Texas 9
Dallas Charter 9, 10, 19, 129
Dalmyn, Tony 53, 54
Damien, Peter 5
Dantzer-Rosenthal, Marya 101, 102
Danylewcyz, Marta 40
Davis, Betty 101
Deadrick, Thomas 87
De Carlo, Sister Rose Marie 119
Deloris Marie, Sister 61
Democratic Party 17, 88
Denov, Dr. Myriam S. 129
Denver, Colorado 8, 96
Department of Justice 15
De Sales High School, Columbus, Ohio 111
Des Plaines, Illinois 120
De Smet, Father Pierre-Jean 89
Dessomes, Andrea 104
Detroit, Michigan 46
Detroit Deadline 47
Devereaux, James 10
Devoy, Father Robert 67, 68
Dickens, Charles 56
Di Liguori, Saint Alfonso 22, 38
Dion, Father Philip E. 33, 34, 36, 37
Dispenza, Mary 20
Divini Illius Magistri 25
Dolan, Archbishop Timothy 16
Dominic, Saint 101
Dominic, Sister 67
Dominic Anne, Sister 40
Dominican High School, Detroit, Michigan 101, 102
Dominican Sisters of Adrian 27, 101, 102
Dominican Sisters of Caldwell 110, 111
Dominican Sisters of Peace 104, 105, 111, 112
Donald, Judge M. Joseph 124, 125
Donatus of Besancon 39
Donoghue, Sister Mary Camilla 60
Dorris, Barbara 93
Doyle, Sister Joan 111
Drexel, Saint Katherine 79
Drexel Hill, Pennsylvania 117, 119
Dubuque, Iowa 29
Duchesne, Saint Philippine 3
Duckro, Paul N. 39, 41, 55
Dundrum, Ireland 57
Duplessis, Maurice 57

Duquesne University 46
Dusseault, Sister Jeanne 50
DuVal, Sister Katherine 100

Edina, Minnesota 98
Edmonds, Washington 108
Edmonton, Alberta, Canada 49, 52
Edwards, Helen 59
Eisenman, Father Sylvester 79
El Salvador 83
Eleta Marie, Sister 81
Enemy Swim Lake, South Dakota 83
Erdely, Pam 97
Erie, diocese of 96
Erie, Pennsylvania 97
Escriva de Balaguer, José Maria 37
Eucharia, Sister 70
Eve 24, 33
Everett, Washington 8

Fall River, Massachusetts 31
Federal Bureau of Investigation 94
Fenton, Linda 67
Feretti, Father A.J. 90
Ferguson, Deborah 59
Fethard, Ireland 57
Finn, Frank 46
Finn, Sister Mary Catherine 45–47
Finnegan, Cait 107
Finnerty, Sister Liette 52
First Amendment 64
Fisher, Fran 29
Fisher, Judith 95, 96, 114
Fisher Catholic High School, Lancaster, Ohio 111
Flathead Indian Reservation, Montana 2, 88, 89
Flavin, Father Cornelius 96
Florida 63, 96, 114
Fontbonne, Mother Saint John 95
Fort Worth, Texas 19
Foster, Father Edward 67
France 6, 37, 76, 89, 95, 101
Francis I 13, 14, 15
Francis of Assisi, Saint 13
Frankel, Vicki 53
Franklin, New Hampshire 48, 49
French Canadians 48, 62, 63
French Revolution 48, 95
Frey, Bishop Gerard 5, 7

Gabriele, Paulo 12
Gabrini, Sister 86
Gaglione, Lori 124
Galatine, Sister Madeline de Paul 60
Galimard, Pierre 36
Gallant, Brother René (Brother Charlie) 90
Garnos, Cooper 87

159

Index

Gass, Marie 28
Gastal, Fey 5
Gastal, Glenn 5
Gatz, Sister Susan 61, 62
Gauthe, Father Gilbert 5, 7
Gelineau, Brother 66, 67
Genevieve Marie, Sister 19
Geoghan, Father John 9
Georgetown University 111
Gerace, Mary Ellen 70
Gerace, Peter R. 70, 72
Gerhardinger, Caroline (Mother Teresa of Jesus) 100
German Americans 83, 101
Giannini, Beverly Margaret (Sister Norma) 120–126, 128
Gillet, Father Louis Florent 115
Gilligan, Mary 40
Giovanna Marie, Sister 18
Girls' High School, Brooklyn, New York 44
Gleeson, Anne 95, 96, 127
Gleeson, Dixon 96
Glen Rock, New Jersey 109
Globe and Mail 54
Good Counsel Academy, Mankato, Minnesota 100, 101
Good Shepherd Convent, Cork, Ireland 1
Gordy, Rose 32
A Gospel of Shame: Children, Sexual Abuse, and the Catholic Church (Burkett and Bruni) 94
Gotti Tedeschi, Ettore 12
Graber, Agnes (Sister Mercedes) 18
Graber, Anne 18
Graber, Katherine 18
Graber, Kay 18
Graber, Martha 18
Graber, Walter 18
Grammond, Father Maurice 10
Grana, Christina 99
Gravel, John 67
Great Plains 76
Green Island, New York 18
Gregory, Judy 70
Gregory, Saint 23
Groer, Cardinal Hans Hermann 10
Gros, Sister Joye 104
Gros Ventre 93
Groton, Connecticut 48
Guam 18

Halstead, Lauro S. 41
Halstead, Margaret M. 41
Hanson, Edward W. 119
Harris, Father Bernard 90
Harvard Extension School 101
Hasbrouck Heights, New Jersey 110
Haswell Road, Watervliet, New York 68

Hazen, Debbie 67
Helena, diocese of 16, 90, 92
Hemingway, Sam 65
Henninger, Sister Jean Patricia 44, 45, 55
Henrietta, Mother 90, 92
Hewankorn, Leland 91
Hickey, Steve 87
Hidalgo, Myra 105, 106
Hill, Clifford 60
Hill, Elizabeth 60
Hill, Patricia 60
Hillside, New Jersey 110
Hoeger, Father Frederick 34, 36
Hollywood, California 37
Holy Cross History Association 54, 55
Holy Cross School, Springfield, Pennsylvania 117–119
Holy Rosary School, Pine Ridge Reservation, South Dakota 78, 87
Holy Union Sisters 31
Horn, Christine 80
Hudson River 70

Idaho 29, 89
Illinois 98
Immacolata School, St. Louis, Missouri 95, 96
Immaculata High School, Manchester, New Hampshire 48
Immaculate Conception School, Everett, Washington 108
Immaculate Heart of Mary Convent, Monroe, Connecticut 45
Independent Reconciliation and Compensation Program 16
Indian Wars 76, 77
Indigenous peoples, Canada 2
indult of exclaustration 45
indult of secularization 53
Innocenzo 6
Inquisition 11, 42
Institute for Works of Religion (Vatican Bank) 12
Iona College 112
Ireland 1, 2, 12, 56, 57
Irish Americans 108, 109, 112, 120
Irish Christian Brothers 107, 112
Iron Wing, D.Z. 82
Italian Americans 112
Italy 43, 89

James Mary, Sister 67
Jane of the Rosary, Sister 67
Jefferson Circuit Court, Kentucky 59
Jersey City, New Jersey 110
Jesus of Nazareth 22, 23, 27, 30, 39, 42, 88
John Marie, Sister 81
John Paul II 8–10, 12, 14, 15, 33

160

Index

John, Sister (Salvatorian) 86
John, Sister (Ursuline) 90, 92
Jordon, Cynthia 53
Joseph, Saint 96
Joseph Michael, Sister 60
Josepha, Mother 31
Juanita, Sister 106
Judeo-Christian tradition 74
Juhrke, Kent 87
Julius III 6

Kansas 30
Karges, Rufina (Mother Loyola) 90–93
Katherine, Sister 86
Kearny, New Jersey 109
Keefe Curb, Rosemary 41
Kelly, Archbishop Thomas C. 104
Kenneally, Marion 31
Kent, Sister Benen 102, 103
Kentucky 18, 58–61, 105
Kerbrat, Father Dominic 52
Kirsch, Father Felix 28, 35
Kistner, Therese Helen (Sister M. Davidica) 81
Klaas, Orice 29, 35
Kobierowski, Sister Janice 45
Kobs, Elese 120, 122
Kobs, Gerald 120–124
Kobs, Terri 122
Kootenai 88
Kostich, Nikola 124
Koszewski (St. Patrick), James 121, 122, 124

La Salle School, Albany, New York 69, 71, 72
Lagenda, Sister 86
Lahey, Bishop Raymond 11
Lake Traverse Reservation, South Dakota 83–85
Lakota 77, 78
Lammers, Father Herman J. 59, 60
Lancaster, Ohio 112
Landry, Sister Lucienne 52
Langdale, Mark 73
Lanning, Kenneth 94
Larsen, Deborah 29, 30
Latin 13, 26
Law, Cardinal Bernard F. 9, 123
lay sisters 3, 80
Le Mans, France 48
Leadership Conference of Women Religious (LCWR) 19, 20, 129
Legionaries of Christ 8
Leo, Father 81
Leontine, Sister 66
Lesbian Nuns: Breaking Silence (Manahan, Keefe Curb) 41
Letourneau, Sister Marguerite 53

Lewis, James C. 118
Liber Gomorrhianus (Damien) 6
Lind, Father Thomas 87
Little Bighorn River, Montana 78
Long Island, New York 29, 37
Lord Dunmore's War 58
Lord's Prayer 37
Loretta, Sister 70, 71
Lorette, Manitoba, Canada 49, 50, 51, 53
Lorraine, Sister 30, 34, 35
Los Angeles, California 40, 78, 99
Losee, Elaine Ann (Sister Mary Regina) 69–73
Lou Gehrig's Disease 107
Louis Hector, Sister 67
Louisiana 89, 105
Louisville, archdiocese of 59, 61, 104
Louisville, Kentucky 58, 59, 62, 104
Lucy Marie, Sister 86
Luther, Martin 20
Lynch, Margaret 32
Lyon, Father George 81

M. Baptista, Sister 81
M. Theophane Sister 81
Maciel Degollado, Father Marcial 8
Madden, Father Michael 67, 68
Madison, Minnesota 100
Mafia 122
magdalene asylums 1, 2, 3
Magdeline of the Redeemer, Sister 66
Magnoni, Greg 108
Main Street, Winnipeg, Manitoba, Canada 51
Maison de croissance 50–54
Maison de la providence Retreat Centre, Ottawa, Ontario, Canada 54
Mallard, Father Daniel 109
Maloney (Robertson), Susanne 69–73
Maloney, Grace 69, 72, 73
Maloney, June 56, 69, 72, 73
Maloney, Willie 69, 70
Manahan, Nancy 41
Manchester, New Hampshire 48
Mandel, Elizabeth 61
Manhattan, New York 113
Manion, Mother Mary Hubert 34
Manitoba, Canada 49, 50, 54, 55
Mankato, Minnesota 100, 101
Marcoux, Paul 123
Mardi Gras 105
Marianites of the Holy Cross 48, 105, 106, 107
Marie Helene, Mother 95
Marion, Sister 90, 92
Marionella Graham, Sister 18
Marks, Patricia 40
Marquette University 46, 123

Index

Marquis, Sister Claire 50
Marty Indian School 81
Mary, Sister 30
Massachusetts 48
Masterson, Mary Jane 37, 40
Mater Christi High School, Queen's, New York 107
Maxwell, Sister Elizabeth 57
Mayo Clinic 103
McCarrick, Cardinal Theodore 14, 15
McDonald, Sister Jane 48–55
McDonald, Rita 122
McGill University 129
McGoey, Father John 32–34
McMahon, Michael 104
McMinnville, Oregon 19
McMurry, William 59, 61
McNeila, John 117, 118
McQuaid Jesuit High School, Rochester, New York 99
Mdewakantons 83
Meagher, Sister Claude 57
Mercy Care Facility, New Orleans, Louisiana 107
Mercy High School, Albany, New York 18
Mercy High School, Riverbend, New York 44
Methodius, Saint 23
Metuchen, diocese of 14
Mexico 76
Miller, Sally 65
Milwaukee, Wisconsin 83, 98, 120–122, 124, 126
Milwaukee, archdiocese of 121, 122, 125
Milwaukee County Courthouse, Milwaukee, Wisconsin 124
Milwaukee County House of Correction, Milwaukee, Wisconsin 125
Minnesota 98, 100, 102
Minnesota River 83
Minnesota Uprising (Little Crow's War) 79, 83
Missionary Oblates of Mary Immaculate 50, 83, 84, 86
Missionary Sisters of the Holy Rosary 30
Mississippi River 76
Missoula County Courthouse, Missoula, Montana 90
Missouri 3, 93
Missouri River 79
mistress of novices 30, 34, 37, 39
Moffat, Father John E. 31, 36
Mohawks 84
Monroe, Connecticut 45
Monroe, Michigan 34, 115
Monroe District Court, Rochester, New York 115
Montana 2, 88, 89
Montana First Judicial Court 90
Montesano, Michael 45
Montpelier, Vermont 63
Montréal, Québec, Canada 48, 62
Moody Blues 117
Mooney, Cardinal Edward 45
Moreau, Father Basile 48
Moreno, Archbishop Manuel 5
Morristown, New Jersey 40
Mortification 36, 37
Most Holy Redeemer School, Evergreen Park, Illinois 121
Mount Angel, Oregon 29, 30, 34
Mount Mercy College, Oakland, Pennsylvania 32
Mount Providence Orphanage, Montréal, Québec, Canada 56, 57
Mullahy, Father Bernard 28
Mullaly, Father Charles J. 27
Mulloy, Father Michael 88
Murphy, Sister Maureen 115
Murtha, Judge J. Garvan 67

Nadeau, Sister Janice 99
Nagle, Nano 1, 57, 70
National Register of Historic Places 93
Native Americans 4, 58, 76, 77, 78, 85, 89, 91, 127
Nebraska 84
New England 48, 62
New Hampshire 48, 49
New Jersey 14, 17, 18, 88
New Orleans, Louisiana 89, 105, 106
New Trier, Minnesota 101
New York 16–19, 31, 45, 63, 72, 88, 101, 107, 113
New York, archdiocese of 14, 112, 113
New York University 111
Newark, archdiocese of 14
Newport, Rhode Island 111
Nigeria 46
Nile River 24
Nolan, Christopher 117, 118
Norbertine Fathers 92
Norfolk, Nebraska 102
North Avenue, Burlington, Vermont 63
North Carolina 18
Northern Cheyenne 78
Notre Dame Academy, Colton, Washington 101
novices 26–40, 46

Oblate Sisters of the Blessed Sacrament 79–82
O'Brien, Cardinal Keith 12
O'Brien, William 65, 67
O'Brien, William "Happy" 119
O'Connor, Cardinal John 15

162

Index

O'Donnell, Patricia 27
O'Fallon, Illinois 106
O'Hara, Mary 46
Ohio River 58
Ohio 98, 105, 111, 112
Oklahoma 30, 77
Omaha, Nebraska 125
Opelousas, Louisiana 105
Opelousas Catholic Middle School, Opelousas, Louisiana 105
Opus Dei 37
Order of Preachers 101
Oregon 89
O'Rourke, Brian 112, 113
Ottawa, Ontario, Canada 11
Our Lady of Charity School, Brookhaven, Pennsylvania 116
Our Lady of Holy Cross College 106
Our Lady of Mount Carmel School, Ridgewood, New Jersey 109
Our Lady of the Visitation Parish School (now Visitation Academy), Paramus, New Jersey 109
Our Lady, Undoer of Knots 107
Our Place-Chez nous 51, 52, 54
Owensboro, Kentucky 59

Pachomius 24
Papal States 43
Papoose House 84
Paramus, New Jersey 109
Parker, Judge Fred I. 64, 65
Parma, Italy 6
particular friendships 39, 40
Patricia Mary Anne, Sister 19
Patriot Rebellions of 1837 and 1838 62
Paul Emmanuelle, Sister 40, 41
Paul VI 6
Pauline Germaine, Sister 66
Paulsen, Father David 16
Pearl Street, Burlington, Vermont 63
Pend d'Oreille 88
Pennsylvania 15, 16, 77, 96–98, 114, 115, 118, 119, 126, 130
Penthouse Magazine 117
Pereira, Sister Anthony Louise 60
Persona Humana: Declaration on Certain Questions Concerning Sexual Ethics 36
Personality and Human Relations 49
Pescia, Italy 42
Pfau, Michael 89
Pfau, Cochran, Vertetis, Amala Law 89
Pharmacology, Biochemistry and Behavior (May 2009) 111
Philadelphia, Pennsylvania 79, 95, 116
Philadelphia, archdiocese of 117, 119
Philadelphia Inquirer 119
Philippe, Father Paul 35, 36

Piasecki, Dr. Elizabeth 122, 124
Pierre, South Dakota 88
Pine Ridge Reservation, South Dakota 77
Pitcavage, Father William 87
Pittsburgh, diocese of 97
Pius XI 6, 25
Pius XII 23, 25, 26, 31
Playboy Magazine 117
Poage, Father Godfrey 26
Pohlen, Father John 84, 85
Poitra, Delia Rose (Sister Mary Francis) 81, 82
Poland 8
Polish Americans 44
Portage Street, Winnipeg, Manitoba, Canada 52
Porte, Cheryl Ann (Sister Ann) 105–107, 114
Portland, Oregon 19
Portland, archdiocese of 10
Portugal 6
Postulants 26, 101
Powers, Sister Mary Ann 60
Pratt, Richard Henry 77
Price, Teresa 29, 32
Priests of the Sacred Heart 87
Priscille, Sister 67
Project Benjamin 122–124
Provera, Father Paulo 34

Québec, Canada 40, 52, 57, 62, 63
Queen of the Angels School, Austin, Minnesota 98

Racketeer Influenced and Corrupt Organizations Act 15
Rada, Andrew 73
Rapid City, diocese of 88
Ratzinger, Cardinal Joseph 11
Red Cloud's War 78
Reformation 10
Regina, Mother 37
Religious Sisters Filippini 40
Renville, Mary-Catherine 84
Republican Party 17, 87
Rhineland, Germany 83
Rhoades, Rebecca 86
Rhoads, Eileen Mary (Sister Francis Therese) 115–119, 126
Richardson, Caity 59, 60
Richardson, Diane 60
Richardson, Gayla 59
Richardson, Kim Michele 59, 60
Richardson, Pamela 59
Ridgewood, New Jersey 109
Ridolfi, Sister Maria Luisa 42, 43
Rivera, Geraldo 7
Robbins, Justice Alfred S. 45

Index

Robertson, Scott 72
Robrecht, Betty 110, 111
Robrecht, Joe 110, 111
Robrecht, Mary 110, 111
Rochais, Father André 49
Rochester, Minnesota 98, 103
Rochester, New York 99
Rochester, diocese of 17, 99
Rockers, Sister Delore 103
Rockville Centre, diocese of 17, 45
Rogers, Carl 49
Rogers Barrett, Marge 31
Rosara Anne, Sister 18
Rose, Sister 70
Rounds, Mike 87
Royal Commission into Institutional Responses to Child Sexual Abuse (Australia) 12
Rupert's Land 83
Russia 76
Ryan, Bishop Edward F. 63
Ryan Commission (Ireland) 12, 57, 58

Sacra Virginitas 23, 31
Sacred Heart Seminary, Detroit, Michigan 46, 47
St. Anne's College, Oxford 22
St. Ann's School, Chicago, Illinois 122
St. Bartholomew School, Wayzata, Minnesota 100
St. Bernard's Industrial School, Dundrum/Fethard, Ireland 57
St. Catherine of Siena Church, Hillside, New Jersey 110
St. Catherine School, Hillside, New Jersey 110
St. Cecelia's School, Kearny, New Jersey 109
St. Christopher Ottillie Children's Services, Long Island, New York 44, 45
St. Colman's Home for Boys and Girls, Watervliet, New York 56, 68–73
St. Frances de Chantal School, the Bronx, New York 112, 113
St. Francis de Sales School, Denver, Colorado 96
St. Francis School, Rosebud Reservation, South Dakota 78, 87
St. Francis's Industrial School, Cashel, Ireland 57
St. Gregory the Great Catholic School, Virginia Beach, Virginia 116, 118
St. Ignatius Mission, Montana 89, 91
St. John's, Newfoundland, Canada 50
St. Joseph's Church, Burlington, Vermont 63
St. Joseph's Indian School, Chamberlain, South Dakota 87

St. Joseph's Orphanage, Burlington, Vermont 62–68
St. Joseph's Parish, Winona, Minnesota 102
St. Joseph's Parish School, Green Island, New York 18
St. Juliana's School, Chicago, Illinois 102, 103
Saint-Laurent, Québec, Canada 48, 51, 52
St. Lawrence Catholic School, Utica, Michigan 102
St. Louis, Missouri 95, 106, 121
St. Louis, archdiocese of 96
St. Louis University 106
St. Margaret Mary School, Louisville, Kentucky 104
St. Margaret Mary School, Rochester, New York 99
St. Mary's Convent, Lancaster, Ohio 112
St. Mary's School, Helena, Montana 91
St. Mary's University 106
St. Maurice Parish, Brooklawn, New Jersey 109
St. Michael School, Minneapolis, Minnesota 100
St. Patrick's Cathedral, New York 14
St. Patrick's Church, Milwaukee, Wisconsin 122
St. Patrick's School, Milwaukee, Wisconsin 120, 122, 123
St. Paul, Minnesota 7, 31, 95
St. Paul's Mission School, Yankton Sioux Reservation, South Dakota 76, 78–83, 88
St. Stanislaus Kostka Elementary School, New York 44
St. Vincent-St. Thomas Orphanage, Louisville, Kentucky 58–62
Salish 88
Sallua, Vincenzo 42
Salois, Gary 91, 93
Salvation Army 51
Salve Regina University 111, 112
Santa Barbara Catholic School, Dededo, Guam 18
Sant'Ambrogio Convent, Rome 42, 43
Santee 83
Satan 23, 24, 34, 38, 39
Savard, Donna 67
Schlosser, Marcene (Sister Mary Cletus) 100, 101
School Sisters of Notre Dame 99–101
Schweich, Mildred Margaret (Sister Ramona) 101
Scotland 12, 56
Scottsdale, Arizona 19
Scranton, Pennsylvania 115
Seattle, Washington 89, 108
Seattle, archdiocese of 108

Index

Seattle Mariners 108
Second Vatican Council 11, 40, 48, 49, 100, 114
Secret of the Holy Office 6
Secreta Continere 6
Seminary of Our Lady of Angels, Albany, New York 33
Senieur, Father Jude 26
sex education 25, 28–38
Shapiro, Josh 15
Sharpe, Louise 71
Shaw, Sister Eileen 109, 110
Shawnee 58
Shekleton, Sister Margaret 84
Shuttle, Donald 67
Siedliska, Mary Francis (Mother Blessed Mary of Jesus the Good Shepherd) 43–45
Simon, J Minos 5
Simon and Garfunkel 117
Sioux 76, 79
Sioux Falls, diocese of 81, 85, 88
Sipe, A.W. Richard 129
Sissetons 83
Sisters, Adorers of the Most Precious Blood 30
Sisters, Home Visitors of Mary 45–47
Sisters of Charity of Montréal (Grey Nuns) 53
Sisters of Charity of Nazareth 58–62
Sisters of Charity of Providence 56, 62–67
Sisters of Charity of St. Elizabeth 32, 109, 110
Sisters of Charity of the Blessed Virgin Mary 29
Sisters of Divine Compassion 112
Sisters of Mercy 18, 19, 32, 107, 120–122, 124–126, 128
Sisters of Providence (St. Mary-of-the-Woods, Indiana) 34, 40, 95
Sisters of St. Francis 19, 43, 87, 98, 102, 103
Sisters of St. Joseph 18, 31, 37, 40, 95–97, 115
Sisters of St. Joseph of Cluny 95
Sisters of the Blessed Sacrament for Indians and Colored People 79–81
Sisters of the Divine Savior (Salvatorians) 83, 84, 86
Sisters of the Good Shepherd 3
Sisters of the Holy Child Jesus 22
Sisters of the Holy Cross 19, 48–55
Sisters of the Holy Family of Nazareth 43–45
Sisters of the Holy Names of Jesus and Mary 108
Sisters of the Immaculate Heart of Mary 37, 40
Sisters of the Presentation of the Blessed Virgin Mary 1, 57, 58, 68–73
Sisters of the Sacred Hearts of Jesus and Mary 1
Sisters of the Third Order of St. Dominic 31
Sisters of the Visitation 83
Sisters, Servants of the Immaculate Heart of Mary 34, 115, 116, 119
Sister's Vow of Chastity (Dion) 33
Sitting Bull 78
Skeabeck, Charlotte (Sister Mary Carmel) 96, 97, 114
Sklba, Auxiliary Bishop Richard J. 121
Smith, Sister Betty 124
Smith, Bryan 89
Smith, Steven R. 87, 88
Society of Jesus (Jesuits) 16, 31, 77, 87, 89, 92
Society of the Sacred Heart 3, 83
Sodeman, Nancy 30
South Dakota 77–79, 83, 88
South Prospect Street, Burlington, Vermont 63
Spain 76
Spalding, Catherine 58, 62
Splenditello 42
Spokane, Washington 108
Stanford University 43
Struck by the Ree 79
Stuppy, Georgene (Sister Dimitri) 98
Survivors' Network of those Abused by Priests (SNAP) 7, 13, 17, 19, 20, 93
Survivors of St. Joseph's Orphanage and Friends 64
Suttmiller, Father Francis 81, 82
Swartz, Patricia 103
Sweeney, Father James 16
Syosset, New York 107
Syracuse, diocese of 17

Tacoma, Washington 108
Tamaki, Blaine 90
Tamaki Law 89
Tavernier, Emilie 56
Tekakwitha, Kateri 84
Tekakwitha Hospital 83
Tekakwitha Indian Home 83–86
Teresa, Sister 86
Teresa of Avila, Saint 42
Theatine Convent of the Mother of God, Pescia, Italy 42
Thieneman, Sister Mary Helen 104, 105
Thomas, Bishop George Lee 90, 92
Throgs Neck, New York 112
Throw Away Child, The (Robertson) 73
Tiffin, Paul 124, 125
Toronto, Ontario, Canada 95
Torresdale, Pennsylvania 44
Trans-Canada Highway 50

Index

Treaty of Fort Laramie 78
Treaty of Hellgate 89
Treaty of Traverse Des Sioux 83
Tripton, Buckinghamshire, England 22
Trotchie, Jackie 91
True Spouse of Jesus Christ, The (Di Liguori) 22
Truth and Reconciliation Commission (Canada) 12
Tucson, diocese of 16
Turk, Midge 27, 37
Turtle Mountain Chippewa 81, 82
Tuscany, Grand Duchy of 42

US Army 76
US Court of Federal Claims 78
US Seventh Cavalry 77, 78
University of Muenster 43
University of Notre Dame 3
Upper Darby District Court, Upper Darby, Pennsylvania 118
Ursuline Academy, Flathead Reservation, Montana 2, 89
Ursuline Sisters 2, 16, 25, 29, 31, 37, 89, 90, 92

Vandever, Joyce 30
Vangheluwe, Bishop Roger 11
Van Zeller, Father Hubert 36
Vatican 9, 12, 13, 14
Veri, Alberta (Sister Bernadine) 97
Vermont 18, 48, 63, 66, 68
Vermont Catholic Charities 64, 67
Victoria, British Columbia, Canada 50
Vietnam 116
Vigneron, Archbishop Allen H. 47
Villa Maria Academy, Erie, Pennsylvania 97
Villa Maria, Chester County, Pennsylvania 115, 116, 119
Virginia 116, 118, 126
Virginia, Mother 73
Virginia Beach, Virginia 116, 118, 119
Virginia Beach Circuit Court, Virginia Beach, Virginia 118
Von Hohenzollern-Sigmaringen, Katherine 42

Von Wuellenweber, Theresa (Mother Mary of the Apostles) 83
vow of chastity 23, 24, 28–33

Wade, Frank 80, 81
Wade, Sandy 80, 81
Wagner, Sister Sharlet 19
Wahpekutes 83
Wahpetons 83
Wanna, Howard 84, 85
Washington, DC 14, 18, 78
Washington State 72, 73, 89
Washita River, Oklahoma 77
Watervliet, New York 68
Watervliet Junior/Senior High School, Watervliet, New York 71
Weakland, Archbishop Rembert 122, 123
Weisberger, Archbishop James 53
West Troy, New York 68
White, Philip 63, 64, 66, 67
Widman, Robert 66–68
Wilfort, Sister Jeanne 48–55
Willet, Sister Stanislaus Kotska 60
Winnipeg, Manitoba, Canada 49, 51, 52
Wisconsin 123, 124, 126
Wisconsin Statute 944.11 124
Wojtyla, Karol 33, 34
Wolf, Ann 39, 41, 55
Wolf, Hubert 43
World Economic Forum 14
World War II 25
Wounded Knee Creek, Pine Ridge Reservation, South Dakota 77
Wuerl, Cardinal Donald 15

Xavier Center, Convent Station, New Jersey 109

Yakima, Washington 89, 90
Yankton Sioux 79
Yorba Linda, California 104

Zenchoff, Mary 31
Zephier, Adele 78, 80, 81
Zephier, Sherwyn 76, 78, 80, 81
Zuccarelli, Lisa 111, 112, 114

www.ingramcontent.com/pod-product-compliance
Ingram Content Group UK Ltd.
Pitfield, Milton Keynes, MK11 3LW, UK
UKHW042016140426
5217IPUK00015B/1206